JANE AUSTEN

IRONY AS DEFENSE AND DISCOVERY

JANE AUSTEN

IRONY AS DEFENSE AND DISCOVERY

BY MARVIN MUDRICK

PRINCETON, NEW JERSEY
PRINCETON UNIVERSITY PRESS
1952

Printed in the United States of America
by Princeton University Press at Princeton, New Jersey

TO BEN LEHMAN

WHO HAD THE TIME AND PATIENCE TO WORK WITH

THIS BOOK AND ITS AUTHOR

PREFACE

THIS book began as an essay to document my conviction that *Emma* is a novel admired, even consecrated, for qualities which it in fact subverts or ignores. Familiarizing myself with the other novels and with Austen criticism and hagiology (these two scarcely separable), I discovered that the conviction had to be extended to take in *all* of Jane Austen's works, that much else remained to be said about them, that even the pertinent things already said* were too fragmentary and isolated to have escaped being buried under the mere mass of cozy family adulation, self-glorifying impressionistic picking-at à *la* Woolf and Forster, and nostalgic latter-day enshrinements of the author as the gentle-hearted chronicler of Regency order. The quantity of conviction has become a book.

The primary debt of the critic of Jane Austen is to the unwearied and self-effacing scholarship of R. W. Chapman, who has provided us with all but one of the primary texts. My other acknowledgments are gratifyingly personal: to Elisabeth Schneider, whose sympathy and luminous example introduced me to the discipline of criticism and to the critical study of the novel; to Mark Schorer, whose advice has been most helpful at various stages of the manuscript; to Milton Orowitz, who has tested and developed by argument many of the critical ideas embodied in this book; and to my wife, whose more immediate suggestions and encouragement throughout

---

* The valuable—if brief—general introductions to Jane Austen are D. W. Harding's "Regulated Hatred: An Aspect of the Work of Jane Austen," *Scrutiny*, VIII (March, 1940), 346-362, and Reginald Farrer's "Jane Austen, *ob.* July 18, 1817," *Quarterly Review*, CCXXVIII (July, 1917), 1-30. Mary Lascelles' book, *Jane Austen and Her Art*, Oxford, 1939, contains much perceptive comment persistently marred by an infusion of outline-softening gentle-Janeism and by her failure to treat the novels as more than aggregations of bits. The valuable introduction to a single Austen work is R. A. Brower's "The Controlling Hand: Jane Austen and 'Pride and Prejudice,'" *Scrutiny*, XIII (September, 1945), 99-111 (to Mr. Brower's incidental pointing out of the simple-complex dichotomy in the novel, I am particularly indebted for having suggested the framework of my chapter on *Pride and Prejudice*).

the writing of the book have appropriately culminated in her insistence on typing the entire manuscript. The debt I acknowledge in the dedication is most immediate and most unpayable of all.

CONTENTS

JANE AUSTEN

IRONY AS DEFENSE AND DISCOVERY

"It seems vain to expect that discourse upon novelists will contain anything new for us until we have really and clearly and accurately seen their books."—PERCY LUBBOCK, *The Craft of Fiction*, New York, 1929, 273.

". . . her books are, as she meant them to be, read and enjoyed by precisely the sort of people whom she disliked; she is a literary classic of the society which attitudes like hers, held widely enough, would undermine."—D. W. HARDING, "Regulated Hatred: An Aspect of the Work of Jane Austen," *Scrutiny*, VIII (March, 1940), 347.

CHAPTER I

THE LITERARY PRETEXT: IRONY
VERSUS SENTIMENT

JUVENILIA

ISTANCE—from her subject and from the reader—was
Jane Austen's first condition for writing. She would
not commit herself. To events, literary or actual, she allowed
herself no public response except the socially conventional or
the ironic; for neither of these endangered her reserve, both
put off self-commitment and feeling, both maintained the distance between author and reader, or author and subject: both
were, primarily, defenses.

Her earliest, and always her characteristic, defense is irony:
throughout her letters and extravagantly in her *juvenilia*, she
observes and defines, without moral or emotional engagement,
the incongruities between pretense and essence, between the
large idea and the inadequate ego. Here, indeed, irony becomes for her a positive agent and appears as the only possible
interpreter of life. Later, as with age and authorship she grew
increasingly aware of the pressures by which society directs
its members out of interpretation of convention into convention
itself, she turned away from irony more and more often to her
alternative defense, convention, until her grand—though temporary—apostasy from irony in *Mansfield Park*. In her letters,
however, where she was not troubled by the responsibility of
authorship, and in her *juvenilia*, the pendulum scarcely swung
from its starting point. Her temperament chose irony at once:
she maintained her distance by diverting herself and her
audience with an unengaged laughter, by setting irony, the
instrument—and, as it happened, the genius—of her temperament, to sharpen and expose all the incongruities between
form and fact, all the delusions intrinsic to conventional art
and conventional society.

If Jane Austen's irony appears at times almost inhumanly
cold and penetrating, and her smile begins to resemble a ric-

1

tus, it may be because we are accustomed to the soft or sentimental alloying of most irony. Sympathy is irrelevant to irony. Jane Austen's compulsion, and genius, is to look only for incongruity; and it delights her wherever she finds it.

She finds it wherever there are people and conventions: her letters to her sister are full of gratified reports on the affectation, the coarseness, the envy, the impropriety of friends and acquaintances. Most often, simple description is enough. "Mrs. Badcock thought herself obliged . . . to run round the room after her drunken Husband.—His avoidance, & her pursuit, with the probable intoxication of both, was an amusing scene." (L I 128, 12 May 1801)* "I had long wanted to see Dr. Britton, & his wife amuses me very much with her affected refinement & elegance." (L II 370, 6 Nov. 1813) "Charles Powlett gave a dance on Thursday, to the great disturbance of all his neighbours, of course, who, you know, take a most lively interest in the state of his finances, and live in hopes of his being soon ruined." (L I 36, 1 Dec. 1798) Sometimes she rearranges for her effect. To impute immorality to one's wife may be mere affectation: "I cannot help thinking from your account of Mrs. E. H. that Earle's vanity has tempted him to invent the account of her former way of Life, that his triumph in securing her might be greater;—I dare say she was nothing but an innocent Country Girl, in fact." (L I 72, 19 Jun. 1799) Incongruity, to seem amusing, must be relieved of guilt; so even immorality shrinks to the dimensions of social error, as Lord Craven, a patron of the Austens, is qualified: "The little flaw of having a Mistress now living with him at Ashdown Park, seems to be the only unpleasing circumstance about him." (L I 106, 8 Jan. 1801) And a friend is excused: "She is . . . so full of kindness for us both, and sends you in particular so many good wishes about your finger, that I am willing to overlook a venial fault; and as Dr. M. is a Clergyman their attachment, however immoral, has a decorous air." (L I 258, 24 Jan. 1809)

These men and women, it appears, are not persons about

* For bibliography of editions used and key to abbreviations, see Appendix I.

whom one feels, but figures in a comedy, whose audience may laugh at every exhibited incongruity of social behavior without becoming involved or responsible. Irony—neutral discoverer and explorer of incongruities—is here exclusively in the service of comedy: of the vision of a world where incongruities have no consequences except in provoking the spectator's laughter.

Irony is not, of course, necessarily comic: it consists in the discrimination between impulse and pretension, between being and seeming, between—in a social setting—man as he is and man as he aspires to be; but of itself it draws no conclusions. It becomes comic when its very neutrality is exploited as a kind of relief from man's conventional response of outrage and involvement toward delusion and error.[1]

It was Jane Austen's first choice to treat life, even in her letters, as material for comedy: not sentimentally, not morally, indeed not tied to any train of consequences, but with a detached discrimination among its incongruities. She was interested in a person, an object, an event, only as she might observe and recreate them free of consequences, as performance, as tableau: her frame was comedy, her defining artistic impulse was irony. Compulsion was also, or became, art. Everywhere she found incongruities between overt and hidden, between professed and acted upon, failures of wholeness which in life have consequences and must be judged but in comedy— and for Jane Austen—are relieved of guilt and responsibility at the moment of perception, to be explored and progressively illuminated by irony.

It is hardly surprising that so active an impulse as Jane Austen's irony could not be contained in letters or talk, but had to overflow into some larger, formal medium. Her early reading, besides, helped to assure this direction, for the Aus-

---

[1] In tragic or satiric irony, on the other hand, this conventional response is not only permitted but powerfully stressed and intensified: the reader is at once involved. In comic irony, the illusion of choice is much stronger. In the comic instant, the shock of relief from involvement predominates; later, the reader feels free, on the basis of the comic artist's evidence, to set his own conditions for involvement.

tens were "great Novel-readers,"[2] and the novels of the time were a treasury of incongruities. It is not surprising, then, that at the age of fourteen[3] she had already produced a burlesque on the popular novels of the latter half of the eighteenth century. Only the quality, the point, the fullness, and the exuberant dismantling thrust of "Love and Freindship" are surprising and extraordinary.

At fourteen, Jane Austen saw her target—the books and their audience—clearly. The great middle-class female audience that wept over Clarissa was not inclined to starve its fresh appetite for vicarious tears. In Richardson, tears are incidental; they are incidental even to Sterne's exposed sensibility: but the literary craving for them, aroused primarily by Clarissa's trials and later extended by Sterne's pathos,[4] was prodigally indulged by more or less ingenuous imitators— with such ruthless directness, in fact, that Dr. Johnson was moved to exclaim to the author of one Richardsonian novel: "I know not, Madam, that you have a right, upon moral principles, to make your readers suffer so much."[5] Jane Austen, reading the new novels that poured off the presses into the circulating libraries, more pertinently felt that the authors, in their adherence to conventions altogether remote from the probabilities of human behavior, had no *artistic* right to make

---

[2] The ethical disrepute into which the novel was falling toward the end of the eighteenth century (for a summary of the facts of this disrepute, see M. Lascelles, *Jane Austen and Her Art*, Oxford, 1939, 51f.) failed to impress the Austens. Jane Austen wrote to her sister: "I have received a very civil note from Mrs. Martin requesting my name as a Subscriber to her Library. . . . As an inducement to subscribe Mrs. Martin tells us that her Collection is not to consist only of Novels, but of every Kind of Literature, &c.&c—She might have spared this pretension to *our* family, who are great Novel-readers & not ashamed of being so." (L I 38, 18 Dec. 1798)

[3] The date "June 13th 1790" is noted at the end of "Love and Freindship." (LF 42)

[4] The female audience passed over *Tristram Shandy* for *A Sentimental Journey* and Shandean humor for pathos, as in Clara Reeve's comment: "Where *Sterne* attempts the Pathos, he is irresistible; the Reviewers have well observed, that though he affected humour and foolery, yet he was greatest in the pathetic style.—His *Maria* and *le Fevre* and his *Monk*, are charming pictures, and will survive, when all his other writings are forgot." C. Reeve, *The Progress of Romance*, London, 1785, II, 31.

[5] G. B. Hill (ed.), *Boswell's Life of Johnson*, New York, 1891, I, 451. The author was Mrs. Frances Sheridan; her book, *The Memoirs of Miss Sidney Biddulph*. See following note.

4

their readers suffer so much, to attempt such a rude infringement of their readers' privacy. At least, she registered her protest—the comic artist's protest of burlesque—against their product.

What these popular authors turned out was, essentially, so fixed and identifiable a blend of Richardson, Sterne, and the picaresque and moralistic elements of Fielding and Smollett, that it should be given a new name: perhaps the lachrymose novel, compounded of sentiment, morality, manners, instruction, sensibility, and adventure.[6] Here at last it shaded off into that other rage of the female audience, the Gothic novel, which demanded gasps instead of tears, and which later, in *Northanger Abbey*, Jane Austen would also examine by the light of irony. In 1790, however, *The Mysteries of Udolpho* was still unwritten, and she concentrated on the flourishing lachrymose novel—on its features in the four great precursors, as well as on the more characteristic examples of Mackenzie's *Man of Feeling* and Fanny Burney's novels, especially those after *Evelina*; most heavily, it is likely, on a very obscure but very characteristic example "By a Young Lady," *Laura and Augustus*,[7] which may also have inspired her to revive the moribund but delightfully vulnerable letter-form for her burlesque.

From Isabel to Laura

How often, in answer to my repeated intreaties that you would give my Daughter a regular detail of the Misfortunes and Adventures of your Life, have you said "No, my freind never will I comply with your request till I may be no longer in Danger of again experiencing such dreadful ones."

Surely that time is now at hand. You are this day 55. If a woman may ever be said to be in safety from the determined

---

[6] Some representative examples: Sarah Fielding's *David Simple* (1744), Charlotte Lennox's *Harriet Stuart* (1751), Mrs. Sheridan's *Sidney Biddulph* (1761), Henry Brooke's *The Fool of Quality* (1765-70), Clara Reeve's *The Old English Baron* (1778), Frances Brooke's *Lady Julia Mandeville* (1782), Sophia Lee's *The Recess* (1785), and Charlotte Smith's *Emmeline* (1788). These novels vary widely in subject and in the emphasis they place upon each of their elements; but all of them demand sensibility and suffering of their protagonists, and tears as the only suitable tribute from their readers. Richardson is the primary influence; the others, especially Sterne, were easily assimilated as soon as they came along.

[7] *Laura and Augustus, An Authentic Story; In A Series of Letters.* By a Young Lady. In Three Volumes. London: 1784.

Perseverance of disagreable Lovers and the cruel Persecutions
of obstinate Fathers, surely it must be at such a time of Life.

Isabel (LF 5)

These paragraphs, which make up the first letter of "Love
and Freindship," already outline every convention of the lachrymose novel, more particularly of the lachrymose novel in
letters. Not that Jane Austen will attack its conventions: she
will, on the contrary, adopt and embody them, so politely and
justly as to avoid, almost, the tone of parody, until she is ready
to apply the slight added strain that brings them down altogether. Jane Austen must take countermeasures: these conventions are, after all, aimed at abolishing the reader's distance; but the ironist is also an artist, and her measures can
satisfy her sense of artistic propriety only if they allow the
unacceptable conventions to argue themselves out of validity.

Truth is the outer convention. The very form of the novel
in letters encourages the author to imply, or to assert, that his
story is true, that he is himself only its editor (so Richardson
designates even his last novel as a selection of documents—
*"The History of Sir Charles Grandison. In a Series of Letters
Published from the Originals.* By the Editor of Pamela and
Clarissa"); and that upon this base lies our obligation to accept any absurdity or irrelevance of pathos it may offer. To
excuse improbability on the ground of truth is not, except in
his prefaces and on his title-pages, a usual trick of Richardson's, but his successors to the female audience are much less
scrupulous: Mackenzie, though abandoning the frame of correspondence, prepares for his episodic improbabilities by de-
claring *The Man of Feeling* nothing more than a remnant of
an authentic document.[8] As the Laura of *Laura and Augustus*
writes, having halted the narrative for a fantastic and tearful
anecdote: ". . . however improbable this circumstance may
appear, yet it is an indubitable fact."[9] Jane Austen, demurely
accepting the letter-form as a license for absurdity and irrelevance, promises in her first letter a series—the elements apparently related to one another only in being presumed to

[8] H. Mackenzie, *The Man of Feeling* (ed. H. Miles), London, 1928, Introduction.
[9] *Laura and Augustus*, II, 179.

6

happen to the same person—of "dreadful" "Misfortunes and Adventures"; each one, after all, is "an indubitable fact." And she proceeds to the inner conventions.

A heroine must live constantly in the midst of "Misfortunes and Adventures." She must be young, at least in her heroic period, and virtuous. The index of virtue is sensibility;[10] and since sensibility thrives on adventure, anything unadventurous or domestic—like a formal courtship, with its mutually admiring quorum of suitor and father—must be proved trivial or wicked. Adventure and sensibility are proper, indeed possible, only to youth, but old age has its value: an older woman —say, one of fifty-five—is beyond the heroic age, but, though of little use for anything else, she may be satisfactory for giving advice on the ground of her accumulated experience. Finally, the young woman—or the young woman grown safely old—will be induced to give a detailed, self-conscious account of her life to some friend: and, since sensibility is infinitely varied and beautiful, the language will be full of circumlocution and ornament. Her account will of course be set to paper, the better to serve its ostensible purpose of inculcating or fortifying morality in others: so the novelist, in this conspiracy of correspondence, laboriously justifies the presence of the reader and the existence of his novel.

In the lachrymose novel, then, convention amounts to personality. For the observing ironist, the incongruity is no longer—as in life—between convention and essence, between the individual as he conforms and the individual as from time to time he involuntarily gives himself away; but between two poles of convention, between the character as he is by literary convention and (explicitly or implicitly) the character as he would appear if we could bring him up against the world's own standard of behavior. Most often, Jane Austen simply—

[10] The lachrymose novelists seem to regard sensibility as a pervasive and sympathetic awareness of feeling, one's own and others'. Sterne, the great propagandist of sensibility, remarked of himself: ". . . my feelings are from the heart, and . . . that heart is not of the worst of molds—praised be God for my sensibility! Though it has often made me wretched, yet I would not exchange it for all the pleasures the grossest sensualist ever felt." L. Sterne, *The Letters of Laurence Sterne*, Oxford, 1927, 68 (Letter to Sir William Stanhope, September 27, 1767).

or at least with only the slightest sharpening of contour—embodies the convention as she has observed it (say, in *Laura and Augustus*), and implies the contrast.

Every character susceptible to vibrations is ready in a moment with his autobiography. So Jane Austen's Laura:

> I informed them of every thing which had befallen me during the course of my life, and at my request they related to me every incident of theirs. (LF 39)

She might just as characteristically have noted:

> Having contracted an acquaintance with one of the nuns the day preceding my quitting Madeira, I received from her as a present a box of candied citron, a work basket and flowers of her own workmanship, with a letter containing the history of her life.

But this is her namesake in *Laura and Augustus*;[11] and here, as elsewhere, only Jane Austen's exposure of clear outline makes the difference.

Adventure and sensibility are proper to a heroine; and what could more patently prefigure them than an exotic ancestry and a cloistered but intellectual upbringing? In "Love and Freindship," Laura is her own example:

> My Father was a native of Ireland and an inhabitant of Wales; my Mother was the natural Daughter of a Scotch Peer by an italian Opera-girl—I was born in Spain and received my Education at a Convent in France. . . . When in the Convent, my progress had always exceeded my instructions, my Acquirements had been wonderful for my age, and I shortly surpassed my Masters.[12] (LF 6)

As for the unfortunate Eliza in *Laura and Augustus*:

> Fontainbleau was the place of my birth, and in giving me life my unfortunate mother expired. She was a native of Italy. I was educated at the convent of the Noblesse in Paris, and received every advantage which the attendance of the most renowned masters could give.[13]

And she turns out later to be the natural daughter of an Eng-

---

[11] *Laura and Augustus*, I, 34.

[12] Emmeline is a similar prodigy: she "had a kind of intuitive knowledge; and comprehended every thing with a facility that soon left her instructors behind her." C. Smith, *Emmeline, The Orphan of the Castle*, London, 1788, I, 5.

[13] *Laura and Augustus*, I, 42.

8

lish Duke. Illegitimacy, that customary romantic stigma—
imagined or actual—of the heroine of the lachrymose novel,[14]
comes ultimately to be displayed as a mark of honor in "Love
and Freindship":

> "We are the sons as you already know, of the two youngest
> Daughters which Lord St Clair had by Laurina an italian
> opera girl. Our mothers could neither of them exactly ascertain
> who were our Fathers, though it is generally beleived that
> Philander, is the son of one Philip Jones a Bricklayer and that
> my Father was Gregory Staves a Staymaker of Edinburgh.
> This is however of little consequence for as our Mothers were
> certainly never married to either of them it reflects no Dis-
> honour on our Blood, which is of a most ancient and un-
> polluted kind. . . . (LF 39)

Virtue ceases to have any meaning except as a synonym
for sensibility, and sensibility becomes the name and vindication of every anarchically self-indulgent impulse. Vanity becomes a high romantic duty. Laura and her Augustus continually preen themselves in the mirror of correspondence:
Laura, complacently reviewing her tearful separation from
her friend Cecilia, remarks how favorably it contrasts with
the "insensibility" of others;[15] Lieutenant Montague, with wonderful inappropriateness to his sex and his vocation, observes
to a fellow officer that "My soul, you know, is full of sensibility,
formed for all the luxury of the melting passion; but it is
equally true, that the sweetest delicacy had ever a place
there."[16] Jane Austen's Laura is as adept—almost—as her
namesake at self-congratulation: "A sensibility too tremblingly
alive to every affliction of my Freinds, my Acquaintance and
particularly to every affliction of my own, was my only fault,
if a fault it could be called." (LF 6) Love at first sight is inevitable for sympathetic minds. "Our love," declares Eliza,
"was pure and disinterested; our souls appeared formed for
each other. On our first interview, our minds secretly acknowledged its counterpart."[17] The Laura of "Love and Freindship"

---

[14] Even Evelina feels the social effect of illegitimacy, though Fanny Burney
spares her readers the fact and justifies her happy ending by making Sir
John Belmont a deserter from marriage rather than a seducer of Evelina's
mother.
[15] *Laura and Augustus*, I, 8.   [16] *Ibid.*, 111.
[17] *Ibid.*, 52.

is not less sure of her eternal bond with Edward when he requests her hand after a few minutes' acquaintance; and they are immediately married by her father, "who tho' he had never taken orders had been bred to the Church." (LF 11)

At moments of crisis, a character exhibits the proper degree of sensibility by weeping, or swooning, or going off into fainting-fits, or running mad, or even dying.[18] In *Laura and Augustus*, every character, at the mere mention of ill-fated love, is ready with tears; and, confronted by his own misfortunes, with the more drastic responses. Eliza's prospective father-in-law dies of repentance after revealing that he is her father also; as for the lovers themselves, "we lay eight days bereft of our senses."[19] When Augustus is "no more," Laura "for six hours . . . was in successive fits";[20] and she awakens only to run mad—" '. . . O! God! he hears me not—Cold! and dead! . . .' "[21] and to drive her mother into convulsions. When, in "Love and Freindship," Edward and Augustus are reunited, their wives are so moved that they "fainted alternately on a sofa." (LF 16) Later Laura and Sophia, having seen a phaeton overturn, arrive to find "Two Gentlemen most elegantly attired but weltering in their blood," (LF 31) who turn out to be Edward and Augustus. "Sophia shreiked and fainted on the ground—I screamed and instantly ran mad—." (LF 31) At Edward's death, Laura achieves a climax of sensibility, which she herself, as a faithful correspondent, must of course minutely describe:

> My Voice faltered, My Eyes assumed a vacant stare, my face became as pale as Death, and my senses were considerably impaired—

[18] Outstanding in this respect is *The Man of Feeling*: tears flow in torrents; in two consecutive pages (162f.), three people die of broken hearts and one man faints; and finally the hero becomes ill of unavowed love and dies in his excess of emotion upon hearing that his love is requited—"He seized her hand—a languid colour reddened her cheek—a smile brightened faintly in his eye. As he gazed on her, it grew dim, it fixed, it closed—He sighed and fell back on his seat—Miss Walton screamed at the sight—His aunt and the servants rushed into the room—They found them lying motionless together.—Her physician happened to call at that instant. Every art was tried to recover them—With Miss Walton they succeeded—But Harley was gone for ever!" (204)

[19] *Laura and Augustus*, I, 68.   [20] *Ibid.*, III, 135.
[21] *Ibid.*, 137.

"Talk not to me of Phaetons (said I, raving in a frantic, in-coherent manner)—Give me a violin—. I'll play to him and sooth him in his melancholy Hours—Beware ye gentle Nymphs of Cupid's Thunderbolts, avoid the piercing shafts of Jupiter—Look at that grove of Firs—I see a Leg of Mutton—They told me Edward was not Dead; but they deceived me—they took him for a cucumber—" (LF 31f.)

Everywhere the claim and value of society—which includes everything outside the tight circle of recognized sensibilities—must be denied. Love, of course, requires no social context. "When we are in love," says Laura, in *Laura and Augustus*, "we forget that there are any other objects, besides that on which our affections are placed. . . ."[22] In "Love and Freind-ship," the lovers Sophia and Augustus are safe from intrusion because they "had . . . taken due care to inform the surround-ing Families, that as their Happiness centered wholly in them-selves, they wished for no other society." (LF 17) Even sym-pathy or sorrow—however violent in its outbreaks—is strictly limited to the tight, self-admiring circle, the slightly extended ego. Laura takes a moment from her love for Augustus to glance out at the world: "I have been here, Cecilia, but one month, and have already been twice alarmed by the cry of murder, which was occasioned by Mr. Snarley's beating his eldest daughter in a most unmerciful manner. This, you may be sure, is very disagreeable to one of my quiet disposition. . . ."[23] Jane Austen's characters are equally unengaged by events outside the circle, even by death or accident. Laura mentions in passing that "trifling circumstance. . . . The death of my Parents . . . ," (LF 20) and she welcomes the overturn-ing of the phaeton as a timely distraction for Sophia's pangs of sensibility. (LF 30) Philander and Gustavus, having stolen nine hundred pounds from their mothers and spent it all, are prevented from returning to them for support only by

[22] *Ibid.*, II, 165.
[23] *Ibid.*, III, 19. Here the incongruity is so obvious, and so little in need of exaggeration or extension for ironic effect, that we begin to suspect ironic intent in the author; but, from the "Young Lady's" characteristic tone, we must conclude that we are importing irony ourselves. Bad art is just dull. Very bad art—at least very bad art of serious intent—becomes amusing because its incongruities between pretension and effect are so sharply visible.

11

"accidentally hearing that they were both starved to Death."
(LF 40)

Far from confusing life and art, the protagonist of sensibility expressly rejects the former and embraces the latter. Social conventions and consequences do not influence him; he acts only according to the punctilio of art—the art of the lachrymose novel. He dwells in a kind of heroic limbo barricaded with novels, now and then impinged upon by the world, but invulnerable to worldly assault. Appropriately, it is the villain of *Laura and Augustus* who pronounces the world's judgment on impractical lovers and the books by which they live: "This comes of people suffering their children to read those ridiculous books called novels";[24] for, in the author's judgment, the lovers act ideally—that is, according to novels—and the world acts wickedly. The lachrymose novelist is not afraid to contrast art with life; and Jane Austen accepts the challenge in her own way. At a corresponding point in "Love and Freindship," she makes her first explicit juxtaposition of literary convention and social convention, and—more crucially— her first departure from the object parodied, as she suddenly confronts the hero with a worldly character not villainous but practical. When Sir Edward insists that Edward marry Dorothea, Edward exclaims:

> ". . . Lady Dorothea is lovely and Engaging; I prefer no woman to her; but know Sir, that I scorn to marry her in compliance with your Wishes. No! Never shall it be said that I obliged my Father. . . ."
>
> Sir Edward was surprised; he had perhaps little expected to meet with so spirited an opposition to his will. "Where, Edward in the name of wonder (said he) did you pick up this unmeaning gibberish? You have been studying Novels I suspect." (LF 10)

How does a character of sensibility survive? Obviously it is beneath Edward's dignity to work for a living. His practical sister, Augusta, asks him whether he will depend on his father's generosity:

> "Never, never Augusta will I so demean myself. (said Ed-

[24] *Ibid.*, I, 127.

ward). Support! What support will Laura want which she can receive from him?"

"Only those very insignificant ones of Victuals and Drink." (answered she).

"Victuals and Drink! (replied my Husband in a most nobly contemptuous Manner) and dost thou then imagine that there is no other support for an exalted mind (such as is my Laura's) than the mean and indelicate employment of Eating and Drinking?"

"None that I know of, so efficacious." (returned Augusta).
(LF 13)

Irony draws the lachrymose premises to their social conclusion. If a penniless lover may not work, or depend on generosity, it follows that he must steal. The two pairs of lovers live for some time on the "considerable sum of money which Augustus had gracefully purloined from his unworthy father's Escritoire" (LF 18); and even after this money is exhausted, they "scorned to reflect a moment on their pecuniary Distresses and would have blushed at the idea of paying their Debts." (LF 18) Unfortunately, society steps in and carries Augustus off to jail. The two girls, their faith in sensibility still unshaken, are sheltered by a cousin of Sophia's at his home in Scotland. There, having exercised their sensibility by persuading his daughter to renounce the suitor approved for her and to elope with someone else, they begin to filch banknotes from their host's private drawer:

. . . as Sophia was majestically removing the 5th Banknote from the Drawer to her own purse, she was suddenly most impertinently interrupted by the entrance of Macdonald himself. . . . Sophia (who though naturally all winning sweetness could when occasions demanded it call forth the Dignity of her sex) instantly put on a most forbiding look, and darting an angry frown on the undaunted culprit, demanded . . . "Wherefore her retirement was thus insolently broken in on?"
(LF 27)

When Macdonald ejects them, their sensibility remains resolutely unimpaired.

Still, Jane Austen means to impair and overthrow sensibility; and her method is only another logical extension of the lachrymose premises. If the protagonist of sensibility must take risks in order to survive, he must take precautions as well,

13

even trifling physical precautions: illness or death, as effectively as lack of money, can block the progress and triumph of any mortal character, however heroic. After the sight of their dying husbands has thrown Sophia into a faint and Laura into a frenzy, Sophia becomes ill, and her friend explains why:

> . . . the bodily Exertions I had undergone in my repeated fits of frenzy had so effectually circulated and warmed my Blood as to make me proof against the chilling Damps of Night, whereas, Sophia lying totally inactive on the ground must have been exposed to all their severity. (LF 33f.)

And Sophia, dying, advises Laura:

> ". . . Beware of swoons Dear Laura. . . . A frenzy fit is not one quarter so pernicious; it is an exercise to the Body and if not too violent, is I dare say conducive to Health in its consequences —Run mad as often as you chuse; but do not faint—" (LF 34)

An uninhibited self-indulgence is fatal. Even sensibility, to survive, must submit to some kind of order; that orderly virtue, discretion, becomes necessary even to a heroine. Yet discretion, once admitted, dominates at last: everything, at last, rounds out to order; in "Love and Freindship," to order wholly unadventurous and domestic. Sensibility is overthrown. Laura completes her story; and though, nostalgically, she still complains about her "melancholy solitude," (LF 42) these are just words: her outlook has changed. Society, not sensibility, is the more comforting, the more indulgent to the ego after all. The world and its tidy oblivions permit her to survive the deaths of her father, her mother, her husband, and her friend; to accept Sir Edward's generous annuity; and to regard people, not with enthusiasm or contempt, but with interest merely. The consistent lachrymose heroine would rather die than qualify her self-indulgence. Laura, on the other hand, discovers the secret of social living: that self-indulgence has the run of the world, provided only it is qualified by the world's one indispensable virtue—discretion.

We are already well beyond R. Brimley Johnson's observation that "Love and Freindship" is a "criticism . . . of art—not

14

of life";[25] the manner of Laura's conversion to respectability implies not only a criticism of life, but an unfavorable one besides. It is true that "Love and Freindship" begins as parody, having an immediate and recognizable occasion in the circulating-library novels which Jane Austen read with such delight. For the parodist, life is simply the unvarying standard, the accepted and inclusive reality, by which he demonstrates the absurdity of bad art: in this sense at least, parody—as a type—is never a criticism of life. For Jane Austen, the accepted reality was the middle-class society of her time.[26] It gave her an orderly set of values to counterpose to those values and categories which she found so amusing, anarchic, and unacceptable in the lachrymose novel. More practically, for a fourteen-year-old girl in a clergyman's household at the turn of the century, it gave her the rock of middle-class convention to base herself upon. So "Love and Freindship" begins as parody, as a criticism of art in terms of life—life, that is, as Jane Austen saw it in the bourgeois world. Yet, having demolished the values of bad art, it ends as a criticism of life, a mocking examination of Laura's freshly claimed middle-class values, and leaves parody conspicuously behind.

A recognition of Jane Austen's wider aim and achievement in "Love and Freindship" brings new obstacles to understanding. "From *Volume the First* onwards," says Miss Lascelles, Jane Austen ". . . very seldom aims merely at this or that wretched novel or novelist. It is her way to strike through a particular novel, or type of novel, to the false conventions that govern it, and through these conventions to the false taste (in writer and reader alike) that have allowed them to come into

[25] R. B. Johnson, "A New Study of Jane Austen," prefixed to *Jane Austen: A French Appreciation*, by L. Villard, tr. Veronica Lucas, London, 1924, 37.

[26] I use the words "middle-class" and "bourgeois," and shall continue to use them through this study, not because they are perfectly accurate here, but because there is no word that peculiarly attaches to the hybrid society of dying feudal tradition and progressively self-assertive bourgeois vigor in which Jane Austen lived. In any case, the new middle-class requisites of money and property were strongly gaining, when they were not merely superimposed, over the feudal requisites of rank and the inherited estate, and the standard of gentility smoothed over the period of transition. We might, perhaps, call her society "genteel," to give it the kind of unity she herself must have seen in it, but its base in her novels is so clearly economic that an economic term seems preferable in most instances.

being."[27] New questions arise. How does Jane Austen decide when taste is false? and is there a target beyond false taste?

In "Love and Freindship," taste appears false whenever it rejects the facts of society, the conventions and values imposed by the middle class upon its members. So Jane Austen points out—by imitation, by exaggeration, by contrast, by logical extension—that the lachrymose novel tends to reject the chief bourgeois values: discretion, financial honesty, a theoretical and professed humanitarianism (however limited in practice), legitimacy, woman's humility and chastity, marriage as a calculated arrangement largely financial. For all these, the lachrymose novel substitutes sensibility and passionate love: values no longer social but personal, and, as Jane Austen demonstrates, liable in themselves to turn the individual obsessively inward away from all social participation or responsibility.

Jane Austen's primary target and incongruity in "Love and Freindship" is the false taste of the lachrymose novelist as it informs his pivotal values, sensibility and passionate love. Yet these values have always been regarded by bourgeois society, above all by the women of that society, as peculiarly feminine, or at least peculiarly adapted to feminine refinement. Why does Jane Austen expose them to such unremitting ridicule? The middle-class woman of the late eighteenth century had good reason to accept and magnify these values. Living in a society dedicated to possession and dominance, with no opportunity for political or economic expression,[28] with no influence, indeed, but such as she might gain by her maneuverability in courtship and marriage and by reading or writing novels in which this maneuverability was exploited, she could hardly fail to examine, claim, and apotheosize—even at the expense of all others—the only values which centered in courtship and marriage, and which could therefore make her feel

---

[27] M. Lascelles, "Miss Austen and Some Books," *London Mercury*, XXIX (April 1934), 530.

[28] In Jane Austen's novels, for example, women do not take part in any discussion of politics or economics. In *Northanger Abbey*, Henry Tilney, talking to his sister and Catherine, "shortly found himself arrived at politics; and from politics, it was an easy step to silence." (111) Mr. Chapman documents this particular manner of the age (E 510).

possessive and dominant. It is significant that an impressive proportion of both lachrymose and Gothic novels—books which disregarded the man's world of property and its cardinal virtue, discretion, or treated them as no more than detestable clogs on sex and sensibility—were written by women; that, in fact, the English novel of the last quarter of the eighteenth century was almost monopolized by women, Fanny Burney and Mrs. Radcliffe being only the preëminent examples; and that Jane Austen was the only woman writer to oppose the tide of feminine sensibility in the novels of the time. The author of "Love and Freindship" has, then, no sympathy for the most cherished values of her sex in her own middle class.

If Jane Austen pushes aside these feminine values, we might expect her to defend the masculine bourgeois values, the very ground of bourgeois taste. Ostensibly, of course, she does. Augusta, Edward's practical sister, and Sir Edward, his forthright father, are approved middle-class types, introduced to set off by their common sense the impractical moonshiny nonsense of the lovers. Later, however, after sense has been allowed to dispose of sensibility, it must itself submit to a quite disconcerting scrutiny. The ironic impulse, freed from parody, turns to consider the sum and end of bourgeois values. The only difference between Laura before and Laura after conversion to the middle class is the quality of discretion, of external tidiness. She no longer yields to faints or frenzies. She no longer expresses violent opinions. She gives up stealing to accept an annuity. She has given up, however, nothing of her egocentrism, of her self-indulgence; for, indeed, society sanctifies these qualities if only they are tempered by discretion. Virtue resides, it seems, not in the anarchy of sensibility, not even in the high moral concepts which man professes, but in order, propriety, tidiness: sympathy and morality are mere conventions, useful as curbs upon, but incongruous with, the personal reality. Even good taste, if one strikes it, gives off a hollow sound. And we find that in her burlesque Jane Austen, having disposed of false taste (false only in its suicidal rejection of social fact and social power), has penetrated to that deeper level of incongruity which she tapped directly in her

17

letters: the social delusion, the incongruity between convention and essence, between the person as society domesticates
him for polite living and the person as he irrevocably is and
occasionally gives himself away.

To ignore this final object of Jane Austen's irony—in "Love
and Freindship," at least—is to misunderstand and moralize
her preference for reality. "Some essential quality in her,"
says Miss Lascelles, "makes her prefer the actual to the illusionary world—prefer it as the prettier and pleasanter
place."[29] In "Love and Freindship," Jane Austen has, of
course, no use for the illusionary world—for anything, that is,
which challenges the probabilities of rural middle-class society. But the actual world is not a prettier or pleasanter place,
it is simply a more orderly place, a wider and more stable
area of reference for the ironic spectator. It is torn by internal
discrepancies even as the world of *Laura and Augustus*; its
moral values, though they may suggest desirable modes of
behavior, exist for man as convenient and flattering abstrac-
tions, too large for the ego to embody or to act upon. Its advantage is an advantage for the ironist only: in society, the
ego—like a child who tends to say the wrong thing in company
—is trained to silence. Jane Austen prefers a world in which
the ego, disciplined against expression, may be safely treated
as a constant of inadequacy: not wicked or weak, but limited,
incapable of fulfilling its social requirements; never threatening—by sensibility or passion—to break out of form and incongruity. In bourgeois society, the ironist never runs out of
situations in which the ego may be stripped of its social pretensions, and exposed in its defenseless inadequacy. Jane
Austen, writing to Cassandra during the Peninsular War,
remarks: "How horrible it is to have so many people killed!—
And what a blessing that one cares for none of them!" (L II
286, 31 May 1811) The ironist matches the bourgeois convention of humanitarianism against its personal reality and
finds that they match badly or not at all: with no bias or pity
toward one or the other, delighting in the durable incongruity
that vindicates her non-commitment. This kind of world is

[29] M. Lascelles, *op.cit.*, 533.

not pretty or pleasant; but it is amusing, it teems with incongruities, and it does not threaten Jane Austen's unpenetrated reserve.

There is a threat, however, in the lachrymose world, the world of the feminine daydream. Jane Austen, born to the middle class of the late eighteenth century, could hardly avoid choosing courtship and marriage as the general subject of her work: the fact is that she had to write about these or nothing, since for the women of her time and class any other area of behavior was presumed to be closed. Yet in courtship and marriage, where she found, again, social forms with the same comically inadequate human content, the lachrymose novelist —revolting against bourgeois discipline—had found sex and sensibility instead, in every superfluity prohibited and damned by the bourgeois world. Consider, for example, what *Laura and Augustus* offers: one case of adultery and another of prospective incest; three pregnancies out of wedlock; one exposed female breast; one half-naked woman; one suspected rape. For all its inept exploitation of feeling and sexual love, *Laura and Augustus* at least testifies that these exist. The bourgeois world is safe for Jane Austen because—formalizing all personal relations—it makes no provision for feeling, which alone can override incongruity and dispose of distance. The illusionary world is unsafe, and must be dismantled, because it not only provides for, but tries to base itself upon, feeling; with an even more specific threat to the wise ironic child-author of "Love and Freindship," upon the great, unknown, adult commitment of sexual love.

It is in her *juvenilia* that Jane Austen takes upon herself the task of dismantling the illusionary world: in the miscellany of burlesques and parodies which she wrote for her family's private amusement and her own; as well as in *Northanger Abbey*, belated instance, in the larger design of her twenties, of the same general tidying-up. This tidying-up ends (it is still going on, residually, in *Sense and Sensibility*)—if we may judge from her later work—by clearing her imagination of everything except the actual, tidy bourgeois world.

In the *juvenilia*, after the exhaustive rereading of the lachrymose novel in "Love and Freindship," her ironic impulse is usually content to relax into briefer and less plotted fantasies, catch-all burlesques on characters and situations incompatible with bourgeois convention. Even in these, however, Jane Austen tends to return to the lachrymose novel, as to an adversary not yet quite subdued.

"Jack and Alice," the longest piece in *Volume the First*,[30] carves a last chunk out of the sentimental hero-type. Charles Adams is "of so dazzling a Beauty that none but Eagles could look him in the Face." (VF 21) At a ball, "The Beams that darted from his Eyes" were "So Strong . . . that no one dared venture within half a mile of them. . . ." (VF 22) Vanity, with Charles also, is a high romantic duty: ". . . I imagine my Manners & Address to be of the most polished kind; there is a certain elegance, a peculiar sweetness in them that I never saw equalled & cannot describe—." (VF 45) Then, turning his candor upon the father of the girl who wishes to marry him, Charles observes: "I look upon you Sir to be a very good sort of Man in the main; a drunken old Dog to be sure, but that's nothing to me. Your Daughter Sir, is neither sufficiently beautifull, sufficiently amiable, sufficiently witty, nor sufficiently rich for me—. I expect nothing more in my wife than my wife will find in me—Perfection." (VF 46)

The curiously mixed "Evelyn," in *Volume the Third*, suffers from stretches of inappropriate serious narrative (the novice novelist becoming impatient with mere parody); but it justifies itself with a final purely parodic flourish of the sentimental virtues: particularly, beauty, generosity, and love. Beauty is, of course, merit:

> This Young Lady . . . was the darling of her relations—From the clearness of her skin & the Brilliancy of her Eyes, she was fully entitled to all their partial affection. Another circumstance contributed to the general Love they bore her, and that was one of the finest heads of hair in the world. (VT 14)

True generosity has no limit, at least when a hero is to

---

[30] By internal evidence (VF vi-viii), *Volume the First* seems to have been written between 1791 and June 3, 1793 (the date written at the end of the manuscript), and therefore to have followed at least the title story of *Love and Freindship.*

benefit by it. So Mr. Gower, a stranger wishing to settle in the hospitable village of Evelyn, is saluted with an offer of everything by the lady of the first house he comes to:

> "Welcome best of Men—Welcome to this House, & to everything it contains. William, tell your Master of the happiness I enjoy—invite him to partake of it—. . . . Then turning to Mʳ Gower, & taking out her purse, "Accept this my good Sir,—. Beleive me you are welcome to everything that is in my power to bestow.—I wish my purse were weightier, but Mʳ Webb must make up my deficiencies—. I know he has cash in the house to the amount of an hundred pounds, which he shall bring you immediately." Mʳ Gower left overpowered by her generosity as he put the purse in his pocket, and from the excess of his Gratitude, could scarcely express himself intelligibly when he accepted her offer of the hundred pounds. (vᴛ 9)

And when Mr. Webb entreats him: " 'Tell us what you wish more to receive, and depend upon our gratitude for the communication of your wishes,' " Mr. Gower replies: " 'Give me your house & Grounds; I ask for nothing else.' " (vᴛ 10)

Mr. Gower is equally lucky in love. The Webbs introduce him to their beautiful daughter, and the hero marries her, and her dowry of ten thousand pounds, the following day. But a family obligation calls him from her, she dies of grief "about 3 hours after his departure," (vᴛ 24) and he returns to marry the hostess at the inn, whom he had met his first day in the village. The Webbs send him thirty pounds in token of their gratitude for his "unexampled generosity in writing to condole with us on the late unlucky accident which befel our Maria," (vᴛ 27) and "Mʳ and Mʳˢ Gower resided many years at Evelyn enjoying perfect happiness the just reward of their virtues." (vᴛ 27)

"Frederick and Elfrida" pays its respects to the splendid diction of the lachrymose novel, by observing "the engaging Exterior & beautiful outside of Jezalinda" (vꜰ 8); and to its picturesque scenery: "a Grove of Poplars which led from the Parsonage to a verdant Lawn enamelled with a variety of variegated flowers & watered by a purling Stream, brought from the Valley of Tempe by a passage underground." (vꜰ 7) "Henry and Eliza" elaborates on the foundling plot: the found-

21

ling heroine is turned out for stealing from her foster-parents, and sheltered by a Duchess; she elopes with the Duchess's prospective son-in-law, is pursued and imprisoned by the Duchess, and at last escapes and returns to her foster-parents, where it is miraculously discovered that she is their own daughter. "Amelia Webster" points out that a heroine can improve on the postal service by providing herself, like Clarissa, with a mailbox in a "convenient old hollow oak," (VF 87) to circumvent any potential captors. "The Generous Curate," subtitled "a moral Tale, setting forth the Advantages of being Generous and a Curate," disposes of the sanctimonious beginning of *Camilla* by the simple method of imitating it. (VF 134f.) "The Beautifull Cassandra" redefines the lachrymose infatuation with noble ancestry: "Her father was of noble Birth, being the near relation of the Dutchess of—'s Butler." (VF 81) The author amuses herself with the cult of inconsequence in the desultory "Adventures of Mr Harley," (VF 73) in the "Memoirs of Mr Clifford" (VF 78ff.); most effectively, in the introduction of the "hero" of "Jack and Alice": "It may now be proper to return to the Hero of this Novel, the brother of Alice, of whom I beleive I have scarcely ever had occasion to speak; which may perhaps be partly owing to his unfortunate propensity to Liquor, which so compleatly deprived him of the use of those faculties Nature had endowed him with, that he never did anything worth mentioning." (VF 44)

Her own social world, the safely amusing world of the letters, is never far out of mind. So, treating grave social errors as trivial or excusable, she mocks at the lachrymose novelist's indulgence of sensibility; but she also, as in her letters, exposes the split in bourgeois man's attitude toward crimes and improprieties, in books or in life: between his conventional response of morally involved outrage and his private response of amoral curiosity (no response of sympathy or understanding being, of course, encouraged by society or admitted by the author). In "Jack and Alice," for example, she gaily presents as her major characters a family whose diversions are gambling and drinking themselves unconscious.

"The Johnsons were a family of Love, & though a little addicted to the Bottle & the Dice had many good Qualities." (VF 22) The heroine, Alice Johnson, is continually engaging herself in pugnacious drunken arguments (VF 29ff., 33 ff.); and after Charles Adams rejects her, "She flew to her Bottle . . ." (VF 47) for consolation. At the ball, "the Bottle being pretty briskly pushed about by the 3 Johnsons, the whole party not excepting even Virtue were carried home, Dead Drunk." (VF 24) Even murder and other high crimes and transgressions are relieved of guilt. In "Sir William Montague," the hero loves a Miss Arundel, who was "cruel; she preferred a Mr Stanhope: Sir William shot Mr Stanhope: the lady had then no reason to refuse him." (VF 76) In "A Letter from a Young Lady," the young lady writes: "I murdered my father at a very early period of my Life, I have since murdered my Mother, and I am now going to murder my Sister. I have changed my religion so often that at present I have not an idea of any left. I have been a perjured witness in every public tryal for these last twelve years; and I have forged my own Will. In short there is scarcely a crime that I have not committed—But I am now going to reform." (LF 136)

Jane Austen returns to direct parody, of an outwardly different kind, in her "History of England," a take-off on Goldsmith's potboiler of the same name. Her purpose, she says, is "to prove the innocence of the Queen of Scotland . . . and to abuse Elizabeth" (LF 96): more generally, to parody Goldsmith's gossip masquerading as history, at the same time that she defends the Yorkists and the Stuarts against Goldsmith's condemnation. We know that Jane Austen possessed and made marginal notes in a copy of Goldsmith's *History*: one of her relatives has anxiously adduced as proof of her warmth of feeling a note she made next to a passage attacking the Stuarts: "A family who were always ill-used, BETRAYED OR NEGLECTED, whose virtues are seldom allowed, while their errors are never forgotten."[31] The question of feeling in

---

[31] M. A. Austen-Leigh, *Personal Aspects of Jane Austen*, London, 1920, 26. This note, according to Miss Austen-Leigh, was written when Jane Austen was twelve or thirteen: another example of her astonishingly early

Jane Austen's work turns, however, not on what she could put into a marginal note at a moment of indignation,[32] but on what her work itself, from its most private beginnings, habitually reveals. If warmth of feeling ever appears in her "History," it is quickly diverted into her habitual pose of amused non-commitment, the same—perhaps a more overt—compulsion to irony, the same safeguarding of distance:

> Henry the 4th ascended the throne of England much to his own satisfaction in the year 1399, after having prevailed on his cousin and predecessor Richard the 2nd, to resign it to him, and to retire for the rest of his life to Pomfret Castle, where he happened to be murdered. It is to be supposed that Henry was married, since he had certainly four sons. . . (LF 85)

During Henry V's reign "Lord Cobham was burnt alive, but I forget what for." (LF 85) As for Richard III:

> It has indeed been confidently asserted that he killed his two Nephews and his Wife, but it has also been declared that he did *not* kill his two Nephews, which I am inclined to beleive true; and if this is the case, it may also be affirmed that he did not kill his Wife, for if Perkin Warbeck was really the Duke of York, why might not Lambert Simnel be the Widow of Richard. (LF 87)

Nothing can be said for Henry VIII

> . . . but that his abolishing Religious Houses and leaving them to the ruinous depredations of time has been of infinite use to the landscape of England in general, which probably was a principal motive for his doing it, since otherwise why should a Man who was of no Religion himself be at so much trouble to abolish one which had for ages been established in the Kingdom. (LF 89)

In Mary's reign, "Many were the people who fell martyrs to the protestant Religion . . . I suppose not fewer than a dozen." (LF 91) Having passionately attacked Elizabeth for her treatment of the Queen of Scotland, the author concludes:

> Oh! what must this bewitching Princess whose only freind was then the Duke of Norfolk, and whose only ones now Mr Whitaker, Mrs Lefroy, Mrs Knight and myself . . . have suffered

---

control of the model eighteenth-century phrase. The "History of England" is dated November 26, 1791—a month before the author's sixteenth birthday.

[32] Even this indignation is, after all, a family affair: Mrs. Austen's family had been firm and celebrated partisans of Charles I. (*Ibid.*, 14ff.)

when informed that Elizabeth had given orders for her Death! (LF 92)

Even indignation must be hedged with irony; religion, too:

> As I am myself partial to the roman catholic religion, it is with infinite regret that I am obliged to blame the Behaviour of any Member of it: yet Truth being I think very excusable in an Historian, I am necessitated to say that in this James I's reign the roman Catholics of England did not behave like Gentlemen to the protestants. (LF 94)

In Charles I's time, it seems that there were only five amiable men:

> The King himself, ever stedfast in his own support—Archbishop Laud, Earl of Strafford, Viscount Faulkland and Duke of Ormond, who were scarcely less strenuous or zealous in the cause. (LF 96)

History, for Jane Austen as for most people, is a world not here and not now. For Jane Austen at sixteen, however, it is also an object of irony, it becomes incongruous and amusing by reason of its very remoteness. Men do not die martyred and murdered; or if they did once, these things happened after all in the distant past, and we cannot be concerned about them in our present bourgeois world, so undemanding and safe in its minor iniquities. It appears, finally, that Jane Austen's purpose is, not to make fun of Goldsmith or to glorify the Stuarts, but to dispose of history as of another unverifiable illusionary world; for history, also, too frequently demands serious partisanship and commitment. Her purpose remains what it was in "Love and Freindship": to clear her imagination of everything except the socially seen and heard, the actual, immediate, ironically vulnerable forms of the bourgeois world.

In three stories among the *juvenilia*, this world already appears with some solidity and extension. Neither "The Three Sisters" nor "Lesley Castle" nor "Catharine or the Bower" rises to the superb assurance of "Love and Freindship"; but in all of them, Jane Austen begins to sacrifice parody for self-sustaining characterization and plot, she moves out to claim and occupy a world already recognizable as the world of the novels.

"Catharine" lapses several times from presentation into flat amateurish description and narrative; but its characters and

situations often have an interest of their own, and more often
as a foreshadowing of characters and situations in the novels.
Its heroine, for example, resembles Elizabeth Bennet in her
forthrightness of opinion:

> ". . . do you call it lucky, for a Girl of Genius & Feeling to be
> sent in quest of a Husband to Bengal, to be married there to a
> Man of whose Disposition she has no opportunity of judging
> till her Judgement is of no use to her, who may be a Tyrant,
> or a Fool or both for what she knows to the Contrary. . . ."
> (VT 56)

and in her habitual playfulness of tone:

> ". . . By the bye are not you in love with him yourself?"
> "To be sure I am replied Kitty laughing, I am in love with
> every handsome Man I see."
> "That is just like me—*I* am always in love with every hand-
> some Man in the World."
> "There you outdo me replied Catherine [Jane Austen's or-
> thography, the reader will have noted, is not absolute] for I
> am only in love with those I *do* see." (VT 92)

She has even a Wickham-like man to fall half in love with,
Edward Stanley, as handsome and charming as Wickham:

> There was a Novelty in his character which to *her* was ex-
> tremely pleasing; his person was uncommonly fine, his Spirits
> & Vivacity suited to her own, and his Manners at once so
> animated & Insinuating, that she thought it must be impossible
> for him to be otherwise than amiable, and was ready to give
> him Credit for being perfectly so. (VT 116)

but with a beau's primping vanity to replace Wickham's self-
seeking shrewdness:

> As Stanley's preparations in dressing were confined to such very
> trifling articles, Kitty of course expected him in about ten
> minutes; but she found that it had not been merely a boast of
> vanity in saying that he was dilatory in that respect, as he
> kept her waiting for him above half an hour. . . .
> "Well said he as he came in, have not I been very quick?
> I never hurried so much in my Life before."
> "In that case you certainly have, replied Kitty, for all Merit
> you know is comparative." (VT 83)

Just so far, there are difficulties. Catharine is too sensible
to imagine herself even half in love with so fractional a person
as Edward Stanley; Wickham, after all, is no fool or mere

social butterfly for Elizabeth to be taken in by. In fact, the general impression one receives from "Catharine" is of a number of miscellaneous characters, more or less entertaining in themselves, but having no discernible relations with each other, or even with themselves from situation to situation. Catharine begins as a mock-sentimental heroine—she retires for periodic consolation to the bower that she and her two friends have built, she eagerly discusses the latest sentimental novels with the Isabella-like Miss Stanley in a scene later rewritten for Gothic novels in *Northanger Abbey* (with another Catherine)—but she very soon becomes the more typical, perhaps more autobiographical, Austen heroine, whose most seductive avatar is Elizabeth Bennet.

The third striking character in "Catharine" is the heroine's aunt, who energetically prefigures Mrs. Norris:

> "Well; *this* is beyond anything I could have supposed. *Profligate* as I *knew* you to be, I was not prepared for such a sight. This is beyond any thing I ever heard of in my Life! Such Impudence, I never witnessed before in such a Girl! And this is the reward for all the cares I have taken in your Education; for all my troubles & Anxieties; and Heaven knows how many they have been! All I wished for, was to breed you up virtuously; I never wanted you to play upon the Harpsichord, or draw better than any one else; but I had hoped to see you respectable and good; to see you able & willing to give an example of Modesty and Virtue to the Young people here abouts. . . ."
> (vt 110f.)

But her extravagant malice seems neither to have affected the personality nor to influence the present actions of the girl she has brought up; again, the author seems to be experimenting with characterization in a vacuum. "Catharine" is, finally, a kind of grab-bag of attractive bits and pieces, of characters like the heroine and her aunt, of very tentative approaches to the perennial situation of the novels, the spirited middle-class girl in search of honorable marriage; a collection of fragments which Jane Austen will have the time and skill to sort and organize later.

"Lesley Castle" contains Jane Austen's first independently achieved character: Charlotte Lutterell. In her first letter,

Charlotte appears complete—gossipy, complacent, house-wifely, with all her affectionate and sensitive impulses smoth-ered in an overriding obsession about food. Having prepared all the food for her sister Eloisa's wedding, she learns that the bridegroom has been injured in a fall and may be dying:

> "Good God! (said I) you dont say so? Why what in the name of Heaven will become of all the Victuals! We shall never be able to eat it while it is good. However, we'll call in the Surgeon to help us. I shall be able to manage the Sirloin myself, my Mother will eat the soup, and You and the Doctor must finish the rest." Here I was interrupted, by seeing my poor Sister fall down to appearance Lifeless upon one of the Chests, where we keep our Table linen. (LF 50)

In her next letter, Charlotte informs her correspondent, Mar-garet Lesley:

> . . . we have every reason to imagine our pantry is by this time nearly cleared, as we left particular orders with the servants to eat as hard as they possibly could. . . . We brought a cold Pigeon pye, a cold turkey, a cold tongue, and half a dozen Jellies with us, which we were lucky enough with the help of our Landlady, her husband, and their three children, to get rid of, in less than two days after our arrival. Poor Eloisa is still . . . very indifferent in Health and Spirits . . . (LF 57)

At Bristol, she meets Mr. and Mrs. Marlowe, with whom she

> . . . spent a very pleasant Day, and had a very good Dinner, tho' to be sure the Veal was terribly underdone, and the Curry had no seasoning. I could not help wishing all dinner-time that I had been at dressing it—. (LF 59)

She contemplates a trip to London:

> I always longed particularly to go to Vaux-hall, to see whether the cold Beef there is cut so thin as it is reported . . . (LF 68)

In the meantime, keeping herself "cool as a cream-cheese," (LF 69) she introduces us to her sister, Eloisa, and mediates obtusely between the snobbish, mercenary Lesley girls and their equally snobbish and mercenary young step-mother.

Sir George Lesley, at fifty-seven still "the Beau, the flighty stripling, the gay Lad, and sprightly Youngster," (LF 47) reads like a first outline of Sir Walter Elliot. His wife, Lady Susan, even more strikingly resembles the later, full-length

Lady Susan,[33] in her spontaneous malice, in her resourceful exploitation of propriety:

> Matilda and Margaret Lesley are two great, tall, out of the way, over-grown girls. . . . They will do very well as foils to myself, so I have invited them to accompany me to London. . . . Besides these two fair Damsels, I found a little humoured Brat, who I beleive is some relation to them, they told me who she was, and gave me a long rigmerole story of her father and a Miss *Somebody* which I have entirely forgot. I hate scandal and detest Children. (LF 62f.)

In "Lesley Castle," Jane Austen establishes for the first time the full atmosphere of a hard, pushing, materialist, feminine world, with all its energies drained into the crucial business of courtship and marriage, or into housewifery, that plausible facsimile of marriage. This much she can project and treat ironically with no fear of involvement.

How, then, does Jane Austen come to present the foil to this world: the character of sensibility no less, treated seriously this time, Eloisa Lutterell? The fact is that Jane Austen never takes any chances with Eloisa in her role as foil. As long as Eloisa is concerned with her lover, we observe her sensibility only at second hand. Toward the end of the story, when Eloisa expresses her feelings directly in her letter to Mrs. Marlowe, these feelings, far from approaching unregulated personal areas, are assimilated—as it must have seemed to the young author—to a wholly explicit social and literary convention; the convention of feminine friendship. So Eloisa writes:

> . . . to have some kind and compassionate Freind who might listen to my sorrows without endeavouring to console me was what I had for some time wished for, when our acquaintance with you, the intimacy which followed it and the particular affectionate attention you paid me almost from the first, caused

[33] Jane Austen's thrift with names, like her characteristic economy of means in subject, situation, and character, is retrospectively obvious in the *juvenilia*, where names familiar in the novels continually appear, often attached to similar characters: Musgrove, Dashwood, Crawford, Willoughby (a faithless lover); the recurring feminine names of Charlotte, Elizabeth, Elinor, Emma, Fanny. (For a critical hypothesis that finds in this economy the key to Jane Austen's methods of composition, see Appendix II.) Interestingly, *Laura and Augustus* mentions two actors named Yates and Crawford (I, 109), and may therefore have maintained a feeble echo in Jane Austen's imagination as late as the theater scenes of *Mansfield Park*.

me to entertain the flattering Idea of those attentions being improved on a closer acquaintance into a Freindship which, if you were what my wishes formed you would be the greatest Happiness I could be capable of enjoying. (LF 72f.)

To which Mrs. Marlowe replies that she intends to fill her letters

... with such lively Wit and enlivening Humour as shall even provoke a smile in the sweet but sorrowfull countenance of my Eloisa.

... I have met your sisters three freinds Lady Lesley and her Daughters, twice in Public since I have been here. . . . But tho' one may be majestic and the other lively, yet the faces of neither possess that Bewitching sweetness of my Eloisas, which her present languor is so far from diminishing. (LF 74f.)

In this gush of irrelevant sentiment, in the abrupt anonymity and adolescent flatness of the style, we are reminded that wise ironic young girls who deride sexual passion may nevertheless dote on other girls; that, moreover, such strong emotional ties as the one between Eloisa and Mrs. Marlowe, or as Emma's infatuation with Harriet, have always been considered safe and conventional in bourgeois society, and certainly unsuggestive of the direct physical commitment of sexual love.

Jane Austen's deflection, here as elsewhere in the *juvenilia*, is away from unmediated contact toward convention. The difference is, not in motive, but in effect. When she examines convention ironically, she produces a sharp, brilliant picture of a limited world, as in "Love and Freindship." When she simply accepts convention—the convention of feminine friendship,[34] for example—we get the collapse of "Lesley Castle" into a pool of self-delusive school-girl yearning (as later the convention of bourgeois morality will warp and shatter the structure of *Mansfield Park*). In either case, she is steadily wary, she must keep her distance from the threat of contact, above all from the ultimate commitment of sex. It is no accident that whenever social maneuvering ceases and lovers must come face to face in a moment of love, Jane Austen makes a joke—as with Emma: "What did she say? Just what a lady

[34] In *Emma*, on the other hand, Jane Austen does not accept this convention; she examines it critically and ironically, as it influences the behavior of two clearly defined characters.

First Ed

Mudrick, Marvin

Jane Austen Irony As Defense

and Discovery

N. Jersey Princeton Univ Press 1952

Fine 5½ x 8½ 267 pp

ought"—or happens to be elsewhere (quite contrary to the literary practice of her age): the conventions of courtship and marriage are here too close to the relations they formalize. Short of this point, however, the conventions may safely be accepted by the citizen or examined by the ironist. Jane Austen prefers to examine. Here too compulsion becomes art: the bourgeois conventions of courtship and marriage, the only area in which her society will recognize a woman's knowledge, become for Jane Austen the characteristic, densely imagined object of her irony. Even in the *juvenilia* they move gradually into the foreground of her attention, until, in "The Three Sisters," Jane Austen gives up parody and concentrates upon them altogether.

Within their social limits, within the patterns of pursuit and capture short of personal involvement, "The Three Sisters" illuminates the conventions of courtship and marriage with a completeness of candor, truth, and irony unparalleled even in Jane Austen's own later work. It would seem that the bourgeois world is her world—and, more particularly, courtship and marriage are her province—because nowhere else, in books or in life, can she find such guarantees of distance, such durable incongruities between form and fact, between moral pretension and material reality, upon which to exercise and fulfill her irony. Irony, beginning as a defensive restriction of outlook, becomes the organizing principle of her art. In "The Three Sisters," the product, whatever its extra-aesthetic motives, is an acutely realized society; it is also, perhaps first of all from the young author's point of view, a society in which involvement is not only unnecessary, but impossible.

In "The Three Sisters," Jane Austen sets out to expose the materialist personality beneath the moral pretension. Her ironic device is to grant this personality an uninhibited articulateness, and so to establish its incongruity with the implied and familiar moral form. Mary Stanhope writes to her friend Fanny:

> I am the happiest creature in the World, for I have received an offer of marriage from Mr Watts. It is the first I have ever had & I hardly know how to value it enough. How

31

I will triumph over the Duttons! . . . He is quite an old Man, about two & thirty, very plain, *so* plain that I cannot bear to look at him. He is extremely disagreable & I hate him more than any body else in the world. He has a large fortune & will make great Settlements on me; but then he is very healthy. In short I do not know what to do. If I refuse him he as good as told me that he should offer himself to Sophia and if *she* refused him to Georgiana, & I could not bear to have either of them married before me. . . . I believe I shall have him. It will be such a triumph to be married before Sophy, Georgiana & the Duttons; And he promised to have a new Carriage on the occasion . . . (vf 104ff.)

In her next letter, still undecided about her answer, Mary is questioned by her mother:

"Ah! I know what you mean; (said I) That old fool Mr Watts has told you all about it, tho' I bid him not. However you shant force me to have him if I don't like it."

"I am not going to force you Child, but only want to know what your resolution is with regard to his Proposals, & to insist upon your making up your mind one way or t'other, that if *you* dont accept him *Sophy* may."

"But will Sophy marry him Mama if he offers to her?"

"Most likely, Why should not she? If however she does not choose it, then Georgiana must, for I am determined not to let such an opportunity escape of settling one of my Daughters so advantageously . . ." The only thing I can think of my dear Fanny is to ask Sophy & Georgiana whether they would have him were he to make proposals to them, & if they say they would not I am resolved to refuse him too, for I hate him more than you can imagine. (vf 1007ff.)

Mary's sister Georgiana, a more prudent and rational materialist, writes to a friend that neither she nor Sophy

. . . attempted to alter my Mother's resolution, which I am sorry to say is generally more strictly kept than rationally formed. (vf 111)

By pretending to favor Mr. Watts themselves, Georgiana and Sophy persuade Mary to assert her priority:

In short my scheme took & Mary is resolved to do *that* to prevent our supposed happiness which she would not have done to ensure it in reality. Yet after all my Heart cannot acquit me & Sophy is even more scrupulous. (vf 115)

Even in repentance Georgiana justifies herself by cutting through to the materialist base of bourgeois morality:

> Consider it well over. Mary will have real pleasure in being a married Woman, & able to chaprone us, which she certainly shall do, for I think myself bound to contribute as much as possible to her happiness in a State I have made her choose. (VF 115f.)

Mr. Watts, as Georgiana records him, believes in turning up all the cards:

> "Fine weather Ladies." Then turning to Mary, "Well Miss Stanhope I hope you have *at last* settled the Matter in your own mind; & will be so good as to let me know whether you will condescend to marry me or not."
>
> "I think Sir (said Mary) You might have asked in a genteeler way than that. I do not know whether I *shall* have you if you behave so odd."
>
> "Mary!" (said my Mother) "Well Mama if he will be so cross. . . ."
>
> "Hush, hush, Mary, you shall not be rude to Mr Watts."
>
> "Pray Madam do not lay any restraint on Miss Stanhope by obliging her to be civil. If she does not choose to accept my hand, I can offer it else where, for . . . it is equally the same to me which I marry of the three." Was there ever such a Wretch! Sophy reddened with anger, & I felt *so* spiteful! (VF 117f.)

They object, of course, not to his opinion, but to the impropriety of expressing it in "polite" society.

After Mary announces a list of her material requirements in marriage, Mrs. Stanhope comments:

> "This is all very reasonable Mr Watts for my Daughter to expect."
>
> "And it is very reasonable Mrs Stanhope that your Daughter should be disappointed." (VF 119)

Mary's expectations continuing to be high, Mr. Watts turns to Sophy,

> ". . . who perhaps may not have raised her's so much."
>
> "You are mistaken Sir in supposing so, (said Sophy) for tho' they may not be exactly in the same Line, yet my expectations are to the full as high as my Sister's; for I expect my Husband to be good tempered & Chearful to consult my Happiness in all his Actions, & to love me with Constancy & Sincerity."

> Mr Watts stared. "These are very odd Ideas truly young Lady. You had better discard them before you marry, or you will be obliged to do it afterwards." (VF 120f.)

Finally, however, he and Mary are reconciled and the marriage settlement is made.

> As soon as he was gone Mary exclaimed "Thank Heaven! he's off at last; how I do hate him!" (VF 123)

To spread the news of her triumph, Mary visits the Duttons with her sisters:

> "You must know Mr Watts is very much in love with me, so that it is quite a match of affection on his side."
> "Not on his only, I suppose" said Kitty.
> "Oh! where there is so much Love on one side there is no occasion for it on the other. However I do not much dislike him tho' he is very plain to be sure."
> Mr Brudenell stared, the Miss Duttons laughed & Sophy & I were heartily ashamed of our Sister. (VF 126)

Again the objection is to expressing such an opinion in company: it is Mr. Watts's rudeness and Mary's naïveté, not their complete amorality, that occasion the younger and politer sisters' shame. Nor should social man stoop from his spectator's discreet eminence to bait vulgarity, as Mr. Brudenell baits Mary:

> He kept his Countenance extremely well, yet it was easy to see that it was with difficulty he kept it. At length however he seemed fatigued and Disgusted with her ridiculous Conversation, as he turned from her to us, & spoke but little to her for about half an hour before we left Stoneham. As soon as we were out of the House we all joined in praising the Person & Manners of Mr. Brudenell. (VF 128)

And the story stops short back at home, where, after another fierce quarrel, Mary and Mr. Watts make another truce and return to their elaborate plans for the wedding.

In such a society, where all relationships are transactions and marriage the most ill-tempered transaction of all, where the only extricable ideal is discretion, it is easy to find the justification of one's ironic reserve, to pride oneself on remaining a spectator, to observe at a distance, to examine without commitment. Making allowance for Mary Russell Mitford's dash of malice, we have evidence that Jane Austen appeared in this role, at least in her spinsterhood, to a personal acquaintance:

> . . . a friend of mine, who visits her now, says that she has stiffened into the most perpendicular, precise, taciturn piece of "single blessedness" that ever existed, and that, till *Pride and Prejudice* showed what a precious gem was hidden in that unbending case, she was no more regarded in society than a poker or a fire-screen, or any other thin upright piece of wood or iron that fills its corner in peace and quietness. The case is very different now; she is still a poker—but a poker of whom every one is afraid. It must be confessed that this silent observation from such an observer is rather formidable . . . a wit, a delineator of character, who does not talk, is terrific indeed![35]

The stiff silence was not, of course, characteristic of her in her youth or with her family, that congenial audience for incongruities;[36] but the perpetual critical observation must always have been. We have not only the impression of Miss Mitford's friend in 1815, but the continuous testimony of Jane Austen's letters and her work—the most convincing testimony, perhaps, in the *juvenilia*, written to be shared only with her family and stored away almost a quarter century before.

Whether her target is *Laura and Augustus* or bourgeois convention, the illusionary world or the real one, she keeps her distance and makes no final, personal choice. Examining the lachrymose novel (to which she returned, in the security of fame and with hilarious effect, as late as 1816[37]) or turning

[35] R. B. Johnson (ed.), *The Letters of Mary Russell Mitford*, New York, 1925, 127 (Letter to Sir William Elford, April 3, 1815). The Janeites triumphantly dismiss this portrait by quoting Miss Mitford's admission that it came from a woman whose family was at law with Jane Austen's brother. My interest is less in its strict authenticity than in its detailed external presentation of an attitude demonstrably central and implicit in Jane Austen's work.

[36] "The family was the unit within which her heart had liberty of choice; friends, neighbours, plays and fame were all objects to be picked up in the course of a flight outside and brought back to the nest for examination. They often laughed over the alien trophies, for they were a hard humorous family." E. M. Forster, *Abinger Harvest*, New York, 1936, 164.

[37] In the "Plan of a Novel," inspired by the impermeable fatuity of the Rev. J. S. Clarke, librarian to the Prince Regent. J. Austen, *Plan of a Novel and Other Notes*, ed. R. W. Chapman, Oxford, 1926: which reprints, among other valuable Austeniana, the complete correspondence between Mr. Clarke and Jane Austen.

to her own middle class, she is from the beginning a spectator; and it is this hard compelled detachment, this conscious shying from emotion, of which her standard admirers are quite ignorant in marveling at the "mildness" and "generosity" of her tone, and which alienates her romantically minded critics, who find her "intolerably sensible,"[38] "vulgar" and "sterile,"[39] who complain of her "triviality"[40] or her "lack of passion"[41] or her quaintness"[42]; who, like Herbert Read, yearn for some apocalyptic death scene in the Heathcliff style.

We may not like Jane Austen's defects and evasions of personality, we may even refuse to recognize them; but the artist, or rather the art, is here to be judged. The fact remains that close observation without sympathy, common sense without tenderness, densely imagined representation without passion may not limit the comic novelist at all, may indeed be the ideal instruments for penetrating the polished surface of the bourgeois world to its unyielding material base. In her *juvenilia* Jane Austen indicates, as in her novels she will prove, that these instruments, far from limiting her to a Burneyan reflection of manners, can reconstitute the whole cold, anxious atmosphere in which the middle class lives and breathes. The first step she must take, however, is to cut off the bourgeois escape, to dispose of all the feverish daydreams (and the germ of feeling that infects them) in which the middle class —especially its unoccupied women—tries guiltily to deny itself. This is the step that Jane Austen takes in the *juvenilia*, in *Northanger Abbey*, and—as a final, if a less confident, morally reinforced tidying-up—in *Sense and Sensibility*.

[38] H. W. Garrod, "Jane Austen: A Depreciation," *Essays by Divers Hands*, London, 1928, VIII, 28.

[39] R. W. Emerson, *Journals of Ralph Waldo Emerson*, Boston, 1913, IX, 336.

[40] A. Meynell, *The Second Person Singular and Other Essays*, Oxford, 1922, 63.

[41] Charlotte Brontë, in C. Shorter, *The Brontës: Life and Letters*, New York, 1908, II, 127f.

[42] H. Read, *English Prose Style*, London, 1932, 120n.

CHAPTER II

THE LITERARY PRETEXT CONTINUED:
IRONY *VERSUS* GOTHICISM

NORTHANGER ABBEY

IRONY, Jane Austen's characteristic response to that curious alien world beyond Steventon, may have turned her toward the eighteenth-century novel as toward a particularly favorable climate for incongruity. Yet it will not account for the fact that she found herself altogether and immediately at home in the novel. Irony is an attitude and an instrument, it brings into view and analyzes; but it does not create or predetermine a medium.

Every medium—even, perhaps above all, the novel, in its often fatally deceptive resemblance to casual, at any rate personal and unfocused, intelligent observation—requires its own special talents; and, for the novel, Jane Austen had these precociously also. Her special talent for thematic narrative is obvious in "Love and Freindship," however limited by the demands of parody; still more, and more variously, in "The Three Sisters." Her talent for recasting and organizing personality in potential depth and development is just as obvious in the barely sketched figures of "Lesley Castle" and "The Three Sisters," and in the remarkable vignette (LF 109ff.) that introduces Lady Greville, first of Jane Austen's predatory female aristocrats. Her irony, as early as in her *juvenilia*, is already operating not only upon the novel, but within the special conditions of the novel.

By 1794, when *The Mysteries of Udolpho* captured the reading public for Mrs. Radcliffe and the Gothic novel, Jane Austen had at least four years of authorship behind her. Having cleared away the lachrymose debris, and in the process grown aware and confident of her literary powers,[1] she may

---

[1] The independent experimentation of the later *juvenilia*, and their evolution toward serious novelistic relationships, seem to reflect Jane Austen's growing confidence in her ability to handle the medium whose extravagances she is burlesquing. Besides, her family audience must always have been

have felt that simple parody, even of so promising and fresh a target as the Gothic novel, was too restrictive for her now; that striking out in novels of her own, which would treat the familiar, verifiable, renewable world, was a more stimulating prospect, for the time being at least. In the next three years, at any rate, she turned from her close preoccupation with parody and wrote two full-length domestic novels.[2]

Meanwhile, however, the Gothic enthusiasm had mounted to a fury,[3] the temptation to dismantle became too strong for the ironist; and *Northanger Abbey* was the result. Yet her talents could no longer be channeled into simple parody. This last formidable assault of hers on the illusionary world could not be as direct and single-minded as that of "Love and Freindship" because the actual world could no longer be implicit or fragmentary as in her burlesques: she had already explored it and staked it out, not just socially as in her letters but artistically also, and she could not or would not exclude it from the focus of attention. *Northanger Abbey*—unlike "Love and Freindship"—is as much domestic novel as parody. Irony overtly juxtaposes the Gothic and the bourgeois worlds, and allows them to comment on each other. The ironic contrast, the juxtaposition of these two sets of values is, in fact, so overt and extensive that the formal unity of the novel depends on

---

appreciative and encouraging: as early as 1797, her father tried to get published, at his own expense if necessary, "a manuscript novel, comprising 3 vols., about the length of Miss Burney's 'Evelina' " (W. and R. A. Austen-Leigh, *Jane Austen: Her Life and Letters*, London, 1913, 97): probably *First Impressions* (see following note).

[2] About these we know, besides that they were written in letters, that their names were *Elinor and Marianne* (which, at least in its final incarnation and probably more markedly in its first, still took off from parody and retained notable parodic elements) and *First Impressions*, that the latter was offered for publication (see preceding note), and that they were later very thoroughly revised into, respectively, *Sense and Sensibility* and *Pride and Prejudice*. *Elinor and Marianne* was written about 1795; *First Impressions* was begun in October 1796 and finished in August 1797. (*Ibid.*, 96.)

[3] Michael Sadleir, having examined the file of catalogues of the Minerva Library, presents statistics which demonstrate that Gothic novels, fairly popular before *The Mysteries of Udolpho* was published but still far outnumbered by novels of sentiment and sensibility, flooded the market in the latter half of the 1790's. (M. Sadleir in J. Austen, *Northanger Abbey*, London, 1930, xiv.)

the author's success in maintaining each one as a distinct, continuous, and self-consistent commentary on the other.

In "Love and Freindship," Jane Austen parodied the lachrymose novel by reproducing its characters and situations and then allowing them both to overreach themselves into absurdity: the action of the parody was single and internal, with no reference but an implicit and general one to the actual world. In *Northanger Abbey*, for the maturing and more conscious artist, the problem of parody has become far more complex.[4] The parody of a novel must itself be a novel: the novelist who shows what is artistically irrelevant and improbable must at the same time show what is relevant and probable. To meet this new standard in *Northanger Abbey*, Jane Austen discards the central technique of "Love and Freindship." Instead of reproducing the Gothic types of character and situation, she presents their anti-types in the actual world, and organizes these into a domestic narrative that parallels or intersects, and at all points is intended to invalidate, the Gothic narrative to which it diligently corresponds. The problem is to write simultaneously a Gothic novel and a realistic novel, and to gain and keep the reader's acceptance of the latter while proving that the former is false and absurd.[5]

It is important to note, at this point, the particular quality and direction of the Gothic world that Jane Austen has under scrutiny in *Northanger Abbey*. Her "Gothicism" derives, not from the stagey sensuality and diabolism of M. G. Lewis's *The*

[4] As it was for Fielding in *Joseph Andrews*; though through a large part of his novel he solved the problem by ignoring it—that is, by dropping parody altogether in favor of his own story.

[5] The implication that *Northanger Abbey* is a work of transition between Jane Austen's youthful parody and her first domestic novels, *Sense and Sensibility* and *Pride and Prejudice*—though these were in first draft earlier (W. and R. A. Austen-Leigh, *op.cit.*, 96)—must be considered. We have evidence that the latter two were thoroughly revised shortly before publication (in 1811 and 1812, respectively). According to Jane Austen's own note, *Northanger Abbey* was probably revised as late as 1803 (NA 12): but there is no evidence of any later revision. It is worth pointing out that the latest Gothic novel mentioned in Isabella's list (NA 40) was published in 1798. In any case, parody—especially of so minutely regulated a form as the Radcliffean novel—imposes so many rigid requirements that the artist's tendency to revise must be much impeded. As they stand, *Northanger Abbey* seems clearly the earliest of the full-length novels: by internal evidence as well, I hope to demonstrate.

Monk,[6] but from that obvious offshoot of the lachrymose novel —the hybrid form which Mrs. Radcliffe developed to its height of effectiveness and popularity, and which had been earlier cultivated in such works as Sophia Lee's *The Recess* (1785) and Charlotte Smith's *Celestine* (1791). In these novels, sensibility is still the index of virtue and the motive of action. The difference is that mere extravagances of pathos, poverty, suffering, and parental misunderstanding are replaced by strangeness and terror—a change of atmosphere rather than of character or motive. For the reader, the only difference is that the gasp replaces the tear as the measurable unit of response. So it is not surprising to meet old friends from the lachrymose novel: the tyrannical father, the importunate and unscrupulous suitor, the hero and heroine of sensibility and of mysterious but noble birth, the confidante (that relic of the epistolary novel), the chaperone—all of them, however, having taken on the dismal coloration of their new surroundings.

Against this world, Jane Austen sets up her own domestic anti-types. As in the Radcliffean novel, the heroine's consciousness, or sensibility, is the center of action; but in *Northanger Abbey* the heroine's function is doubled with the doubling of the action. There is irony even in its internal point of view: in the fact that its two worlds must originate, converge, and be finally discriminated in the limited consciousness of that most ingenuous and domestic heroine, Catherine Morland. The double burden seems almost too much for so lightweight a mind.

Of course, the author helps. At the outset, nobody but the author knows that Catherine is a potential Gothic heroine:

> No one who had ever seen Catherine Morland in her infancy, would have supposed her born to be a heroine. Her situa-

[6] Published in 1796, and followed by a library of blood-and-sin novels culminating in C. R. Maturin's *Melmoth the Wanderer* (1820) and—with no appreciable change of medium—in Byron's dramas. Jane Austen was quite aware of this form: see the list of novels which Isabella urges Catherine to read (NA 40), and which Michael Sadleir summarizes and comments upon in his excellent essay on eighteenth-century Gothicism: *The Northanger Novels*, The English Association, Pamphlet No. 68, Oxford, 1927; but she never handled it, ironically or otherwise. It was not nearly so easy to handle with ironic detachment as the more ladylike variety of Gothic novel.

tion in life, the character of her father and mother, her own person and disposition, were all equally against her. Her father was a clergyman, without being neglected, or poor, and a very respectable man, though his name was Richard[7]—and he had never been handsome. He had a considerable independence, besides two good livings—and he was not in the least addicted to locking up his daughters. (NA 13)

Moreover, Catherine "had a thin awkward figure, a sallow skin without colour, dark lank hair, and strong features." (NA 13) Nor are her abilities those of a heroine:

> She never could learn or understand anything before she was taught; and sometimes not even then, for she was often inattentive, and occasionally stupid. (NA 14)

> The day which dismissed the music-master was one of the happiest of Catherine's life. Her taste for drawing was not superior; though whenever she could obtain the outside of a letter from her mother, or seize upon any other odd piece of paper, she did what she could in that way, by drawing houses and trees, hens and chickens, all very much like one another.[8] (NA 14)

As she grows up and becomes "almost pretty," she begins to occupy, without yet being aware of, her role:

> . . . from fifteen to seventeen she was in training for a heroine; she read all such works as heroines must read to supply their memories with those quotations which are so serviceable and so soothing in the vicissitudes of their eventful lives.[9] (NA 15)

Unfortunately,

> She had reached the age of seventeen, without having seen one amiable youth who could call forth her sensibility; without having inspired one real passion, and without having excited even any admiration but what was very moderate and very transient.

[7] Another indication that *Northanger Abbey* is in detail, as well as in spirit, the earliest of the novels, the closest to the family-diversion atmosphere of the *juvenilia*. The name "Richard" was a private family joke: "Mr. Richard Harvey's match is put off till he has got a Better Christian name, of which he has great Hopes. Mr. Children's two Sons are both going to be married, John & George—. They are to have one wife between them; a Miss Holwell, who belongs to the Black Hole at Calcutta." (LI 15, 15 Sept. 1796).

[8] Miss Lascelles has pointed out that this whole introduction of Catherine Morland is a close parody of Charlotte Smith's *Emmeline, The Orphan of the Castle* (1788), that midway marker between the lachrymose and the Gothic novels. M. Lascelles, *Jane Austen and Her Art*, Oxford, 1939, 60.

[9] One of the most conspicuous symptoms of the lachrymose and Gothic novels is their rash of portentous quotations: invariably on the title-page, and abundantly scattered through the text.

This was strange indeed! But strange things may be generally accounted for if their cause be fairly searched out. There was not one lord in the neighbourhood; no—not even a baronet. There was not one family among their acquaintance who had reared and supported a boy accidentally found at their door—not one young man whose origin was unknown. Her father had no ward, and the squire of the parish no children. (NA 16)

Catherine's luck changes when Mr. and Mrs. Allen, a childless couple in the village, invite her to accompany them to Bath. Even now, Mrs. Morland fails to act as a heroine's mother should:

> Cautions against the violence of such noblemen and baronets as delight in forcing young ladies away to some remote farmhouse, must, at such a moment, relieve the fulness of her heart. Who would not think so? But Mrs. Morland knew so little of lords and baronets, that she entertained no notion of their general mischievousness, and was wholly unsuspicious of danger to her daughter from their machinations. (NA 18)

So the party leaves: and Catherine, entrusted to the care of Mrs. Allen, happily anticipates the excitements of a resort.

Jane Austen never lets us doubt her dual intention in the narrative. She places before us both what a character should be if he were to conform to the Gothic mode, and what he really is. As long as Catherine, still uninstructed by Isabella, remains incapable of manufacturing her own illusionary world to offset the real one, the author will manufacture it for her. Here, for example, is what Mrs. Allen should be:

> It is now expedient to give some description of Mrs. Allen, that the reader may be able to judge, in what manner her actions will hereafter tend to promote the general distress of the work, and how she will, probably, contribute to reduce poor Catherine to all the desperate wretchedness of which a last volume is capable—whether by her imprudence, vulgarity, or jealousy—whether by interrupting her letters, ruining her character, or turning her out of doors.[10] (NA 19f.)

And here is what she is:

---

[10] In this description of a wicked chaperone, which could apply pretty closely to, say, Mrs. Jewkes in *Pamela*, the continuity of sentimental impetus in the eighteenth-century novel—from Richardson through the lachrymose novelists to Mrs. Radcliffe—is clear enough. The sentimental types remain strikingly constant, though their milieu becomes progressively remote and improbable.

. . . one of that numerous class of females, whose society can raise no other emotion than surprise at there being any man in the world who could like them well enough to marry them. She had neither beauty, genius, accomplishment, nor manner. The air of a gentlewoman, a great deal of quiet, inactive good temper, and a trifling turn of mind, were all that could account for her being the choice of a sensible, intelligent man, like Mr. Allen. (NA 20)

Unlike the Gothic chaperone, she is neither wicked nor vigilant. She is content to let Catherine walk and visit where she pleases, to bring her to balls, and always to sit placidly by, whether later with a gossipy friend, or at first serenely deploring the fact that Catherine has not been asked to dance and so helping the author (for Catherine is still unaware of her role in the parallel story) to define the Gothic convention that the hero and heroine, drawn toward each other by a natural affinity, scorn so artificial a method as the formal introduction.

Nevertheless, this is the method by which Catherine meets Henry Tilney: they are introduced by the master of ceremonies at the ballroom. Henry is not even of mysterious birth or vocation. Mr. Allen finds out before the evening is ended that he is a clergyman, and "of a very respectable family in Gloucestershire." (NA 30) And it soon becomes apparent not only that Henry fancies himself as an anti-hero, but that he will take over a large part of what has been up till now the author's function: to provide a non-committal running ironic commentary on the hypocrisy of social conventions and the incredibility of the literary conventions that parallel them. Not only is Henry within the two actions of the story, but he becomes our chief observer and interpreter of both.

Henry prides himself on his worldliness and his lack of sentimentality; and—like his author—he expresses either only through irony. Anything falsely emotional, like social conversation, inspires him to burlesque:

. . . forming his features into a set smile, and affectedly softening his voice, he added, with a simpering air, "Have you been long in Bath, madam?"

"About a week, sir," replied Catherine, trying not to laugh.

"Really!" with affected astonishment.

"Why should you be surprised, sir?"

"Why, indeed!" said he, in his natural tone—"but some emotion must appear to be raised by your reply, and surprize is more easily assumed, and not less reasonable than any other. . . ." (NA 26)

Later on, after Catherine has been thoroughly indoctrinated by Isabella and her own reading into the Gothic world, he will tease her with a minutely detailed burlesque on its improbabilities. In the meantime, he is cocksurely articulate about the wearing qualities of women's clothes and of their letters, about imprecision of language, about dancing and marriage, about the beauties of landscape. He is always informed and confident, and almost always flippant to the verge of, but saved by a lively irony from, cynicism. His role in Catherine's unsentimental education is clear. To become her chief mentor, all he needs beyond his personality is to be attracted by her; and Jane Austen herself, having made Catherine impeccably ignorant, guarantees that much:

> . . . in justice to men . . . though to the larger and more trifling part of the sex, imbecility in females is a great enhancement of their personal charms, there is a portion of them too reasonable and too well informed themselves to desire any thing more in woman than ignorance. (NA 111)

It is Isabella Thorpe, however, who first explicitly introduces the Gothic theme. Isabella parades herself as a heroine; and Catherine, dazzled, is quite willing to play the confidante to this paragon of beauty and sensibility:

> The progress of the friendship between Catherine and Isabella was quick as its beginning had been warm, and they passed so rapidly through every gradation of increasing tenderness, that there was shortly no fresh proof of it to be given to their friends or themselves. They called each other by their Christian name, were always arm in arm when they walked, pinned up each other's train for the dance, and were not to be divided in the set; and if a rainy morning deprived them of other enjoyments, they were still resolute in meeting in defiance of wet and dirt, and shut themselves up, to read novels together. (NA 36f.)

The Mysteries of Udolpho, appropriately, is the first novel that Isabella brings Catherine to read; and she promises her also *The Italian* and seven other Gothic romances that she names.[11] Plunged into all this self-conscious heroism, Catherine has no difficulty in accepting Isabella's protestations of affection, altruism, and constancy:

> ". . . I wish you knew Miss Andrews, you would be delighted with her. She is netting herself the sweetest cloak you can conceive. I think her as beautiful as an angel, and I am so vexed with the men for not admiring her! I scold them all amazingly about it."
>
> "Scold them! Do you scold them for not admiring her?"
>
> "Yes, that I do. There is nothing I would not do for those who are really my friends. I have no notion of loving people by halves, it is not my nature. My attachments are always excessively strong. I told Capt. Hunt at one of our assemblies this winter, that if he was to tease me all night, I would not dance with him, unless he would allow Miss Andrews to be as beautiful as an angel . . . ." (NA 40)

Catherine is moving steadily toward the Gothic world. Not only has she read the right books, but she has met her own particular hero (who, having left Bath "mysteriously," can be mooned over) and an authentic heroine. She has many occasions to match her sensibility with Isabella's, and to find it adequate:

> . . . they followed their chaperons, arm in arm, into the ballroom, whispering to each other whenever a thought occurred and supplying the place of many ideas by a squeeze of the hand or a smile of affection. (NA 52)

Her ingenuousness and ignorance have prevented her from suspecting Isabella's indefatigable coquetry, her malice toward women, her large foolish generalizations about men. Of course, Catherine does not yet imagine that she—not Isabella—has been destined for the role of heroine; even now that the atmosphere of literary sensibility is strongly established, she needs at least a villain or two, and a recognizable Gothic setting, to precipitate her into self-delusion.

It is typical of the explicitly realistic ground of Jane Austen's parody in *Northanger Abbey* that Catherine seems, not an hallucinated puppet,[12] but a credibly impressionable

---

[11] M. Sadleir (*op.cit.*) demonstrates how representative these romances are of the leading Gothic trends.

[12] Like the heroines of other burlesque novels of the late eighteenth century. See Miss Lascelles' summary, *op.cit.*, 16f.

and ingenuous young girl, with enough common sense to require at least a show of evidence before she draws the Gothic conclusions. Catherine finds her villains, not simply because she is looking for them, but because the author finds villains in actual life and allows her a few. For all the malice, hypocrisy, treachery, and general wickedness at Udolpho, Jane Austen finds very satisfactory counterparts at Bath. What her irony does here, as elsewhere, is to diminish scale, to puncture the grandiose pretensions of the Gothic villains, to demonstrate what villainy is like when transferred to the everyday, middle-class, social world. In this juxtaposition of Gothic type and actual anti-type, the latter is undeniably villainous also: only, like the rest of the actual world, on a much smaller and more disposable scale. The ironist finds no iniquity at Bath, but there is enough contemptibleness and to spare.

Consider John Thorpe, Jane Austen's anti-type for the unwelcome suitor. Certainly, he is importunate and unscrupulous enough to carry the Gothic role; but there is nothing sinister about him. He is simply exasperating, vulgar, rude, and foolish. The author is quick to put her own social tag on him:

> He . . . seemed fearful of being too handsome unless he wore the dress of a groom, and too much like a gentleman unless he were easy when he ought to be civil, and impudent when he might be allowed to be easy. (NA 45)

He cannot let off boasting of the quality of his possessions: the speed of his horse, the durability of his gig, his skill at billiards. One of his favorite epithets, which he applies to whomever he suspects of having money, is "rich as a Jew." (NA 63, 96) He has a relish for profanity and financial transactions:[13]

> "My horse! oh, d— it! I would not sell my horse for a hundred. . . ." (NA 47)
> ". . . He asked fifty guineas; I closed with him directly, threw down the money, and the carriage was mine." (NA 46)

All these traits prepare the reader, if not Catherine (she is,

[13] Jane Austen's only character who does. John Thorpe is, in fact, her only quite unmannerly character (unmannerly, that is, to a society becoming middle-class, reconciled to money but not to trade or to marketplace language). When she illustrates vulgarity later, she works it more subtly into the framework of manners, which are used as a defense, rather than violated, by the character.

naturally, prejudiced in favor of Isabella's brother), for Thorpe's villainy. Not that he abducts or tortures Catherine when she declines his attentions; he does not even connive with her father at marrying her against her will. His world and his talent are too limited for spectacular achievements; but he does as much mischief as he can.

He keeps forcing his presence and his garrulity on Catherine, in spite of her at first passive and later even obstinately active preference for other company. He has no scruple against lying to get her—or anyone else—to do or think as he wishes, and no feeling of guilt when caught in a lie. While Catherine is waiting to be visited by Henry and his sister, Thorpe tells her that he has seen them driving off elsewhere; later, when Catherine, driving with him, catches sight of them on their way to meet her, he is, in fact, only pleased with the success of his maneuver. His general offensiveness is so marked that Catherine herself, overawed at first by his continual, loud brashness and by his sister's authority, finds him tiring, and his hints at a proposal—her ingenuousness being reinforced by her reluctance to listen to him—comprehensible only as more rattling palaver. And finally—in accord with his function as anti-type to the villainous suitor—his boasting, his lying, his treachery, and his lack of scruple are all involved in his confidences to General Tilney, upon which the whole culminating Gothic adventure and its realistic aftermath depend.

The most interesting novelistic fact about all these characters is that—whatever else they may be—they are consistently, even rigidly, functional. They perform the special tasks of parody within a domestic setting, of action beside action: they behave as the author knows that bourgeois types behave, and in their behavior they suggest the corresponding Gothic types by being so different, by displaying the Gothic qualities reversed or contracted. Mrs. Allen, for example, is the Gothic chaperone reversed: Mrs. Allen all placid, submerged inertia and unconcern (a less well married Lady Bertram); the Gothic chaperone always deeply concerned, motivated—depending on whether the author needs her for a "good" or a "bad" character—either by an anxious propriety or by a busy malevolence. Isabella is the heroine's confidante reversed: sensibility into vulgarity, sympathy into egocentrism, chastity into man-chasing, thoughtfulness into frivolity. Thorpe, on the other hand, is the unwelcome suitor *contracted*: he too plagues the heroine and threatens her future happiness with his importunities, but his methods are ludicrously petty by comparison.

They are, then, consistently functional characters, and their function is to illustrate Jane Austen's double irony: that the Gothic world does not correspond to human nature as it may be seen at Bath; and that human nature as it may be seen at Bath is not necessarily more agreeable or more trustworthy than the Udolpho variety, though it *is* necessarily more limited. It remains to be considered whether these characters, or the rest, are more than functional, whether they go beyond merely illustrating the ironic intent of the novel.

One figure that seems more than merely functional is Henry Tilney. He is, of course, the Gothic hero reversed: he does not treat the heroine with solemn respect, he fails to fall in love with her at first sight, he does not even rescue her at any critical moment from a villain's clutches. Positively, however, he is witty, lively, talkative, didactic, and his common sense does rescue Catherine finally from delusion. He seems, in fact, the only perceptive person in the book; and he closely resembles, except for a few details of dress and appearance, the author herself.

This resemblance is more than superficial: his irritation with the use of words like "nice" and "amazing" to signify general approval of everything from looks to people, his defense of novel-reading, his delight in spinning out a worldly judgment or a circumstantial burlesque. Behind these characteristics, and uniting them all, is the impetus of irony, the unrelaxing wariness against a personal involvement.

Henry is constitutionally incapable of making a statement unqualified by irony. He can judiciously mock Catherine's opinion that history is a torment to little children:

"That little boys and girls should be tormented . . . is what no one at all acquainted with human nature in a civilized state can deny; but in behalf of our most distinguished historians, I must observe, that they might well be offended at being supposed to have no higher aim; and that by their method and style, they are perfectly well qualified to torment readers of the most advanced reason and mature time of life. I use the verb 'to torment,' as I observed to be your own method, instead of 'to instruct,' supposing them to be now admitted as synonimous." (NA 109)

In his eagerness to turn everything to ironic profit, he can even be unkind when his sister misunderstands Catherine's solemn announcement that "something very shocking indeed, will soon come out in London." (NA 112)

" . . . my stupid sister has mistaken all your clearest expressions. You talked of expected horrors in London—and instead of instantly conceiving, as any rational creature would have done, that such words could relate only to a circulating library, she immediately pictured to herself a mob of three thousand men assembling in St. George's Fields; the Bank attacked, the Tower threatened, the streets of London flowing with blood, a detachment of the 12th Light Dragoons, (the hope of the nation,) called up from Northampton to quell the insurgents, and the gallant Capt. Frederick Tilney, in the moment of charging at the head of his troop, knocked off his horse by a brickbat from an upper window. Forgive her stupidity. The fears of the sister have added to the weakness of the woman; but she is by no means a simpleton in general." (NA 113)

When his sister asks him to apologize, he replies:

"Miss Morland, I think very highly of the understanding of all the women in the world—especially of those—whoever they may be—with whom I happen to be in company."

"That is not enough. Be more serious."

"Miss Morland, no one can think more highly of the understanding of women than I do. In my opinion, nature has given them so much, that they never find it necessary to use more than half." (NA 113f.)

Henry Tilney is the willfully ironic and detached spectator as no one except the author herself is in any other of Jane Austen's novels. Whenever he speaks, he speaks from the outside, to amuse, to parry, to lead on, to instruct, to humble; never plainly and straightforwardly, or unwarily, to reveal or engage himself. Even when Catherine, obviously anxious, questions him about his brother's attentions to Isabella (who is now betrothed to her brother James), he can only put her off, reinforcing his irony with evasiveness, and relenting briefly into a final, false assurance that nothing is wrong. (NA 150ff.) As for the few times in the novel when, according to the exigencies of the plot, we must be made aware of his increasing affection for Catherine, he cannot speak except in irony (NA 132f., 206); and on the occasion of his visiting the Morlands' home to propose to Catherine—when irony seems inappropriate, besides, because of Catherine's recent indignities at the hands of his father—the author, wisely enough, keeps him silent, wrapped in a cloud of indirect expression and conventional novelistic explanations. The living Henry never made the trip at all.

To introduce this sort of spectator-character, especially into a novel like *Northanger Abbey*, is an obvious convenience for the novelist. In any novel, such a character may unify the action, and with the advantage over the author of being within it, by examining it totally. In an overtly double action like that of *Northanger Abbey*, since the novel's unity depends upon our sharp discrimination, simultaneously with our awareness of correspondence and symmetry, between two self-consistent worlds, a character like Henry Tilney—familiar with both worlds, and aware of all their correspondences and differences—helps to unify the novel from within, to fortify the author's own observations and implications, which are likely in themselves to have an air of imposition. In personal terms, moreover, Henry makes an ideal foil for Catherine: irony and straightforwardness, sophistication and naïveté, confidence and timidity, information and ignorance.

One disadvantage is that such a character, by his very superiority of awareness and insight, may in contrast make the other characters look too confined and predictable. He may damage or destroy the illusion of their personal freedom, may come to seem himself no more than an arbitrary self-projection by the author. The other characters may seem, not personal, but functional only, without will. In a combination of Gothic novel and domestic novel like *Northanger Abbey*, where the gallery of characters is obliged at the same time to illustrate one rigorously defined set of values and to suggest the other, such a failure of will becomes more probable yet.

It is not merely what Henry says and thinks about the other characters that makes us suspect him, but his position of relative immunity in an atmosphere contagious with irony. Jane Austen does make fun of his youthful pedantry from time to time, she lets him fall in love with Catherine out of gratitude for Catherine's attachment to him (NA 243), and out of a didactic delight in her ignorance; but that is the sum of the charges. Otherwise, he is allowed to know about as much as the author does, to pass similar judgments, to respond with a similarly persistent and inviolable irony toward all characters and events that come within his range. The effect of Henry's resemblance to the author is, finally, to make us wonder just how present the author is; or, rather, to strengthen our impression that she is present intrusively, in the need to assert her own non-commitment, and at the expense of the personal depth and independence of her characters.

There is, of course, besides this compulsion, the fact of her inexperience: among her large-scale works in the forms in which they survive,[14] *Northanger Abbey* is probably the earliest.[15] At any rate, *Northanger Abbey* has its share of the common literary property upon which even a novelist of genius is likely to draw in early work: characters like James Morland, who exists only to be deceived by Isabella; Eleanor Tilney, a wraith of female gentility hardly more substantial than Catherine's Gothic imaginings; Mr. Allen, who might as well have stayed home in Fullerton for all that we see or learn of him at Bath. This is the kind of failure to which the author is liable simply by being a novice, however precocious and brilliant, and more especially by undertaking so complex a scheme.

The other kind of failure in *Northanger Abbey* is peculiar to the author: a product of inexperience and compulsion at once. Jane Austen's compulsion toward irony persists throughout the novels until *Persuasion*, but she learns to accommodate

[14] Except for the revised chapters of *Persuasion* (J. Austen, *Two Chapters of Persuasion*, ed. R. W. Chapman, Oxford, 1926), no manuscript of the novels survives.
[15] For such evidence as there is, see above note 5.

it more and more skillfully to the requirements of her story. After *Northanger Abbey*, there are no all-knowing Henry Tilneys: the only privileged spectator is the author, and character and situation tend to establish and contain their own level of irony. In *Northanger Abbey*, however, the irony—always somewhat excessive for its material—is besides repeatedly expressed and spotlighted by the author from the outside. Jane Austen has yet neither the mature skill to direct wholly within the action of her novel, nor the social qualms to replace by bourgeois morality, her characteristic response of irony to all the phenomena she is willing to recognize. In *Northanger Abbey*, she cannot help intruding to assert her own detachment, not simply from society as in her letters, or from the illusionary world as in her youthful burlesques, but from the events and the people that she herself has created.

This enforced detachment justifies itself, with her pleasant characters, by denying them any depth or complexity of feeling; and, with her unpleasant ones, by denying them not only feeling but any favorable qualities at all. There is, of course, the thematic need of invalidating the Gothic world by a detached observation and exposure; but Jane Austen goes further and in her flippancy tends now and then to suspend our belief or interest in her domestic world as well. In *Northanger Abbey*, her irony is too often in excess of the immediate need.

We can never believe, for example, that Catherine or her troubles are of much moment because the author so deliberately makes light of them. This depreciation begins mildly enough, as part of the specific parody of romantic love. Catherine, having fallen in love, perversely fails to lose either appetite or sleep; on the contrary, her reaction takes the form of an

> . . . extraordinary hunger, and when that was appeased, changed into an earnest longing to be in bed; such was the extreme point of her distress; for when there she immediately fell into a sound sleep which lasted nine hours, and from which she awoke perfectly revived, in excellent spirits, with fresh hopes and fresh schemes. (NA 60)

After a while, however, Jane Austen's early remark that Catherine is quite ignorant and unworldly seems as much an excuse for the author's condescension as a foreshadowing of the character's behavior. Parody tends here to become an affirmation of superiority. Catherine is never allowed to display a sensitivity that might engage our sympathy or transcend her author's ironic vigilance. She fails to measure up, not only to the idea of a Gothic heroine, but even to our idea of an interesting person. Unrelieved as it is, her naïveté begins to resemble dullness. She is too easily hoodwinked by Isabella. Even the impossible Mr. Thorpe she finds tolerable for a time. Her wide-eyed infatuation with Henry becomes tedious because we are not allowed to believe that it is anything more. Whenever we suspect that she deserves our concern—as when Thorpe tricks her into giving up an afternoon with Henry— the author takes pains to undeceive us:

> And now I may dismiss my heroine to the sleepless couch, which is the true heroine's portion; to a pillow strewed with thorns and wet with tears. And lucky may she think herself, if she get another good night's rest in the course of the next three months. (NA 90)

Catherine is the center of the action: yet she is neither the borrowed heroine of a pure burlesque, like Laura in "Love and Freindship," nor as interesting and complex a person as she would have to be—intellectually or emotionally—to sustain the necessary tensions at the center of a realistic novel. We can neither treat her as a joke, nor take her at the value her position in the novel requires. She is credible enough; she functions amusingly in her dual role; but she is too simple and too slight, too narrowly a symbol of the author's rejection of romantic nonsense, to assert the claim of personal feeling and value beyond mere function. Jane Austen's rejection of romance develops into a rejection—at least, the spectator's implicit rejection—of personality: whatever value or autonomous feeling the action even begins to suggest for Catherine is immediately drowned in the author's irony.

To the other characters, Jane Austen denies even a suspicion of depth. They are ironically defined at the beginning in terms of their function, and allowed thereafter to act only on the basis of this definition. Mrs. Allen sits gossiping forever; Isabella pursues and jilts men and women equally; Thorpe swears to his improbable achievements and extends his lying as a matter of course; only General Tilney is permitted for a time to evade definition, for the sake of the plot: but none of them ever gives a hint of compunction or self-knowledge, of penetrability past or latent. They have no history; they are flatly in the present, beneath the author's irony.

Still, the most striking evidence of Jane Austen's compelled detachment lies, not in the behavior of her characters, but in her own explicit intrusions into the story, as in her treatment of Catherine sleepless with tears (NA 90): in her own imposed direction, tone, and commentary. She cannot yet adjust her ironic attack nicely to the strength of its object, the flimsy and false-fronted Gothic world; she overreaches into her own realistic world and shakes that also, dangerously. She can never, for example, quite moderate her attack on the literary platitudes about affection. We have seen how she disposes of Catherine in love and in the disappointments of love. In her friendship with Isabella, Catherine is just as severely treated: the two girls supply "the place of many ideas by a squeeze of the hand or a smile of affection" (NA 52); and Catherine, having found so good a friend at the Pump-room, considers "that building . . . so favourable for the discovery of female excellence, and the completion of female intimacy, so admirably adapted for secret discourses and unlimited confidence, that she was most reasonably encouraged to expect another friend from within its walls." (NA 60) The irony here is especially loaded and supererogatory because at Isabella's earliest appearance we are put to no trouble at all to discover her motives from her words alone: the fact that Catherine is ingenuous to be deceived by her requires no underlining. As for friendship between those two inoffensive, aging vegetables, Mrs. Allen and Mrs. Thorpe, the author cannot restrain her contempt. At an unexpected meeting in Bath,

> Their joy . . . was very great, as well it might, since they had been contented to know nothing of each other for the last fifteen years. (NA 31f.)

And Mrs. Allen is later

. . . never satisfied with the day unless she spent the chief of it by the side of Mrs. Thorpe, in what they called conversation, but in which there was scarcely any exchange of opinion, and not often any resemblance of subject, for Mrs. Thorpe talked chiefly of her children, and Mrs. Allen of her gowns. (NA 36) It is not that Jane Austen fails to illustrate her characters by incident for the most part, but that she cannot resist establishing her distance from them in her own voice as well, as if she does not trust—or is not yet aware of—the power of her art alone, without the arbitrary expression of her will, to cut down and isolate the middle-class world for detached examination and so to safeguard her against involvement.

Function and commentary are the two dimensions of *Northanger Abbey*; and though we may be on the verge of a third now and then—as when Catherine apologizes in the eager rush of explanation to Henry:

"Oh! Mr. Tilney, I have been quite wild to speak to you, and make my apologies. You must have thought me so rude; but indeed it was not my own fault,—was it, Mrs. Allen? Did not they tell me that Mr. Tilney and his sister were gone out in a phaeton together? and then what could I do? But I had ten thousand times rather have been with you; now had not I, Mrs. Allen?" (NA 93f.)

or when we share the Tilneys' sense of strain in their father's presence and in his unctuousness toward Catherine—the author always pulls herself up in time.

It is true that General Tilney arouses enough interest in his nature and his motives to show promise of a personal dimension. Functionally, of course, he is not only effective but crucial. Without him, there would be no suspense and no climax, Gothic or otherwise. We wonder from his first appearance about this impressive-looking father of whom his otherwise lively and irreverent son never speaks. We wonder even more at his sudden courtliness toward Catherine in the midst of hints about his irascibility and in the face of information from Henry and Eleanor that he would never allow his son Frederick to marry a girl like Isabella, without "consequence and fortune." (NA 208) And, conveniently, he lives in an abbey—made over but still with traces of antiquity—in a room of which Catherine, her head turned by too much Gothic reading and by growing evidence of the General's willful bad temper, conjures up her night-terrors of a mysterious manuscript and a murdered or imprisoned wife. Without the suspense aroused by our uncertainty about him, the Gothic episode in *Northanger Abbey* would in fact have no realistic scaffolding at all.

Yet, having borrowed[16] and fitted in so useful a character, Jane Austen seems concerned, ultimately, much less to make him consistent than to keep him at his function. It is not that she might not have done both at once; but, in his case at least, her desire to do the latter inhibits her ability to do the former. General Tilney keeps escaping into his own life; but he must be cut down to size, he must be converted into a small piece of amusement for the author-spectator. So, in the end, we are not even allowed to observe his climactic—and, perhaps, impressive—rage at being deceived about the Morlands' affluence. We are merely expected to believe that a man of great, almost monomaniacal pride and ambition of place, of unbending severity, who considers "consequence" as well as "fortune" indispensable to any prospective member of his family, who by the harshness of his authority has driven his otherwise independent-spirited children into frightened submission, whom we never see humble himself to anyone else, would treat with the most fatuous, pliant, immoderate deference a very young girl "without consequence" solely in the belief that she will bring his son a large dowry. There may be somewhere such a commingling of traits; but Jane Austen does nothing to make it seem probable, to ease and vindicate the transition between the General with Catherine and the General without her. The final explanation of the General's conduct amounts to a betrayal, for it involves dropping out of sight most of what we have learned about him. The two lines of his conduct remain as disparate as they ever were, and the one element that kept them simultaneously acceptable—the author's skillful implication that they would be resolved in the

---

[16] The General derives, of course, from the tyrannical father or guardian; Catherine specifically compares him to Mrs. Radcliffe's Montoni. (NA 187)

end—has been sunk in her desire to leave him contemptible only, to cram him back into the limits of his function: the tyrannical parent contracted.

Catherine, too, shows signs of by-passing her function: into a plain matter-of-factness, without the intervention of the Gothic climax called for in the formal design of *Northanger Abbey*. Catherine, like the General, has got away somewhat from her author and threatens to become unmanageable. It is not strange, therefore, that the Gothic episode, in which she is returned and rigidly fitted to her function, is the most inflexible and uncreative episode in the book. It is pat and single-textured; atmospherically unprepared and discontinuous with the rest of the novel; too literally a carrying-out of the Radcliffean terror episode, and of Henry's amusing prophecy. Most injuriously, however, it sacrifices Catherine's consistency to her function. It demands too abrupt a transition from Catherine the matter-of-fact ingénue to Catherine the self-appointed Gothic heroine: we can see, in retrospect, the accumulation of evidence—the directed reading, the abbey, the mysterious and forbidding widower, the bedroom with its Gothic paraphernalia—by which the author has attempted to rationalize the change; but we can hardly believe that Catherine's present imaginative credulity is a natural development out of her previous unimaginative credulity. The key to Catherine's nature is, not credulity, but matter-of-factness, whether she is quite lost in Isabella's innuendoes about a vanished clergyman-lover of her own (NA 36) or bewildered by Henry's evasiveness about the relations between Isabella and his brother. (NA 150ff.) Catherine is incapable of discovering implications: she is credulous only because she believes exactly what people say, not because she draws false and sentimental inferences from what they say or do.

In *Northanger Abbey*, function is the only field for Jane Austen's irony. When her characters begin to slip away from her into attitudes unforeseen by function, to solicit sympathy or understanding, her only recourse is to force them back, by inconsistency of conduct or her own authoritative commentary, into the limits of their function. Her skill and tact in directing realistic characters—so different from the easily disparaged puppets of "Love and Freindship"—have not yet developed to the point of tempering and assimilating the disparagement, the often arbitrary reduction of scale, the assumption that nothing need be taken seriously, upon all of which her irony in *Northanger Abbey* blandly insists. The denouement of the novel represents also the climax of this insistence. If Henry and Catherine are separated by General Tilney's unyielding will (which function has not accounted for and cannot deal with), our story, dear reader, is after all only a story and we can pull a viscount out of the hat:

> The anxiety, which in this state of their attachment must be the portion of Henry and Catherine, and of all who loved either, as to its final event, can hardly extend, I fear, to the bosom of my readers, who will see in the tell-tale compression of the pages before them, that we are all hastening together to perfect felicity. The means by which their early marriage was effected can be the only doubt; what probable circumstance could work upon a temper like the General's? The circumstance which chiefly availed was the marriage of his daughter with a man of fortune and consequence . . . . (NA 250)

So, carried back to the belatedly introduced hero of "Jack and Alice,"[17] and conveniently ignoring the realistic ground of *Northanger Abbey*, the author dismisses her absurd finishing-off as a joke. It seems that Eleanor's husband, the viscount,

> . . . was really deserving of her; independent of his peerage, his wealth, and his attachment, being to a precision the most charming young man in the world. Any further definition of his merits must be unnecessary; the most charming young man in the world is instantly before the imagination of us all. Concerning the one in question therefore I have only to add— (aware that the rules of composition forbid the introduction of a character not connected with my fable)—that this was the very gentleman whose negligent servant left behind him that collection of washing-bills, resulting from a long visit at Northanger, by which my heroine was involved in one of her most alarming adventures. (NA 251)

And, in a final flourish of unconcern, she leaves the reader with a choice of morals:

[17] See p. 22, this study.

. . . I leave it to be settled by whomsoever it may concern, whether the tendency of this work be altogether to recommend parental tyranny, or reward filial disobedience. (NA 252)

This is rejection outright, and from without. Jane Austen's irony is no longer able even to make a pretense of coping internally with its materials: she shrugs off altogether the artist's responsibility toward them. They are disposed of, and we must ask no questions. She might have found the key to the plausible development and resolution of the story elsewhere, she might perhaps have elaborated the double action out of this more consistent and more characteristically youthful aspect of Catherine:

. . . the inexplicability of the General's conduct dwelt much in her thoughts . . . why he should say one thing so positively, and mean another all the while, was most unaccountable! How were people, at that rate, to be understood? Who but Henry could have been aware of what his father was at? (NA 211)

But irony comes too close to relinquishing its office here, too close in fact to defining its threat to human relationships, as in a mirror in which hypocrisy and irony come to much the same thing, weapons against commitment; and the author shies away, back to parody, to the predictable anti-types who, having demolished the Gothic delusion by their own inadequacy to its demands, must now be reduced to faceless inconsequence and dismissed in turn. The novelist gives way to the parodist; and irony, here as in "Love and Freindship," as in all the *juvenilia*, hardens perceptibly into rejection: in *Northanger Abbey*, into a rejection not only of the illusionary world, but of the realistic characters who disprove it—indeed, of the whole realistic basis of the novel. Irony overrides the artist, and becomes rejection unlimited.

CHAPTER III

THE LITERARY PRETEXT CONCLUDED:
IRONY AND CONVENTION *VERSUS* FEELING

SENSE AND SENSIBILITY

EVEN when, in *Sense and Sensibility*, Jane Austen sets for herself her first mature novelistic problem, she cannot quite dispense with parody. Here, of course, parody does not direct the narrative, as it does in the *juvenilia* or in *Northanger Abbey*. In *Sense and Sensibility*, on the contrary, it seems the last embedded relic of her earliest style, an incongruous survival; it operates, besides, under a new, restrictive attitude; but the arresting fact is that here, in the midst of elements either far more complex or altogether different, it survives at all.

It survives most fully in the title of the novel. The parody, as the title suggests, returns us to one of Jane Austen's earliest targets, the novel of sensibility. The immediate target now is the sensibility of Marianne Dashwood, who was

> . . . eager in every thing; her sorrows, her joys, could have no moderation. She was generous, amiable, interesting: she was every thing but prudent. (ss 6)

There is, at once, an obvious break with the tone and method of the *juvenilia*. The vivacity, the disinterested focus on scene and action, of "Love and Freindship" are here remarkable by their absence. At once Jane Austen's tone is didactic and reproving; and there is at the outset no representation, only summary and judgment. The object of parody must now be explicitly condemned before we may observe it in action. When family misfortune overwhelms the impressionable Marianne and her mother, between whom there is, we are told, a "strikingly great" (ss 6) resemblance, we have no scene, and no evidence except what is summarized in the brief and moral report by the author. Mother and daughter

> . . . encouraged each other . . . in the violence of their affliction. The agony of grief which overpowered them at first, was vol-

untarily renewed, was sought for, was created again and again.
They gave themselves up wholly to their sorrow, seeking in-
crease of wretchedness in every reflection that could afford it,
and resolved against ever admitting consolation in future.
(ss 7)

Having first, then, fixed for us our attitude toward sensibility, Jane Austen permits us to see and hear Marianne herself:

". . . I could not be happy [says Marianne] with a man whose
taste did not in every point coincide with my own. He must
enter into all my feelings; the same books, the same music
must charm us both. . . ." (ss 17)

When the Dashwoods are obliged to leave Norland,

"Dear, dear Norland!" said Marianne, as she wandered alone
before the house on the last evening of their being there; "when
shall I cease to regret you!—when learn to feel a home elsewhere!—Oh! happy house, could you know what I suffer in
now viewing you from this spot, from whence perhaps I may
view you no more!—And you, ye well-known trees!—but you
will continue the same.—No leaf will decay because we are re-
moved, nor any branch become motionless although we can
observe you no longer! . . ." (ss 27)

Elinor's calm in the absence of her suitor remains, for Marianne, incomprehensible:

". . . Elinor, in quitting Norland and Edward, cried not as I
did. Even now her self-command is invariable. When is she
dejected or melancholy? When does she try to avoid society, or
appear restless and dissatisfied in it?" (ss 39)

When Elinor remonstrates with her for a breach of manners,
Marianne replies that

". . . if there had been any real impropriety in what I did, I
should have been sensible of it at the time, for we always know
when we are acting wrong, and with such a conviction I could
have had no pleasure." (ss 68)

On the two sisters' visit to Cleveland, the "consciousness of
being only eighty miles from Barton," (ss 302) their present
home, "and not thirty from Combe Magna," (ss 302) the
unfaithful Willoughby's estate, compels Marianne to enter
the Palmers' house

. . . with an heart swelling with emotion . . . and before she
had been five minutes within its walls, while the others were

61

busily helping Charlotte shew her child to the housekeeper, she quitted it again, stealing away through the winding shrubberies, now just beginning to be in beauty, to gain a distant eminence; where, from its Grecian temple, her eye, wandering over a wide tract of country to the southeast, could fondly rest on the farthest ridge of hills in the horizon, and fancy that from their summits Combe Magna might be seen.

In such moments of precious, of invaluable misery, she rejoiced in tears of agony to be at Cleveland. . . . (ss 302f.)

Even such flat and unpromising, often dispirited, parody as this, however, Jane Austen must contain now within her stiff, specific disapproval. Having parted with Willoughby, Marianne

. . . was without any power, because she was without any desire of command over herself. (ss 82)

She would, indeed,

. . . have thought herself very inexcusable had she been able to sleep at all the first night. . . . She would have been ashamed to look her family in the face the next morning, had she not risen from her bed in more need of repose than when she lay down in it. But the feelings which made such composure a disgrace, left her in no danger of incurring it. She was awake the whole night, and she wept the greatest part of it. She got up with an headache, was unable to talk, and unwilling to take any nourishment; giving pain every moment to her mother and sisters, and forbidding all attempt at consolation from either. Her sensibility was potent enough! (ss 83)

The fact is that parody has always been, for Jane Austen, the simplest reaction to feeling, the easiest irony. If she is older (*Sense and Sensibility* was revised for publication as late as her thirty-sixth year) and in general more seriously responsive to her medium, she still maintains her decisive remoteness from feeling. Being older, she is also, however, more responsive to the pressures of the marriage-and-money society in which she has become a spinster without means, and which must by its nature react to feeling with an invincible antipathy. In her impulse to parody, Jane Austen hardly differs now from the precocious author of "Love and Freindship." In this she has not changed because she has had no reason to change. The first change and novelty is in her *handling* of parody: in her forced yielding to social convention, in the di-

rect and unequivocal disapproval with which she circumscribes her amusement, and assures her readers that feeling—
at least an excess of it—is not merely amusing, but morally
wrong. Marianne, we are informed again and again, is, more
than an object of irony, a very bad example.

In the presentation of Marianne Dashwood, Jane Austen's
irony—as parody, its easiest form—tends for the first time to
dissolve away in social uneasiness. Moreover, the character of
Marianne focuses another development of Jane Austen's
irony: away from parody, toward a free and responsible consideration of the individual, toward the questions of personal
decision and personal value.

Juvenile parody aside (and in its fragmentariness and irrelevance it may be quickly set aside), Marianne makes her
own decisions and has her own value. She is no cardboard
cutout as in the *juvenilia* or pleasant vacuity like Catherine
Morland, ready to have her light head turned by the giddiest
fiction. Marianne is not hallucinated or a fool; her difficulties
arise from a youthful and inexperienced, a bold but incomplete
awareness. In this at least, she resembles Elizabeth Bennet.
Like Elizabeth, she is alert, sensitive, intelligent; and, like
Elizabeth, she is inclined to generalize too facilely, to have
strong first impressions and stick by them, to fill up the gaps
in her knowledge of people with approval or distaste, to be
persuaded not by absurd fiction but by plausible reality.
Marianne's problem, and the mature ironic problem of *Sense
and Sensibility*, is the interpretation of personality: the discrimination, not crudely of fact from fiction—as for Catherine
Morland—but of substance from plausibility. The problem,
though its solution is complicated for Marianne by her ardor,
her eager susceptibleness to first impressions, is an adult one;
and on the whole she does very well with it, hardly less well
than Elinor—or than the author herself.

As interpreters of personality, these three tend, indeed, to
agree surprisingly. They differ in attitude, in degree of patience; the author has, of course, an advantage in information
over both the sisters: yet their *judgments* coincide altogether
on most of the characters in the novel—on the John Dash-

woods, the Middletons, the Palmers, Mrs. Ferrars, the Misses Steele.

Elinor, Marianne, and the author all present for us, frequently and in various lights, the unmistakable John Dashwoods. The author introduces the pair at once as they are:

> He was not an ill-disposed young man unless to be rather cold-hearted, and rather selfish, is to be ill-disposed: but he was, in general, well respected; for he conducted himself with propriety in the discharge of his ordinary duties. Had he married a more amiable woman, he might have been made still more respectable than he was:—he might even have been made amiable himself; for he was very young when he married, and very fond of his wife. But Mrs. John Dashwood was a strong caricature of himself;—more narrow-minded and selfish. (ss 5)

When the lady and her husband, without allowing Elinor, Marianne, and their mother even a decent period of mourning, move into Norland after Mr. Henry Dashwood's death, the author and her heroines clearly agree on the moral quality of the act and of the actors. The author confirms our judgment by observing for us alone the superb scene in which Mrs. John Dashwood persuades her husband—or allows him to persuade himself—that they are too poor to afford a gift to his father's wife and children:

> Mrs. John Dashwood did not at all approve of what her husband intended to do for his sisters. . . . It was very well known that no affection was ever supposed to exist between the children of any man by different marriages; and why was he to ruin himself, and their poor little Harry, by giving away all his money to his half sisters?
>
> "It was my father's last request to me," replied her husband, "that I should assist his widow and daughters."
>
> "He did not know what he was talking of, I dare say; ten to one but he was light-headed at the time. . . ."
>
> ". . . he . . . requested me, in general terms, to assist them. . . . Perhaps it would have been as well if he had left it wholly to myself. He could hardly suppose I should neglect them. But as he required the promise, I could not do less than give it: at least I thought so at the time. . . ." (ss 8f.)

So the masterly reciprocal rationalizations proceed, until Mr. Dashwood suggests a small annuity:

> "To be sure," said she, "it is better than parting with fifteen

hundred pounds at once. But then if Mrs. Dashwood should live fifteen years, we shall be completely taken in."

"Fifteen years! my dear Fanny: her life cannot be worth half that purchase."

"Certainly not; but if you observe, people always live for ever when there is any annuity to be paid them; and she is very stout and healthy, and hardly forty. An annuity is a very serious business; it comes over and over every year, and there is no getting rid of it. . . ."

"It is certainly an unpleasant thing," replied Mr. Dashwood, "to have those kind of yearly drains on one's income. One's fortune, as your mother justly says, is *not* one's own. . . ."

"Undoubtedly; and after all you have no thanks for it. They think themselves secure, you do no more than what is expected, and it raises no gratitude at all. . . ." (ss 10f.)

Indeed, Mr. Henry Dashwood, having left "all the china, plate, and linen" (ss 13) to his widow, did *more* than was proper, according to his daughter-in-law:

". . . Your father thought only of *them*. And I must say this: that you owe no particular gratitude to him, nor attention to his wishes, for we very well know that if he could, he would have left almost every thing in the world to *them*."

This argument was irresistible. It gave to his intentions whatever of decision was wanting before. . . . (ss 13)

The scene has no moral aura, no social uneasiness at all, and it is far beyond parody: it refracts only the author's unengaged delight in the monumental self-deception of respectability, man and wife; it is already very near the high, sustained, lethal irony of *Emma*. In the novel, moreover, it reproduces a mode of thought familiar and abhorrent to both Elinor and Marianne. Both *know* the John Dashwoods; and Elinor's sense brings her no more quickly or surely to the knowledge than Marianne's sensibility.

The difference is, of course, between Elinor's notion of propriety and Marianne's. Elinor—here, at least, the social façade of her author's irony—is always courteous and agreeable toward her brother, whatever his provocations of mercenariness and blind complacency:

As soon as they were out of the house, his enquiries began.

"Who is Colonel Brandon? Is he a man of fortune?"

"Yes; he has very good property in Dorsetshire."

65

"I am glad of it. He seems a most gentlemanlike man; and I think, Elinor, I may congratulate you on the prospect of a very respectable establishment in life."

"Me, brother! what do you mean?"

"He likes you. I observed him narrowly, and am convinced of it. What is the amount of his fortune?"

"I believe about two thousand a-year."

"Two thousand a-year"; and then working himself up to a pitch of enthusiastic generosity, he added, "Elinor, I wish with all my heart, it were *twice* as much, for your sake." (ss 223)

As for Marianne, she can regard her brother with disgust, with contemptuous silence, but never with smooth civility. Elinor, following John Dashwood along the single track of his bankteller's mind, has occasion to be

. . . very thankful that Marianne was not present, to share the provocation. (ss 226)

Even after the collapse of her hopes, and remembering her resolution to be kind and forbearing to everyone, Marianne cannot suppress a burst of indignation when her brother remarks approvingly on Mrs. Ferrars' decision concerning her son, the undutiful son who declines the well-dowered wife his mother has chosen for him:

". . . so far would she be from affording him the smallest assistance, that if he were to enter into any profession with a view of better support, she would do all in her power to prevent his advancing in it."

Here Marianne, in an ecstasy of indignation, clapped her hands together, and cried, "Gracious God! can this be possible!"

"Well may you wonder, Marianne," replied her brother, "at the obstinacy which could resist such arguments as these. Your exclamation is very natural."

Marianne was going to retort, but she remembered her promises, and forebore. (ss 267)

Finally, despite Elinor's request and her own new humility, Marianne refuses even to pay the John Dashwoods a courtesy call:

This was an obligation . . . which not only opposed . . . [Elinor's] own inclination, but which had not the assistance of any encouragement. . . . Marianne, not contented with absolutely refusing to go herself, was very urgent to prevent her sister's going at all. . . . (ss 293f.)

The author presents her damaging evidence, and her two heroines—always implicitly, and at several points expressly— make their agreement clear. Sir John and Lady Middleton, to whose cottage Elinor, Marianne, and their mother move, we soon discover to be, respectively, solicitous and elegant; but also, both of them, stupid and boring:

> They were scarcely ever without some friends staying with them in the house, and they kept more company of every kind than any other family in the neighbourhood. It was necessary to the happiness of both; for however dissimilar in temperament and outward behaviour, they strongly resembled each other in that total want of talent and taste which confined their employments, unconnected with such as society produced, within a very narrow compass. Sir John was a sportsman, Lady Middleton a mother. He hunted and shot, and she humoured her children; and these were their only resources. (ss 32)

When the author, appropriately, brings Mrs. John Dashwood and Lady Middleton face to face, the former finds the latter

> . . . one of the most charming women in the world!
> Lady Middleton was equally pleased with Mrs. Dashwood. There was a kind of cold hearted selfishness on both sides, which mutually attracted them; and they sympathised with each other in an insipid propriety of demeanour, and a general want of understanding. (ss 229)

Marianne, on the other hand, soon has more than enough of the Middletons, who—in their horror of being alone with each other—insist that the girls and their mother dine frequently at Barton Park:

> "Why should they ask us? . . . The rent of this cottage is said to be low; but we have it on very hard terms, if we are to dine at the park whenever any one is staying either with them, or with us." (ss 109)

Upon Lucy Steele's exclamation, "What a sweet woman Lady Middleton is!" (ss 122)

> Marianne was silent; it was impossible for her to say what she did not feel, however trivial the occasion; and upon Elinor therefore the whole task of telling lies when politeness required it, always fell. (ss 122)

When Sir John, trying to tease Marianne about Willoughby, remarks:

"I see how it will be. You will be setting your cap at him now, and never think of poor Brandon."

"That is an expression, Sir John," said Marianne, warmly, "which I particularly dislike. I abhor every common-place phrase by which wit is intended; and 'setting one's cap at a man,' or 'making a conquest,' are the most odious of all. Their tendency is gross and illiberal; and if their construction could ever be deemed clever, time has long ago destroyed all its ingenuity."

Sir John did not much understand this reproof; but he laughed as heartily as if he did. . . . (ss 45)

Lady Middleton, of course, does not like the girls at all; so Jane Austen observes in a comment perhaps as much defensive of her own ironist's isolation in society, as pertinent to her story:

Because they neither flattered herself nor her children, she could not believe them good-natured; and because they were fond of reading, she fancied them satirical: perhaps without exactly knowing what it was to be satirical; but *that* did not signify. It was censure in common use, and easily given. (ss 246)

And poor Marianne, having received Willoughby's cruel letter, cries out in despair:

". . . I cannot stay to endure the questions and remarks of all these people. The Middletons and Palmers—how am I to bear their pity? The pity of such a woman as Lady Middleton! Oh! what would *he* say to that!" (ss 191)

The Middletons and the Palmers are related, for Elinor and the author as well as for Marianne, by more than the fact that the ladies are sisters. They are, of course, all four of them and the John Dashwoods also, individuals with a dull or unpleasant history; but as couples they are even closer, they are indeed identical as they collectively represent Marianne's great enemy, the cold unconscious final indignity of prudent middle-class marriage.

Setting off the Palmers' brand of indignity is its effect upon Marianne's gentle and quite unironic ally, her mother; the first response to the Palmers is Mrs. Henry Dashwood's:

He entered the room with a look of self-consequence, slightly bowed to the ladies, without speaking a word, and, after briefly surveying them and their apartments, took up a newspaper from the table and continued to read it as long as he staid.

Mrs. Palmer, on the contrary, who was strongly endowed

68

by nature with a turn for being uniformly civil and happy, was hardly seated before her admiration of the parlour and every thing in it burst forth.

"Well! what a delightful room this is! I never saw anything so charming! Only think, mama, how it is improved since I was here last! I always thought it such a sweet place, ma'am! (turning to Mrs. Dashwood,) but you have made it so charming! Only look, sister, how delightful every thing is! How I should like such a house for myself! Should not you, Mr. Palmer?"

Mr. Palmer made her no answer, and did not even raise his eyes from the newspaper.

"Mr. Palmer does not hear me," said she, laughing, "he never does sometimes. It is so ridiculous!"

This was quite a new idea to Mrs. Dashwood, she had never been used to find wit in the inattention of any one, and could not help looking with surprise at them both. (ss 106f.)

From this point on, the pattern repeats itself amusingly, in different settings and situations, but without development. Though Elinor later exposes her own (and the author's) explanation and judgment of the marriage, and especially of Mr. Palmer:

His temper might perhaps be a little soured by finding, like many others of his sex, that through some unaccountable bias in favour of beauty, he was the husband of a very silly woman, —but she knew that this kind of blunder was too common for any sensible man to be lastingly hurt by it.—It was rather a wish of distinction she believed, which produced his contemptuous treatment of every body, and his general abuse of every thing before him. (ss 112)

though Elinor becomes more explicit and much less ironic still later, we have already seen the Palmers for ourselves; we are prepared already for Marianne's cry, "The Middletons and Palmers—how am I to bear their pity?"; and we wait only for new circumstances to induce and emphasize their predictable reaction, the pattern of conventional mediocrity immediately obvious and finally so painful to Marianne.

The shadow of Mrs. Ferrars falls early, when Mrs. John Dashwood, her daughter, alluding to Elinor's interest in Edward Ferrars,

. . . took the first opportunity of affronting her mother-in-law
. . . talking to her so expressively of her brother's great expec-

tations, of Mrs. Ferrars's resolution that both her sons should marry well, and of the danger attending any young woman who attempted to *draw him in*; that Mrs. Dashwood could neither pretend to be unconscious, nor endeavour to be calm. (ss 23)

Quite properly, the ogress herself does not appear until her malevolence has been well established. When she appears at last, she is ready in all her arrogant ill-nature to devour Elinor for her presumptuous attitude toward Edward:

> She was not a woman of many words: for, unlike people in general, she proportioned them to the number of her ideas; and of the few syllables that did escape her, not one fell to the share of Miss Dashwood, whom she eyed with the spirited determination of disliking her at all events. (ss 232)

Now, as always, Marianne makes her feelings clear by her resoluteness against feigning. The conversation at the John Dashwoods' dinner party lags by

> Want of sense, either natural or improved—want of elegance—want of spirits—or want of temper. (ss 233)

When it lights desperately on the comparative heights of two little boys, only one of them present, everyone offers his own opinion to the parents and grandparents except Marianne, who,

> . . . when called on for her's, offended them all, by declaring that she had no opinion to give, as she had never thought about it. (ss 234)

And the inevitable uninhibited outburst comes after Mrs. Ferrars contemptuously passes over a screen painted by Elinor to praise the talent of the heiress Miss Morton, Edward's prospective bride:

> Marianne could not bear this.—She was already greatly displeased with Mrs. Ferrars; and such ill-timed praise of another, at Elinor's expense . . . provoked her immediately to say with warmth,
> "This is admiration of a very particular kind!—what is Miss Morton to us?—who knows, or who cares, for her?—it is Elinor of whom *we* think and speak."
> And so saying, she took the screens out of her sister-in-law's hands, to admire them herself as they ought to be admired.
> Mrs. Ferrars looked exceedingly angry, and drawing herself up more stiffly than ever, pronounced in retort this bitter philippic; "Miss Morton is Lord Morton's daughter." (ss 235f.)

It is not surprising that the Misses Steele, especially Lucy, gain the favor of Mrs. Ferrars, at least before the latter learns of Lucy's secret engagement to Edward. So Elinor

> . . . could not but smile to see the graciousness of both mother and daughter towards the very person—for Lucy was particularly distinguished—whom of all others, had they known as much as she did, they would have been most anxious to mortify; while she herself, who had comparatively no power to wound them, sat pointedly slighted by both. But while she smiled at a graciousness so misapplied, she could not reflect on the mean-spirited folly from which it sprung, nor observe the studied attentions with which the Miss Steeles courted its continuance, without thoroughly despising them all four. (ss 232f.)

The community of mean minds—" 'So dull, so wretchedly dull!' " (ss 243) exclaims Marianne—organizes itself spontaneously. Lady Middleton, even under the burden of accepting the Steele girls as guests, loves her cousins almost instinctively:

> Their dress was very smart, their manners very civil, they were delighted with the house, and in raptures with the furniture, and they happened to be so doatingly fond of children that Lady Middleton's good opinion was engaged in their favour before they had been an hour at the Park. She declared them to be very agreeable girls indeed, which for her ladyship was enthusiastic admiration. (ss 119)

Mrs. John Dashwood, who receives them next,

> . . . had never been so much pleased with any young women in her life . . . had given each of them a needle book, made by some emigrant; called Lucy by her christian name; and did not know whether she should ever be able to part with them. (ss 254)

As for Mrs. Ferrars, after the first rage of seeing her scheme for Edward's prudent marriage thwarted by the penniless Lucy, even after Lucy's unexpected elopement with her younger son, she too is soon completely won over. Lucy's

> . . . selfish sagacity . . . which had at first drawn Robert into the scrape, was the principal instrument of his deliverance from it; for her respectful humility, assiduous attentions, and endless flatteries, as soon as the smallest opening was given for their exercise, reconciled Mrs. Ferrars to his choice, and re-established him completely in her favour.

71

The whole of Lucy's behaviour in the affair, and the prosperity which crowned it, therefore, may be held forth as a most encouraging instance of what an earnest, an unceasing attention to self-interest, however its progress may be apparently obstructed, will do in securing every advantage of fortune, with no other sacrifice than that of time and conscience. (ss 375f.)

The foppish and absurd Robert Ferrars, whose nonsense Elinor does not challenge at their single meeting because "she did not think he deserved the compliment of rational opposition," (ss 252)

. . . was proud of his conquest, proud of tricking Edward, and very proud of marrying privately without his mother's consent. What immediately followed is known. They passed some months in great happiness at Dawlish; for she had many relations and old acquaintance to cut—and he drew several plans for magnificent cottages;—and from thence returning to town, procured the forgiveness of Mrs. Ferrars, by the simple expedient of asking it, which, at Lucy's instigation, was adopted. The forgiveness at first, indeed, as was reasonable, comprehended only Robert; and Lucy, who had owed his mother no duty, and therefore could have transgressed none, still remained some weeks longer unpardoned. But perseverance in humility of conduct and messages, in self-condemnation for Robert's offence, and gratitude for the unkindness she was treated with, procured her in time the haughty notice which overcame her by its graciousness, and led soon afterwards, by rapid degrees, to the highest state of affection and influence. Lucy became as necessary to Mrs. Ferrars, as either Robert or Fanny; and while Edward was never cordially forgiven for having once intended to marry her, and Elinor, though superior to her in fortune and birth, was spoken of as an intruder, *she* was in every thing considered, and always openly acknowledged, to be a favourite child. (ss 376f.)

The author does not, however, leave her mean minds without the implication that meanness is its own reward:

They settled in town, received very liberal assistance from Mrs. Ferrars, were on the best terms imaginable with the Dashwoods; and setting aside the jealousies and ill-will continually subsisting between Fanny and Lucy, in which their husbands of course took a part, as well as the frequent domestic disagreements between Robert and Lucy themselves, nothing could exceed the harmony in which they all lived together. (ss 377)

And Jane Austen's ironic implication is, of course, Marianne's constant serious judgment—that the hypocrite and the mercenary need only be left to themselves to find their own station, populous and conventional, in hell. The honest person checks their advances and leaves them to themselves, and to their tricks. Elinor has her reasons for keeping silent about Lucy's engagement to Edward, especially in their presence; but when, alone with her sister, she plays Lucy's trick of bland dissimulation, she is, from Marianne's standpoint, on the enemy's ground and deserves the same judgment:

> "What can bring her here so often!" said Marianne, on . . . [Lucy's] leaving them. "Could she not see that we wanted her gone!—how teazing to Edward!"
>
> "Why so?—we were all his friends, and Lucy has been the longest known to him of any. It is but natural that he should like to see her as well as ourselves."
>
> Marianne looked at her steadily, and said, "You know, Elinor, that this is a kind of talking which I cannot bear. If you only hope to have your assertion contradicted, as I must suppose to be the case, you ought to recollect that I am the last person in the world to do it. I cannot descend to be tricked out of assurances, that are not really wanted."
>
> She then left the room . . . (ss 244)

leaving meanness (so dissimulation would have seemed to her, even had she divined Elinor's true motives) to itself.

The code is a strict one, and Marianne makes no allowances. She dislikes the Misses Steele,

> . . . and to the invariable coldness of her behaviour towards them, which checked every endeavour at intimacy on their side, Elinor principally attributed that preference of herself which soon became evident in the manners of both, but especially of Lucy. . . . (ss 127)

Lucy confides in Elinor because she can count on receiving every social allowance, because she can taunt Elinor about Edward with an ingenuous air as false and insulting to Elinor's intelligence as it is invulnerable to her courtesy; but also because—as Marianne suspects—Elinor's courtesy, accosted and tantalized by meanness, is liable to contract on occasion into a cold hypocrisy hardly distinguishable from its object. So Elinor not only listens to Lucy's confidences, but solicits them with an air as ingenuous and false as Lucy's own:

> "I should be undeserving of the confidence you have honoured me with, if I felt no desire for its continuance, or no farther curiosity on its subject. I will not apologize therefore for bringing it forward again." (ss 146)

The feminine jockeying that follows serves to enlighten Elinor about Edward and Lucy; but the claws are as evident in Elinor's leading questions as in Lucy's calculated answers:

> Lucy here looked up; but Elinor was careful in guarding her countenance from every expression that could give her words a suspicious tendency. (ss 147)

The end—information—seems to justify the method. Lucy protests the constancy of Edward's love for her; and what Elinor cynically thinks:

> "All this . . . is very pretty; but it can impose upon neither of us." (ss 148)

does not deter her at all from pressing her interrogation with the most imperturbable civility:

> "But what," said she after a short silence, "are your views? or have you none but that of waiting for Mrs. Ferrars' death, which is a melancholy and shocking extremity? . . ." (ss 148)

Yet the point is not so much that Elinor must learn these things by some method or other, as that she exploits Lucy's own method without hesitation, even with eagerness; that dissimulation, no longer distinguishable from courtesy, becomes a positive pleasure, sanctified by custom and most useful in social emergencies. Nor does Jane Austen, here or elsewhere, present Elinor ironically. This, then, is approved behavior, this is sense as it shows itself superior to sensibility. To Elinor's behavior, the implied and foolish alternative is Marianne's—not just tactlessness or self-righteous candor, but a basic opposition to lying and the forms of lying. In this instance, however, the reader finds himself not so firmly on Elinor's side as the author, by her deliberate protective exclusion of Elinor from the focus of irony, always intends him to be. The views of author and reader begin to diverge.

Marianne has, of course, her hastes and impatiences of

judgment. She recognizes only two categories of people: the worthy, who are honest and sensitive, and the unworthy, who are dishonest and insensitive; and she will admit no permutations. Sensitivity becomes, in fact, nearly equivalent to virtue; and insensitivity, to wickedness. So she sees Lucy and Anne Steele as one, though Anne is nothing but a silly garrulous spinster, as innocent of Lucy's malice as of her shrewdness.

With Anne, the injustice is trivial; but with Mrs. Jennings it becomes more serious. For Marianne, sensitivity—or, in the idiom of her time, sensibility—is a large quality: she might have defined it as a passionate, discriminating, instantaneous sympathy for worthy people and beautiful things. She is sure that she has it; and her mother, and Elinor (probably, though Marianne has occasional sharp doubts), and Willoughby. She will settle for nothing less, she regards anything less with impatience and contempt.

Mrs. Jennings has no sensibility—certainly little enough discrimination. She loves her daughters, frosty Lady Middleton and foolish Mrs. Palmer, equally and unqualifiedly. She is even incapable of taking offense from her offensive son-in-law, Mr. Palmer, when he remarks to his wife:

"I did not know I contradicted any body in calling your mother ill-bred."

"Aye, you may abuse me as you please," said the good-natured old lady, "you have taken Charlotte off my hands, and cannot give her back again. So there I have the whip hand of you." (ss 112)

Her gossipy good nature needs no encouragement. She is pleased with Sir John, pleased with the Steele girls, pleased with Edward, pleased with Colonel Brandon and his love for Marianne:

". . . Well, Colonel, I have brought two young ladies with me, you see—that is, you see but one of them now, but there is another somewhere. Your friend Miss Marianne, too—which you will not be sorry to hear. I do not know what you and Mr. Willoughby will do between you about her. Aye, it is a fine thing to be young and handsome. . . ." (ss 163)

She is pleased enough with Elinor and Marianne to invite

them to stay with her at her London house for an indefinite period:

> ". . . I thought it would be more comfortable for them to be together; because if they got tired of me, they might talk to one another, and laugh at my odd ways behind my back. . . ." (ss 154)

and to bustle about the two of them there like a mother-hen. When Willoughby's treachery is revealed, she exclaims with genuine, if unappreciated, concern:

> ". . . I have no notion of men's going on in this way: and if ever I meet him again, I will give him such a dressing as he has not had this many a day. But there is one comfort, my dear Miss Marianne; he is not the only young man in the world worth having; and with your pretty face you will never want admirers. Well, poor thing! I won't disturb her any longer, for she had better have her cry out at once, and have done with it. . . ." (ss 192)

And it is appropriate that her abundantly optimistic mind leaps at once to Colonel Brandon's improved chances:

> ". . . 'tis a true saying about an ill wind, for it will be all the better for Colonel Brandon. He will have her at last; aye, that he will. Mind me, now, if they an't married by Midsummer. Lord! how he'll chuckle over this news! . . ." (ss 196)

In the face of such pushing unmanageable cheerfulness, Marianne is for a long time unwilling to accept its sincerity or value:

> Her heart was hardened against the belief of Mrs. Jennings's entering into her sorrows with any compassion.
> "No, no, no, it cannot be," she cried; "she cannot feel. Her kindness is not sympathy; her good nature is not tenderness. All that she wants is gossip, and she only likes me now because I supply it." (ss 201)

True, Mrs. Jennings is not altogether undiscriminating. She dislikes Mrs. John Dashwood for her obvious coldness toward Elinor and Marianne. (ss 229) She is indignant about Willoughby's treatment of Marianne. She bluntly declares to John Dashwood that his mother-in-law has acted meanly in disinheriting Edward for his engagement to Lucy (ss 267ff.); and here she articulates in her own manner the feelings that Marianne suppresses, remembering her promise of self-control.

Marianne must have been aware of this, just as she is finally aware of Mrs. Jennings' devoted attendance upon her in her grave and prolonged illness; and, when the time of departure comes, she takes

> . . . so particular and lengthened a leave of Mrs. Jennings, one so earnestly grateful, so full of respect and kind wishes as seemed due to her own heart from a secret acknowledgment of past inattention. . . . (ss 341)

Thus Mrs. Jennings is recognized by Marianne at last, and it is clear that Marianne has so far enlarged her definition of worthiness as to include a sympathy by no means synonymous with sensibility. Yet Marianne's notion of sensibility remains; and we have yet learned nothing to make it appear trivial or invalid, or seriously inadequate as a criterion of human value. As such a criterion, it is tested—so the author, and Elinor, manifestly intend us to believe—by the personality and the ultimate decision of Willoughby.

No hero enters a story more romantically than Willoughby. To sweep into his arms a lovely girl who has just turned her ankle, and carry her to the pretty cottage which is her home: the circumstances alone are enough to predispose us—and Marianne, Elinor, and their mother—in his favor. No hero, besides, is given the benefit of a more attractive appearance and manner:

> Elinor and her mother rose up in amazement at their entrance, and while the eyes of both were fixed on him with an evident wonder and a secret admiration which equally sprung from his appearance, he apologized for his intrusion by relating its cause, in a manner so frank and so graceful, that his person, which was uncommonly handsome, received additional charms from his voice and expression. (ss 42)

The most engaging description the author presents of Marianne coincides with another highly favorable view of Willoughby, when he returns the next day to inquire about her recovery:

> . . . her smile was sweet and attractive, and in her eyes, which were very dark, there was a life, a spirit, an eagerness which could hardly be seen without delight. From Willoughby their expression was at first held back, by the embarrassment which the remembrance of his assistance created. But when this

passed away, when her spirits became collected, when she saw
that to the perfect good-breeding of the gentleman, he united
frankness and vivacity, and above all, when she heard him declare that of music and dancing he was passionately fond, she
gave him such a look of approbation as secured the largest
share of his discourse to herself for the rest of his stay. (ss 46)
They are soon talking with an enthusiasm and familiarity so
unusual—and perhaps, conventionally, so suspect—for a
formal first meeting that Elinor cannot refrain from teasing
her sister as soon as Willoughby leaves. Whether or not
Elinor is even partly serious now on the side of sense and
cautious bourgeois convention, Marianne's retort is a powerful defense of sensibility:

". . . I have been too much at my ease, too happy, too frank. I
have erred against every common-place notion of decorum; I
have been open and sincere where I ought to have been reserved, spiritless, dull, and deceitful:—had I talked only of
the weather and the roads, and had I spoken only once in ten
minutes, this reproach would have been spared." (ss 48)

What is wrong with enthusiasm, familiarity, a quick sharing of tastes, an instantaneous sympathy between a handsome,
cultivated young man and an ardent and beautiful girl? Elinor
does not know yet, except that the situation develops too
rapidly, that a courtship should proceed more gradually toward love and betrothal, that Marianne and Willoughby are
too shut off from the rest of the world in their discovery of
each other, that when they have time for the rest of the world
they both are much too frank and unconventional in their
judgments of it. Colonel Brandon is a dullard, Mrs. Jennings
a vulgar gossip, the others at Barton Park unmentionable.
They claim special privileges for lovers: Marianne—ignoring
convention and the expense of upkeep—may accept as a gift
a horse from Willoughby's stables; she may accompany Willoughby unchaperoned on a visit to the wealthy old woman
who has made him her heir (acts considered not immoral, it
must be remembered, but at worst suspiciously unconventional, in the context of class and time). For Elinor, the lovers
are denying their social obligations. And Elinor deplores,
though she cannot yet come to a decisive adverse judgment.

Even Elinor does not accuse Marianne or Willoughby of deliberate unkindness. They are thoughtless of everyone else, they talk a complete language, and those who do not they scorn in order to emphasize their own happy and unlimited communication. Marianne, at seventeen, begins

> ... to perceive that the desperation which had seized her at sixteen and a half, of ever seeing a man who could satisfy her ideas of perfection, had been rash and unjustifiable. (ss 49)

But when she feels she has hurt Elinor or her mother, she is immediately contrite, "softened in a moment." (ss 48) She is never vindictive, just youthfully unsympathetic, and still more so now in the excitement of first love, toward the obtuse and the insensitive, those—as she sees them now—incapable of falling passionately in love. As for Willoughby, Elinor's single objection is that

> In hastily forming and giving his opinion of other people, in sacrificing general politeness to the enjoyment of undivided attention where his heart was engaged, and in slighting too easily the forms of worldly propriety, he displayed a want of caution which Elinor could not approve, in spite of all that he and Marianne could say in its support. (ss 49)

The charge is, then, that they are young and incautiously, thoughtlessly—though deeply—in love; and there is no other charge, so far, against either Marianne or Willoughby.

It is not long, however, before we are provided with a group of new, impressive, and increasingly somber charges against Willoughby. We have learned, till now, only that he and Marianne, to all appearances, are deeply in love; that the strong exclusiveness of their feeling has allowed Marianne, at least, to confide in no one else; and that they are handsome and sensitive young persons disdainful of convention and stupidity, which they tend to equate. This is all we know, or have reason to suspect.

The first more disquieting fact is Willoughby's announcement that he is leaving for London and will not be likely to return for a year or more; and the disquiet is multiplied by Willoughby's obvious strain in notifying Elinor and her mother, and by Marianne's violent grief. There is no question of a quarrel, or of cooling affection. The explanation may be that Mrs. Smith has sent her heir away on business of hers in order to save him from marriage with an unpropertied girl, and that Willoughby has not, for the time being, dared refuse. So Elinor hopes, in spite of her suspicions, as she cries to her optimistic and reproachful mother:

> "I love Willoughby, sincerely love him; and suspicion of his integrity cannot be more painful to yourself than to me. . . ." (ss 81)

For some time, the situation does not alter much. We learn very little because our only source of information is Elinor, and Marianne is not confiding in her now. From what we do learn, the disquiet remains, but it is tempered with hope. We hear nothing about Willoughby; but Marianne, after the first shock of his departure, does not seem despondent at all. When Edward visits the sisters, his matter-of-factness moves Marianne to recall pensively that there was *someone* on whom her sensibility was not lost. (ss 88) Mrs. Palmer's remark that her home at Cleveland is near Willoughby's estate arouses excited interest, not pain, in Marianne. (ss 111) When Mrs. Jennings invites the sisters to her house in London, Elinor permits her first negative impulse to be overruled by Marianne's eagerness to accept—clearly in order to see Willoughby again. (ss 153ff.) No sooner have they arrived at Mrs. Jennings' than Elinor observes her sister rapidly writing and dispatching a letter, on the face of which she "thought she could distinguish a large W." (ss 161)—and Elinor is pleased because she knows that no well-bred girl writes to a man to whom she is not formally engaged.

The disquiet begins now to intensify; our disquiet also, for Marianne. Neither Willoughby, nor a letter from him appears. About a week later, when the sisters return from a morning drive, his card is on the table:

> "Good God!" cried Marianne, "he has been here while we were out." (ss 169)

When Elinor, in the tightening anxiety, accuses Marianne of lacking confidence in her, the accusation is strongly returned:

> "Nay, Elinor, this reproach from *you*—you who have confidence in no one!"

"Me!" returned Elinor in some confusion; "indeed, Marianne, I have nothing to tell."

"Nor I," answered Marianne with energy, "our situations then are alike. We have neither of us any thing to tell; you because you communicate, and I, because I conceal nothing." (ss 170)

We learn, then, that even Marianne's secrecy, which had seemed one of the least excusable traits of her relationship with Willoughby, has been largely a defense, a smarting reaction against Elinor's own secrecy about Edward, Lucy, and herself; and our sympathy moves still closer to Marianne.

When, finally, at a party to which Elinor accompanies the increasingly troubled Marianne, Willoughby appears, his cold courtesy, his total failure of kindness are almost as overpowering to the reader as to Marianne; and the picture of the passionate and beautiful girl, in an agony of doubt and bewilderment, takes its place beside the scene in *Persuasion* at the White Hart Inn as Jane Austen's most affecting representation of feeling—here, not mature and diffused as with Anne Elliot, but youthful, concentrated, sickeningly desperate:

"But have you not received my notes?" cried Marianne in the wildest anxiety. "Here is some mistake I am sure—some dreadful mistake. What can be the meaning of it? Tell me, Willoughby; for heaven's sake tell me, what is the matter?" (ss 177)

and in its acute continuance after the party, at home, when Elinor entreats her sister to make an effort against her grief:

"I cannot, I cannot," cried Marianne; "leave me, leave me, if I distress you; leave me, hate me, forget me! but do not torture me so. . . ." (ss 185)

It must be borne steadily in mind that the author intends to impress upon us these crucial conclusions: that Marianne, however winning and lovely (and she is perhaps more winning and lovely even than Jane Austen had originally planned), must appear to have been made unhappy because sensibility—unlike Elinor's sense—fatally damages the judgment (this is, in fact, the theme of the book); that it is Marianne's sensibility which has caused her critical misjudgment of Willoughby; and that only by renouncing sensibility as a guide can she become settled and happy.

Now there is no question, finally, of Willoughby's duplicity and depravity. As he informs Elinor later, his first intention was only to trifle with Marianne. After he has begun to feel a real affection for her, he abandons her for an heiress because his potential benefactress, outraged by one of his (presumably many) amorous adventures, decides to disinherit him. He never gives Marianne the benefit of an explanation, nor anyone else for that matter, until Marianne is apparently on her deathbed. He is a waster and a coward, at our first introduction to him temporarily disguised by his wit, demeanor, and intelligence. Certainly, Marianne—however accurately she has judged others—has made a mistake about Willoughby.

A question still remains. Has it been Marianne's *sensibility* that was responsible for her mistake? Judgment, on the basis of partial evidence, is difficult for anyone. In *Pride and Prejudice*, the problem of Wickham—a character strikingly similar to Willoughby—is clouded and complicated by the problem of Darcy: we—and Elizabeth—know by the expressed terms of their intense mutual dislike that one of them is honest and the other not; and we must wait on further evidence before we can ultimately decide about either. Even so, we do not feel that in Elizabeth's early infatuation with Wickham her judgment has been ruined by her sensibility. We feel only that she is youthfully confident on the basis of partial evidence; and Elizabeth soon has Darcy's letter, and many events besides, to enlighten her before she has committed herself. Marianne, on the other hand, has none of these aids to judgment. Why should Willoughby not be what he appears? There is no Darcy in the vicinity: only poor, mute, aging, hat-in-hand Colonel Brandon. There is no letter, and no event except love-making—until the catastrophe.

What, moreover, do the other main characters think of Willoughby? Marianne's mother, of course, is enchanted with him. "Why," she asks Marianne, before Willoughby has yet made his gallant entrance, "should you be less fortunate than your mother . . ." (ss 18): that is, in achieving a blissful marriage founded on passionate love? And Willoughby seems to fulfill her prophecy. Edward does not know his prospective brother-in-law. Colonel Brandon knows Willoughby, and has better reasons than jealousy for disliking him; but he never tells anyone until it is too late. Elinor's attitude is the most curious of all.

Elinor has misgivings about Willoughby, but they exclusively concern his failure to attend to social forms. (ss 49) He—as well as Marianne—is unconventional; and their separate impulses to condemn or ignore convention reinforce each other. Yet Elinor has no inkling of Willoughby's motives, and she doubts neither his attachment nor its honorable end in marriage. Elinor too, even without sensibility, makes the mistake of considering Willoughby a very eligible bachelor. Later, of course, after he has treated Marianne so cruelly face to face and in his letter, and especially after Colonel Brandon has made his belated disclosure, Elinor sees Willoughby as a monster of debauchery and deceit. By all odds, however, her most unexpected and interesting reaction to him occurs during and after his long concluding interview with her.

She starts out feeling only impatience and anger with his presumptuousness: several times she asks him to leave, and only his fierce insistence on being heard overcomes her disinclination to listen. (ss 317ff.) So she listens to the tedious eighteenth-century tale of extravagance, debts, and loose living, relieved (and made somewhat credible) only by Willoughby's uncontrolled galling regret for what he has lost with Marianne. He has really loved Marianne; and, ostensibly, it is the recognition of this fact that softens Elinor's attitude toward him. We are not surprised by a softening, a more evident charity; but Elinor's change of heart—once she need no longer regard him as a monster—goes far beyond this.

Her first moral reflection is really a vindication of Marianne:
Her thoughts were silently fixed on the irreparable injury which too early an independence and its consequent habits of idleness, dissipation, and luxury, had made in the mind, the character, the happiness of a man who, to every advantage of person and talents, united a disposition naturally open and honest, and a feeling, affectionate temper. (ss 331)

Doubtless; and it was this potential Willoughby—made actual for a time by excitement and then love—that Marianne saw quite clearly, that her sensibility, far from blinding her, *helped* her to see clearly.

When Willoughby leaves at last, sped by Elinor's good wishes, he leaves Elinor to a "croud of ideas," (ss 333) most of them astonishingly imprudent for a protagonist of sense:

> She felt that his influence over her mind was heightened by circumstances which ought not in reason to have weight; by that person of uncommon attraction, that open, affectionate, and lively manner which it was no merit to possess; and by that still ardent love for Marianne, which it was not even innocent to indulge. But she felt that it was so, long, long before she could feel his influence less. (ss 333)

Even the arrival of her anguished mother at Marianne's bedside hardly diverts these musings. Elinor, in a state of agitation as much erotic as compassionate, cannot drive "Willoughby, 'poor Willoughby,' as she now allowed herself to call him," (ss 334) from her thoughts long enough to fall asleep:

> . . . she would not but have heard his vindication for the world, and now blamed, now acquitted herself for having judged him so harshly before. But her promise of relating it to her sister was invariably painful. She dreaded the performance of it, dreaded what its effect on Marianne might be; doubted whether after such an explanation she could ever be happy with another; and for a moment wished Willoughby a widower. (ss 334f.)

So, in her persistent vicarious lover's revery, she wishes Mrs. Willoughby dead and Willoughby Marianne's husband, before she can spare even a thought for her former favorite, Colonel Brandon, for "*his* sufferings and *his* constancy." (ss 335) When her mother, relieved by Marianne's recovery and bursting with the news of Colonel Brandon's profession of love for Marianne, declares that the Colonel will in any case be a better husband for her than Willoughby would have been, Elinor—though silently—"could not quite agree with her" (ss 338); and, as their conversation is interrupted,

> . . . Elinor withdrew to think it all over in private, to wish suc-

cess for her friend, and yet in wishing it, to feel a pang for Willoughby. (ss 339)

This is Elinor's last pang for her sister's lover; and, while the story is being tidied up into its prudent conclusion, we tend to forget the contradiction of attitudes, explicit and implicit, here involved. Elinor is her author's conscience: she clearly and frequently directs the reader toward the judgments he must make, she establishes the moral atmosphere, the right of sense against her sister's wrong of sensibility, and she—unlike all the other characters in the novel—is totally shielded from her author's irony or social disapproval. Yet as surely as we are intended to condemn Willoughby after his disclosure, we must nevertheless at this very point observe Elinor—and presumably the author—almost in love, and quite amorally in love, with him. Not only does irony fail here for the moment, but the conscience of the novel, the formal conscience of the rural gentry, becomes embarrassingly transparent; and through the flagrant inconsistency of her heroine Jane Austen is herself revealed in a posture of yearning for the impossible and lost, the passionate and beautiful hero, the absolute lover.

The revelation is momentary, and must give way to the triumph of the formal conscience: to its embodiment, the *consistent* Elinor; and to the conscientious suitors, Edward Ferrars and Colonel Brandon, the men who live by form.

Adherence to form is, first of all, their most crucial trait from the standpoint of the plot. It is this trait which generates the dual suspense of the entire novel: whether Elinor's love for Edward will ultimately and happily be returned, whether Marianne's rapid and unreserved attachment will be vindicated. If Edward might break his secret engagement to the girl he no longer even likes or at least confide his problem to the girl he now loves, Elinor would be spared most of the anxiety that shadows her; if Colonel Brandon might for a moment qualify or set aside his code, which permits him to fight a duel with Willoughby but not to tell Marianne's family the truth about her prospective husband, Marianne's mistake would have been evident much earlier, at least to Elinor, and perhaps with considerably less, surely with less prolonged and bewildered, suffering for Marianne. But Edward and the Colonel are honorable, and honor is adherence to form: to formal betrothals, to the convention of personal reticence, to the gentleman's code which may call the evildoer to account on behalf of his past victims but not, apparently, of his future ones. Every action must be referred to that peculiar complex of persistent feudal and supervening bourgeois conventions which to Jane Austen's class seemed the base and guarantee of social order; and the highest virtue is adherence to social forms at whatever personal cost. This virtue Edward and Colonel Brandon—and Elinor (except during her regretful daydream about Willoughby)—infallibly have.

It is, in fact, the only self-evident virtue, or attraction, of either suitor. The trouble with both is not that they are honorable, but that their honor does not prevent them from seeming limited and insipid social figures, just as Marianne's and Willoughby's inattention to form does not prevent them from seeming vivacious and likable individuals.

Edward Ferrars is Elinor's own choice: Elinor often assures her dubious sister that he is an intelligent and upright young man, that "his mind is well-informed, his enjoyment of books exceedingly great, his imagination lively, his observation just and correct, and his taste delicate and pure." (ss 20) There is no question about Elinor's opinion; but the author never produces the evidence upon which it is purportedly founded. In the action of the novel, whatever Edward says or does makes him seem very damp company. When he meets and presumably falls in love with Elinor, the author does not give him a word or a scene; and even Elinor is soon aware of his frequent "want of spirits" and "dejection of mind." (ss 22) On his first speaking appearance, during his visit to Elinor at Barton Cottage,

> His coldness and reserve mortified her severely; she was vexed and half angry . . . . (ss 89)

A discussion of shyness with Elinor and Marianne causes him to sit "for some time silent and dull." (ss 95) Elinor, however, is still eager to explain his dullness away, as the result, probably, of his fear of being disinherited (and Elinor's sense regards this, of course, as a most legitimate fear):

> His want of spirits, of openness, and of consistency, were most usually attributed to his want of independence, and his better knowledge of Mrs. Ferrars's disposition and designs. (ss 101f.)

When she learns of his secret engagement to Lucy, she is delighted to excuse everything: he is, after all, only the honorable victim of convention. And we, too, are ready now to observe him in a more understanding light, to accept new evidence and revaluate the old. But nothing new happens. When Edward next appears, breaking in, awkwardly enough, on Elinor and Lucy together, our impression of his clumsy and characterless reserve in any personal situation is unhappily reinforced. Elinor may have "gloried in his integrity," (ss 270) in his refusal, that is, to renounce his engagement to an avaricious, self-sufficient girl whom he now glumly dislikes; but even this "integrity" is something we only hear about. The Edward we see and hear for ourselves is insistently the person whose meetings with Elinor cause them to sit down together "in a most promising state of embarrassment," (ss 288) and who customarily leaves "with rather an attempt to return . . . [Elinor's] good will, than the power of expressing it." (ss 290) Even when Edward is honorably free to ask Elinor to marry him, the author cannot present his ecstasy and triumph except as a matter of hearsay:

> How soon he had walked himself into the proper resolution, however, how soon an opportunity of exercising it occurred, in what manner he expressed himself, and how he was received, need not be particularly told. This only need be said;—that when they all sat down to table at four o'clock, about three hours after his arrival, he had secured his lady, engaged her mother's consent, and was not only in the rapturous profession of the lover, but in the reality of reason and truth, one of the happiest of men. (ss 361)

To all of which we may be excused for repeating Elinor's words on another occasion:

> "All this . . . is very pretty; but it can impose upon neither of us." (ss 148)

upon neither the reader nor, it is likely, the author. There is simply no evidence. Edward ventures finally to explain his youthful infatuation with Lucy; and that is all, except for marriage and the author's word on their happy thereafter. The temptation is, then, irresistible to reject Elinor's—and the author's—notion of Edward, and to turn thankfully to Marianne's sensibility, which from the very outset judges, though with generous allowances on Elinor's behalf, that Edward is as "spiritless" and "tame" as his manner in reading Cowper. (ss 17)

If Edward Ferrars is dull, Colonel Brandon is a vacuum. Introducing him, the author describes him as "silent and grave" (ss 34); and this is the liveliest account we have of him. He is a colorless, aging bachelor, and Marianne's response to the suggestion of his being in love with her seems quite just and charitable:

> ". . . he is old enough to be *my* father; and if he were ever animated enough to be in love, must have long outlived every sensation of the kind. It is too ridiculous! When is a man to be safe from such wit, if age and infirmity will not protect him?" (ss 37)

Nor does Elinor's objection that the Colonel

> ". . . merely . . . chanced to complain yesterday (a very cold damp day) of a slight rheumatic feel in one of his shoulders." (ss 38)

explain why, though cheerlessly reticent on all other matters, he is so unperceptive, in the company of the young and romantic girl he loves, as to publicize such an unromantic ailment. We are told that

> In Colonel Brandon alone, of all her new acquaintance, did Elinor find a person who could in any degree claim the respect of abilities, excite the interest of friendship, or give pleasure as a companion. (ss 55)

But abilities, interest, and pleasure are things that Elinor alone finds in the Colonel, that exist nowhere in the Colonel outside Elinor's mind. His actual appearances are a series of solemn silences, wistful allusions to Marianne's opinion against "second attachments," hesitations and abortive beginnings in conversation, until even Elinor is reduced to impatience by his inarticulateness. (ss 172) His wordless devotion during

Marianne's illness does at last move kind-hearted Marianne to regard him with a "pitying eye," (ss 216) which is precisely what it deserves. He offers Edward Ferrars the living of Delaford, a favor for which everyone is duly grateful, and which labels the Colonel philanthropist as well as old bachelor. After another period of mooning at Delaford, he comes to Barton, at a time when events seem for the first time disposed to give him a chance with Marianne,

> . . . in a temper of mind which needed all the improvement in Marianne's looks, all the kindness of her welcome, and all the encouragement of her mother's language, to make it cheerful. Among such friends, however, and such flattery, he did revive. (ss 369f.)

Revive, one may ask, to what? As with Edward, we are never shown any life which the Colonel, freed from anxiety, might resume; and the author is not enlightening when she gives us the summary account of another offstage marriage, without a proposal that we are permitted to hear (could we believe our ears in hearing the proposal of a Colonel Brandon to a Marianne Dashwood?) or a bridegroom who can even mildly engage our interest.

There is a single occasion on which Colonel Brandon speaks at some length: when he tells all regarding Willoughby. Here, doubtless, we are intended to observe the Colonel in his true light as a nobly feeling man, by contrast with the revealed infamy of his rival. The sad fact is, however, that just at this point Jane Austen's control of her subject collapses utterly. Indeed, she here represents in its pure state what has been till now one of the prime targets of her irony, the primly salacious core of the sentimental novel; and the scene is littered, not uproariously as in "Love and Freindship" but quite unironically, with those sure-fire tear-jerking puppets of the Mackenzian novelist—the ruined female victims and bastard offspring of dissolute gentlemen. By the time Colonel Brandon has concluded his obstetrical report on Eliza One:

> ". . . So altered—so faded—worn down by acute suffering of every kind! hardly could I believe the melancholy and sickly figure before me, to be the remains of the lovely, blooming, healthful girl, on whom I had once doated. . . ." (ss 207)

and Eliza Two, impregnated by Willoughby, the effect may verge on hilarity or acute boredom; but in any case the author has buried Colonel Brandon, not only as a man of feeling, but as a sympathetic, largely even as a credible, character.

If we need a judgment on the Colonel Brandon who remains, we find that even silly Mrs. Palmer, so anxious to put in a good word for everyone, sums him up accurately:

".. . He is such a charming man, that it is quite a pity he should be so grave and so dull. . . ." (ss 115)

And Willoughby's judgment—in which Marianne concurs, at least in the beginning—is the final one:

"Brandon is just the kind of man . . . whom every body speaks well of, and nobody cares about; whom all are delighted to see, and nobody remembers to talk to." (ss 50)

The alternatives to Willoughby are the alternatives to feeling. Edward Ferrars and Colonel Brandon represent, in fact, the antidote to feeling, the proposition that the only cure for a passionate heart is to remove it. Now it is true that Jane Austen begins with the notion of sensibility as it appears in the Mackenzian novel, as a foolish, exaggerated, literary, indeed an emotionless emotionalism: a notion which instigates the tired parody of a sensibility character that Marianne seems at first. Much more significantly, however, Marianne through the main action of the novel is not this at all: She is a person of strong, complex, and abiding passion, which Jane Austen nevertheless insists on equating with Mackenzian sensibility, and which she ultimately exorcises altogether. Not merely *false* feeling, but feeling itself, is bad: not because it leads to misjudgment[1] (we have seen that it had nothing to do even with Marianne's misjudgment of Willoughby, and that Marianne is in general a more trustworthy judge of people than her sister), not because it invariably leads to unhappiness (we must take Mrs. Henry Dashwood's word that her romantic marriage was a very happy one), not because it gives Marianne a false or one-sided view of the world (for she sees the

---

[1] Miss Lascelles is clearly ignoring the facts when she observes that ". . . the misjudgement of people which causes Marianne so much suffering springs directly from her romantic vision of the world, as this from her reading." (M. Lascelles, *Jane Austen and Her Art*, Oxford, 1939, 64f.)

other side, but simply disregards it unless it blocks her). Irony and social forms are good because they enable one to remain detached, from oneself as from others; and feeling is bad because it is a personal commitment.

Irony, which has till now been Jane Austen's defense against feeling, is here reinforced and ultimately superseded by another defense, more official if less artistic: social convention, the code of a society which makes no provision, because in stabilizing itself it is otherwise employed, for feeling. Yet it is Jane Austen who has created Marianne, the "burning heart of passion,"[2] even if she buries her finally in the coffin of convention. Against her own moral will and conscious artistic purpose, the creator makes her creature wholly sympathetic—because, one must conclude, Marianne represents an unacknowledged depth of her author's spirit. Still, because it is an aspect which, even outside herself, Jane Austen will not acknowledge to be good, Marianne must be humiliated and destroyed. Irony and social convention turn out to be Jane Austen's defenses, not only against the world, but against herself, against the heart of passion. Irony is her defense as an artist, the novelist who organizes her work so firmly and totally as to leave us without a sense of loss for the personal commitment she will not make; and convention is her defense as the genteel spinster when the artist is overcome, perhaps by some powerful social or domestic pressure, perhaps by the pressure of a theme too close to commitment or of an insurgent sympathetic committing character like Marianne.

So Elinor rebukes Marianne by implying that in her still disappointed love for Edward she is as unhappy as Marianne but has kept silent because of "what I owed to my dearest friends" (ss 264) (an implication for which one would be hard put to find evidence in the novel, where Elinor seems amorously moved only by Willoughby); and Marianne begins her recantation:

"Oh! Elinor," she cried, "you have made me hate myself for ever.—How barbarous have I been to you!—you, who have

---

[2] The phrase is George Moore's, quoted by R. W. Chapman, in *Jane Austen: Facts and Problems*, Oxford, 1948, 193.

been my only comfort, who have borne with me in all my misery, who have seemed to be only suffering for me! . . ." (ss 264)

In consequence of her almost mortal illness, Marianne moves closer and closer to identity with Elinor, until at last she atones altogether for what she has been, and virtually *becomes* Elinor:

> ". . . Do not, my dearest Elinor, let your kindness defend what I know your judgment must censure. My illness has made me think—It has given me leisure and calmness for serious recollection. . . ." (ss 345)

She concludes in a missionary forgiving spirit which encompasses not only Mrs. Jennings, but the Middletons, the Palmers, the Steeles, as far as the John Dashwoods. And the author leaves this submissive Marianne in the arms of Colonel Brandon, wealthy, propertied, honorable, the very symbol of social forms and of their climax in prudent middle-class marriage, and therefore her natural unalterable contrary.

In spite of the genteel moralist who has taken charge of the novel, the novelist proper comes enough alive before the end to recall that she has embarked on a comedy; but her attempt to bring us back to the presumed even tenor of reality is too abrupt and half-hearted to convince. The daylight to which she returns us, of Edward and Elinor settled at Delaford Rectory, especially of poor muted transformed Marianne's eventual acceptance (again, without the peril of dialogue) of the Colonel:

> Marianne Dashwood was born to an extraordinary fate. She was born to discover the falsehood of her own opinions, and to counteract, by her conduct, her most favourite maxims. She was born to overcome an affection formed so late in life as at seventeen, and with no sentiment superior to strong esteem and lively friendship, voluntarily to give her hand to another!—and *that* other, a man who had suffered no less than herself under the event of a former attachment, whom two years before, she had considered too old to be married,—and who still sought the constitutional safeguard of a flannel waistcoat! (ss 378)

and even of Willoughby's unromantic ability to enjoy life a little despite his wickedness and stupid choice:

> . . . that he was for ever inconsolable, that he fled from society, or contracted an habitual gloom of temper, or died of a broken

heart, must not be depended on—for he did neither. He lived to exert, and frequently to enjoy himself. (ss 379)
this daylight of reality, as the author wrenches us back to the (never firmly established) parodic frame of reference and to the good humor she hopes it embodies, is very gray. We may be assured that everyone turns out to be prudently happy, with even a share of domestic satisfaction left for the villain. But we are not to be reconciled. Marianne, the life and center of the novel, has been betrayed; and not by Willoughby.

CHAPTER IV

IRONY AS DISCRIMINATION

PRIDE AND PREJUDICE

IN *Pride and Prejudice*, for the first time, Jane Austen allows her heroine to share her own characteristic response to the world. Elizabeth Bennet tells Darcy:

". . . Follies and nonsense, whims and inconsistencies do divert me, I own, and I laugh at them whenever I can. . . ." (PP 57)

The response is not only characteristic of Elizabeth and her author, but consciously and articulately aimed at by both of them. Both choose diversion; and both, moreover, look for their diversion in the people about them. Elizabeth, despite her youth and the limitations of a rural society, is—like the author of "Lesley Castle" and "The Three Sisters"—a busy "studier of character," as Bingley leads her to affirm:

"You begin to comprehend me, do you?" cried he, turning towards her.

"Oh! yes—I understand you perfectly."

"I wish I might take this for a compliment; but to be so easily seen through I am afraid is pitiful."

"That is as it happens. It does not necessarily follow that a deep, intricate character is more or less estimable than such a one as yours."

"Lizzy," cried her mother, "remember where you are, and do not run on in the wild manner that you are suffered to do at home."

"I did not know before," continued Bingley immediately, "that you were a studier of character. It must be an amazing study."

"Yes; but intricate characters are the *most* amusing. They have at least that advantage." (PP 42)

"Character" gains a general overtone: with Elizabeth's qualifying adjective, it becomes not only the summation of a single personality, but the summation of a type, the fixing of the individual into a category. So Elizabeth sets herself up as an ironic spectator, able and prepared to judge and classify, already making the first large division of the world into two sorts of people: the simple ones, those who give themselves away out of shallowness (as Bingley fears) or perhaps openness (as Elizabeth implies) or an excess of affectation (as Mr. Collins will demonstrate); and the intricate ones, those who cannot be judged and classified so easily, who are "the most amusing" to the ironic spectator because they offer the most formidable challenge to his powers of detection and analysis. Into one of these preliminary categories, Elizabeth fits everybody she observes.

Elizabeth shares her author's characteristic response of comic irony, defining incongruities without drawing them into a moral context; and, still more specifically, Elizabeth's vision of the world as divided between the simple and the intricate is, in *Pride and Prejudice* at any rate, Jane Austen's vision also. This identification between the author and her heroine establishes, in fact, the whole ground pattern of judgment in the novel. The first decision we must make about anyone, so Elizabeth suggests and the author confirms by her shaping commentary, is not moral but psychological, not whether he is good or bad, but whether he is simple or intricate: whether he may be disposed of as fixed and predictable or must be recognized as variable, perhaps torn between contradictory motives, intellectually or emotionally complex, unsusceptible to a quick judgment.

Once having placed the individual in his category, we must proceed to discriminate him from the others there; and, in the category of simplicity at least, Elizabeth judges as accurately as her author. Jane Austen allows the "simple" characters to have no surprises for Elizabeth, and, consequently, none for us. They perform, they amuse; but we never doubt that we know what they are, and why they act as they do.

We know Mrs. Bennet, for example, at once, in her first conversation with her husband, as she describes the newcomer at Netherfield Park:

". . . A single man of large fortune; four or five thousand a year. What a fine thing for our girls." (PP 3f.)

And the author curtly sums her up at the end of the first chapter:

She was a woman of mean understanding, little information, and uncertain temper. When she was discontented, she fancied herself nervous. The business of her life was to get her daughters married; its solace was visiting and news. (PP 5)

Two subjects dominate her life and conversation: the injustice of the entail by which Mr. Bennet's estate will descend to his closest male relative rather than to his immediate family, and the problem of getting her daughters married. Out of these fixed ideas, untempered by any altruism, circumspection, wit, or intellect, derive all of her appearances and her total function in the story. The matter of the entail serves mainly to introduce Mr. Collins and to complicate the second and stronger fixed idea; it also provides Mr. Bennet with opportunities to bait his wife:

> "About a month ago I received this letter . . . from my cousin, Mr. Collins, who, when I am dead, may turn you all out of the house as soon as he pleases."
>
> "Oh! my dear," cried his wife, "I cannot bear to hear that mentioned. Pray do not talk of that odious man. I do think it is the hardest thing in the world, that your estate should be entailed away from your own children; and I am sure if I had been you, I should have tried long ago to do something or other about it." (PP 61f.)

The problem of getting her daughters married, however, involves her much more directly in the tensions and progress of the narrative. It is her irrepressible vulgarity in discussing Jane's prospective marriage to Bingley which convinces Darcy that any alliance with Mrs. Bennet's family—for his friend or for himself—would be imprudent and degrading:

> . . . Mrs. Bennet seemed incapable of fatigue while enumerating the advantages of the match. His being such a charming young man, and so rich, and living but three miles from them, were the first points of self-gratulation. . . . It was, moreover, such a promising thing for her younger daughter, as Jane's marrying so greatly must throw them in the way of other rich men. . . .
>
> In vain did Elizabeth endeavour to check the rapidity of her mother's words, or persuade her to describe her felicity in a less audible whisper; for to her inexpressible vexation, she could perceive that the chief of it was overheard by Mr. Darcy,

96

who sat opposite to them. Her mother only scolded her for being nonsensical!

"What is Mr. Darcy to me, pray, that I should be afraid of him? I am sure we owe him no such particular civility as to be obliged to say nothing *he* may not like to hear." (PP 99)

Having decided that Darcy is too haughty to pursue any of her daughters, she goes out of her way, in fact, to offend him. When Darcy and Elizabeth exchange opinions on the limits of a country life, Mrs. Bennet cannot forbear adding her own comment:

> "The country," said Darcy, "can in general supply but few subjects for such a study. In a country neighbourhood you move in a very confined and unvarying society."
> "But people themselves alter so much, that there is something new to be observed in them forever."
> "Yes, indeed," cried Mrs. Bennet, offended by his manner of mentioning a country neighbourhood. "I assure you there is quite as much of *that* going on in the country as in town."
> Every body was surprised; and Darcy, after looking at her for a moment, turned silently away. (PP 42f.)

Her feeling toward Mr. Collins swings between extremes of deference and indignation, according as she must consider him a profit or a loss: a suitor, or the holder of the entail. When he is quite unknown to her except as the latter, she detests him. When, in his letter, he barely hints at courting one of the Bennet girls during his coming visit, she thaws almost at once:

> "There is some sense in what he says about the girls however; and if he is disposed to make them any amends, I shall not be the person to discourage him." (PP 83)

When, on appearing, he seems quite bent on marriage,

> Mrs. Bennet . . . trusted that she might soon have two daughters married; and the man whom she could not bear to speak of the day before, was now high in her good graces. (PP 71)

After Elizabeth, in spite of Mrs. Bennet's strenuous pleading, has turned him down and he marries Charlotte Lucas instead, she can see him only as she saw him at first, gloating—and with a wife now to help him gloat—over the entail:

". . . And so, I suppose, they often talk of having Longbourn when your father is dead. They look upon it as quite their own, I dare say, whenever that happens." (PP 228)

Her obsession with material security overrides every consideration of kindness or solicitude toward her husband and her daughters. She sends Jane on horseback to Netherfield on the chance that she may be caught in a rainstorm and obliged to stay overnight; and, when news comes next morning that Jane is ill, Mrs. Bennet is quite unperturbed, even by her husband's sharpest sarcasm:

"Well, my dear," said Mr. Bennet . . . "if your daughter should have a dangerous fit of illness, if she should die, it would be a comfort to know that it was all in pursuit of Mr. Bingley, and under your orders."

"Oh! I am not at all afraid of her dying. People do not die of little trifling colds. She will be taken good care of. As long as she stays there, it is all very well. I would go and see her, if I could have the carriage." (PP 31f.)

Forced to surrender the hope that Bingley will return to Jane, Mrs. Bennet remarks:

". . . Well, my comfort is, I am sure Jane will die of a broken heart, and then he will be sorry for what he has done." (PP 228)

Yet, though she can regard Jane's death as a potential comfort, though she can speak of her husband's death as if it is imminent, and only as it means that she will be turned out of her house by Mr. Collins, she is not at all prepared to contemplate her own:

"Indeed, Mr. Bennet," said she, "it is very hard to think that Charlotte Lucas shall ever be mistress of this house, that *I* shall be forced to make way for *her*, and live to see her take my place in it!"

"My dear, do not give way to such gloomy thoughts. Let us hope for better things. Let us flatter ourselves that *I* may be the survivor."

This was not very consoling to Mrs. Bennet, and, therefore, instead of making any answer, she went on as before . . . (PP 130)

She fears one thing finally: her own physical discomfort, of which death—when her husband maliciously thrusts its image before her—must seem the severest and most frightening variety. An inadequate mind to begin with, marriage to a man who treats her with contempt only, preoccupation with the insistent material concerns imposed by society upon a woman of her class—they have all combined in Mrs. Bennet's single continuously operating motive: to be herself secure and comfortable, and to fortify her own security by getting her daughters settled in prudent marriage, that condition symbolic of material well-being. For Mrs. Bennet, everything in life reduces itself to the dimensions of this motive; everything except her daughter Lydia.

Lydia is, of course, Mrs. Bennet as she must remember herself at the same age:

> Lydia was a stout, well-grown girl of fifteen, with a fine complexion and good-humoured countenance; a favourite with her mother, whose affection had brought her into public at an early age. She had high animal spirits, and a sort of natural self-consequence, which the attentions of the officers, to whom her uncle's good dinners and her own easy manners recommended her, had increased into assurance. (PP 45)

The coming of a militia regiment to Meryton has determined the course of her life, as far ahead as she cares to look. Her sister Kitty is a willing and easily led ally. They can think of nothing but dancing and flirtation, the excitement of a uniform, the sense of importance at hearing and repeating officer gossip, the perspective of innumerable balls and dress parades into the future. When the regiment is ordered to Brighton, their world seems ready to collapse, and Mrs. Bennet is scarcely less despairing:

> "Good Heaven! What is to become of us! What are we to do!" would they often exclaim in the bitterness of woe. "How can you be smiling so, Lizzy?"
> Their affectionate mother shared all their grief; she remembered what she had herself endured on a similar occasion, five and twenty years ago.
> "I am sure," said she, "I cried for two days together when Colonel Millar's regiment went away. I thought I should have broke my heart."
> "I am sure I shall break *mine*," said Lydia. (PP 229)

But Lydia, at least, is spared by receiving an invitation from her good friend, the colonel's wife, to accompany the regiment to Brighton. Parting from Lydia, Mrs. Bennet

> ... was diffuse in her good wishes for the felicity of her daughter, and impressive in her injunctions that she would not miss the opportunity of enjoying herself as much as possible; advice, which there was every reason to believe would be attended to ... (PP 235)

One of Jane Austen's triumphs in *Pride and Prejudice* is her refusal to sentimentalize Lydia (as well as Mrs. Bennet) once she has fashioned her to a hard and simple consistency. Lydia is a self-assured, highly sexed, wholly amoral and unintellectual girl. When she runs off with Wickham, nothing can lower her spirits or drive her to shame—not all the disapproval of society, not the horror and shame of her family (though her mother, of course, is neither horrified nor ashamed). She has done what she wanted to do; and if her uncle or father or someone else must pay Wickham to persuade him to legalize the union, that is their worry, not hers. She is not defiantly, but simply, impenitent: she recognizes no authority to which penitence or concealment is due. If marriage is valued by some, so much the better; if, for no effort on her part, it gives her a social precedence and dignity, she will take these, though she did not ask for them and could have lived without them. And, again, her defender is her mother, who, when the married pair return to Longbourn,

> ... stepped forwards, embraced her, and welcomed her with rapture; gave her hand with an affectionate smile to Wickham, who followed his lady, and wished them both joy, with an alacrity which allowed no doubt of their happiness. (PP 315)

Elizabeth may be "disgusted, and even Miss Bennet . . . shocked," but

> Lydia was Lydia still; untamed, unabashed, wild, noisy, and fearless. (PP 315)

What Elizabeth designates as Lydia's "susceptibility to her feelings," (PP 317) what the author has called her "high animal spirits," (PP 45) is Lydia's only motive, as it must once have been Mrs. Bennet's also; but Lydia has not abandoned it out of prudence or fear, has even seen it assume the unanticipated respectability of marriage:

100

"Well, mamma . . . and what do you think of my husband? Is not he a charming man? I am sure my sisters must all envy me. I only hope they may have half my good luck. They must all go to Brighton. That is the place to get husbands. What a pity it is, mamma, we did not all go."

"Very true; and if I had my will, we should. . . ." (PP 317)

And Lydia never repents; neither mother nor daughter even recognizes that there is anything to repent.

Mr. Collins and Lady Catherine, though "simple" also, differ from Lydia and Mrs. Bennet at least to the extent that Elizabeth can observe them more freely, without the sense of shame and responsibility she must feel toward her mother and sister. Mr. Collins is, indeed, so remote from Elizabeth's personal concerns that she and the reader can enjoy him as a pure fool, unweighted by moral import. The fact that he is a clergyman underscores his foolishness and moral nullity:

". . . I have been so fortunate as to be distinguished by the patronage of the Right Honourable Lady Catherine de Bourgh, widow of Sir Lewis de Bourgh, whose bounty and beneficence has preferred me to the valuable rectory of this parish, where it shall be my earnest endeavour to demean myself with grateful respect towards her Ladyship, and be ever ready to perform those rites and ceremonies which are instituted by the Church of England. As a clergyman, moreover, I feel it my duty to promote and establish the blessing of peace in all families within the reach of my influence; and on these grounds I flatter myself that my present overtures of good-will are highly commendable, and that the circumstance of my being next in the entail of Longbourn estate, will be kindly overlooked on your side, and not lead you to reject the offered olive branch. . . ."[1] (PP 62f.)

[1] One is tempted to believe that Henry Austen, though he was Jane's "favourite brother" (W. and R. A. Austen-Leigh, *Jane Austen: Her Life and Letters*, London, 1913, p. 48), may have provided her with a model for at least Mr. Collins' style in letters. On the acquittal of Warren Hastings (godfather of Henry's cousin Eliza), Henry wrote to Hastings: "Permit me . . . to congratulate my country and myself as an Englishman; for right dear to every Englishman must it be to behold the issue of a combat where forms of judicature threatened to annihilate the essence of justice." (*Ibid.*, 79.) And he wrote to the publisher John Murray concerning *Emma*: ". . . The politeness and perspicuity of your letter equally claim my earliest exertion. . . . Though I venture to differ occasionally from your critique yet I assure you the quantum of your commendation rather exceeds than fall short of the author's expectation and my own. . . ." (*Ibid.*, 310.)

" '. . . Can he be a sensible man, sir?' " Elizabeth asks; and her father replies:

> "No, my dear; I think not. I have great hopes of finding him quite the reverse. There is a mixture of servility and self-importance in his letter, which promises well. I am impatient to see him." (PP 64)

Mr. Bennet's expectation of amusement is fulfilled many times over. "Mr. Collins was not a sensible man," (PP 70) as the author begins a superfluous descriptive paragraph; and his fatuity, sycophancy, conceit, and resolutely unprejudiced wife-hunting are given ample range. Wherever he goes, whatever he does, he remains unshakably foolish. Elizabeth's declining his proposal, once he can believe that it is not to be ascribed to the "usual practice of elegant females," (PP 108) clouds his jauntiness for a moment; but he recovers soon enough to propose as fervently to Charlotte Lucas three days later, and when he leaves Longbourn he wishes his "fair cousins . . . health and happiness, not excepting my cousin Elizabeth." (PP 124) As he likes to be useful to Lady Catherine, so he is useful to the plot: he provides a place for Elizabeth to visit, where she can observe Lady Catherine and see Darcy again; he draws out his "affable and condescending" patroness for Elizabeth's edification; he serves as a medium through which Lady Catherine's opinions on events in the Bennet family are graciously transmitted to the Bennets. And always he remains firm in the conviction of his importance and dignity, of his place at the center—or a little off the matriarchal center—of the universe, whether he is almost walking on air in contemplation of the advantage of Rosings:

> Words were insufficient for the elevation of his feelings; and he was obliged to walk about the room, while Elizabeth tried to unite civility and truth in a few short sentences. (PP 216)

or warning Elizabeth against a "precipitate closure" (PP 363) with Darcy's suit, or offering his clerical opinion on Lydia and Wickham:

> ". . . I must not . . . refrain from declaring my amazement, at hearing that you received the young couple into your house as soon as they were married. It was an encouragement of vice; and had I been the rector of Longbourn, I should very stren-

uously have opposed it. You ought certainly to forgive them as a christian, but never to admit them in your sight, or allow their names to be mentioned in your hearing. (PP 363f.)

Like Mr. Collins, Lady Catherine is chiefly amusing because of the incongruity between the importance she assumes to herself and the actual influence she exercises upon the story. At first glance, she is, of course, far more formidable than Mr. Collins:

> Her air was not conciliating, nor was her manner of receiving them, such as to make her visitors forget their inferior rank. (PP 162)

She has her worshipful courtier in Mr. Collins, who, dining at Rosings, "looked as if he felt that life could furnish nothing greater." (PP 163) And she is confident of having her judgments explicitly followed:

> ... delivering her opinion on every subject in so decisive a manner as proved that she was not used to have her judgement controverted. . . . Elizabeth found that nothing was beneath this great Lady's attention, which could furnish her with an occasion of dictating to others. (PP 163)

Yet, in the story at least, she never does what she thinks she is doing or wishes to do. It is true—as Elizabeth remarks—that "Lady Catherine has been of infinite use, which ought to make her happy, for she loves to be of use." (PP 381) She is useful to the story; but only in ways she is unaware of and would repudiate with outrage if she knew of them. By her insulting condescension toward Elizabeth, she helps Darcy to balance off his distaste of Mrs. Bennet's not dissimilar shortcomings. She provokes Elizabeth into asserting her own independence of spirit, even to the point of impertinence. In her arrogant effort to dissuade Elizabeth from accepting Darcy, she gives Elizabeth the opportunity to set her own proud value upon herself as an individual, and later, having angrily brought the news to Darcy, encourages him to believe that Elizabeth may not refuse him a second time. Lady Catherine is a purely comic figure, not because she is not potentially powerful and dangerous in the authority that rank and wealth confer upon her, but because she is easily known for what she is, and because the lovers are in a position—Darcy by his own rank and wealth, Elizabeth by her spirit and intelligence—to deny her power altogether.

This quality of powerlessness is, indeed, peculiar to Elizabeth's, and the author's, whole category of simplicity: not merely in Mrs. Bennet, Lydia, Mr. Collins, and Lady Catherine, but in the predictably malicious Miss Bingley, in single-postured simpletons like Sir William Lucas and Mary Bennet, down to an unrealized function like Georgiana Darcy. They are powerless, that is, at the center of the story. They cannot decisively divert Elizabeth's or Darcy's mind and purpose because they cannot cope with the adult personality that either of the lovers presents. They are powerless, ultimately, because they are not themselves adult. They convince us of their existence (except, perhaps, Georgiana and Mary), sometimes even brilliantly; but they are not sufficiently complex or self-aware to be taken at the highest level of seriousness. Elizabeth's judgment of them is, then, primarily psychological, not moral: they have not grown to a personal stature significantly measurable by moral law. However Elizabeth may console Bingley that a "deep, intricate character" may be no more "estimable than such a one as yours," (PP 42) the fact is that though she finds simplicity comfortable or amusing, it is only intricacy, complexity of spirit, that she finds fascinating, deserving of pursuit and capture, susceptible to a grave moral judgment.

It may be objected that Jane Bennet belongs in the category of simplicity also, and that Elizabeth, nonetheless, loves and admires her sister above anyone else. Both statements are true; but the latter is true only in a very special sense. There is something maternal, something affectionately envious, something of the nature of a schoolgirl passion in Elizabeth's feeling for Jane. Jane is gentle, sweet, forbearing, incapable of vindictiveness, incapable almost of believing ill of anyone:

". . . You are a great deal too apt . . . to like people in general. You never see a fault in any body. All the world are good and agreeable in your eyes. I never heard you speak ill of a human being in my life."

"I would wish not to be hasty in censuring any one; but I always speak what I think." (PP 14)

Elizabeth may counter with a remark on her sister's "good sense":

> "I know you do; and it is *that* which makes the wonder. With *your* good sense, to be so honestly blind to the follies and nonsense of others! . . ." (PP 14)

Yet it is this honest blindness, not the good sense, that we observe in operation. Jane believes good of everyone, not out of any rational or intuitive knowledge beyond Elizabeth's, but out of a total incapacity to accept the possibility of evil until it quite bluntly proclaims itself. She is a good person because she is by nature too easy and temperate to be otherwise. The difference between her natural, uncomplex, unintuitive, almost unseeing goodness and Elizabeth's conscious, reasoned, perpetual examination into motive—this is a difference not merely between individuals, but between altogether different orders of mind. Elizabeth loves Jane as Jane is a kind and loving sister, she envies Jane her facile solution—or her plain ignorance— of the problems of interpreting personality, she even plays the schoolgirl to her older sister as confidante; but Elizabeth never doubts that Jane's opinions of others have no objective value, and that Jane's response toward people and society is much too simple, even too simple-minded, to be hers. So Elizabeth, as Jane defends Bingley's sisters against her charge of snobbery,

> . . . listened in silence, but was not convinced; their behaviour at the assembly had not been calculated to please in general; and with more quickness of observation and less pliancy of temper than her sister, and with a judgment too unassailed by any attention to herself, she was very little disposed to approve them. (PP 15)

The surest proof of Elizabeth's, and the author's, attitude toward Jane is the lover they are both delighted to supply her with. Bingley is a person of secondary order far more obviously than Jane. He is handsome, very amiable and courteous, lively, properly smitten by Jane almost at first glance. That, and his considerable wealth, make up the extent of his charms. It is significant that Elizabeth never has a twinge of feeling for him, except as he seems a fine catch for her sister. In his conversation with Elizabeth at Netherfield, he fears that he gives himself away out of shallowness (PP 42); and, despite Elizabeth's graceful denial, he does. There is nothing below the surface. His strong-willed friend, Darcy, leads him about by the nose. Though he is supposed to have fallen seriously in love with Jane, the merest trick of Darcy's and his sister's is enough to send and keep him away from her. As Darcy explains:

". . . Bingley is most unaffectedly modest. His diffidence had prevented his depending on his own judgment in so anxious a case, but his reliance on mine, made every thing easy. . . ." (PP 371)

"Modest" is a charitable word here. Darcy has been equally successful, moreover, in turning about and persuading Bingley that Jane *is* in love with him; whereupon

Elizabeth longed to observe that Mr. Bingley had been a most delightful friend; so easily guided that his worth was invaluable. . . . (PP 371)

It is true that Jane pines over Bingley for a long time. She is a sincere and faithful lover; but our admiration of this trait tends to diminish as we think about the object of her love. Jane and Bingley provide us, then, with one of the book's primary ironies: that love is simple, straightforward, and immediate only for very simple people. Jane and Bingley could, of course, have served very well as a pair of story-book lovers, tossed romantically on a sea of circumstances not only beyond their control but beyond their understanding. In the pattern of the novel, however, they have their adult guardians and counterparts—Jane in her sister, Bingley in his friend—to haul them in when the sea gets too rough; and though, like the standard lovers of romance, they will never have to worry about growing up, we are obliged, by the presence of Elizabeth at least, to admit that it *is* possible—perhaps even preferable—for lovers to be complex and mature.

To this point Elizabeth's judgment is as acute and ironic as her author's. Elizabeth, indeed, is far more aware of distinctions in personality than any of the author's previous heroines: Catherine Morland, Elinor or Marianne Dashwood. In *Northanger Abbey*, the author could not allow her heroine

106

to be aware from the outset since her story developed precisely out of Catherine's unawareness of distinctions (a quality suggested, perhaps, by Jane Austen's early tendency to assert an arbitrary omniscience over the objects of her irony). In *Sense and Sensibility*, Jane Austen, yielding for the first time to the moral pressures inevitable upon a woman of her time and class, allowed Elinor only the solemn and easy discriminations of bourgeois morality, and finally smothered the threatening spark of Marianne's much livelier and more observing consciousness. In *Pride and Prejudice*, however, there is no compulsion—personal, thematic, or moral—toward denying the heroine her own powers of judgment. There is, on the contrary, a thematic need for the heroine to display a subtle, accurate, a perceiving mind. In *Pride and Prejudice*, as in the previous novels, Jane Austen deals with the distinction between false moral values and true; but she is also dealing here with a distinction antecedent to the moral judgment—the distinction between the simple personality, unequipped with that self-awareness which alone makes choice seem possible, and the complex personality, whose most crucial complexity is its awareness, of self and others. This distinction, which in her youthful defensive posture Jane Austen has tended to make only between her characters and herself, she here establishes internally, between two categories of personality within the novel. The distinction is, in fact, one that every character in *Pride and Prejudice* must make if he can; and the complex characters—Elizabeth and Darcy among them—justify their complexity by making it, and trying to live by its implications, through all their lapses of arrogance, prejudice, sensuality, and fear. Elizabeth is aware because, in the novel's climate of adult decision, she must be so to survive with our respect and interest.

Yet the distinction must be made in a social setting, by human beings fallible, if for no other reason, because of their own social involvement. The province of *Pride and Prejudice* —as always in Jane Austen's novels—is marriage in an acquisitive society. Elizabeth herself, being young, attractive, and unmarried, is at the center of it; and it is this position that sets her off from such an external and imposed commentator as Henry Tilney. Her position of personal involvement subjects her, moreover, to a risk of error never run by the detached Mr. Tilney. She can tag and dismiss the blatantly simple persons very well; it is when she moves away from these toward ambiguity and self-concealment, toward persons themselves aware enough to interest and engage her, that her youth and inexperience and emotional partiality begin to deceive her.

They deceive her first with Charlotte Lucas. The two girls have been good friends. Charlotte, according to the author, is a "sensible, intelligent young woman," (pp 18) and she shares Elizabeth's taste for raillery and social generalization. Even when Charlotte offers her altogether cynical views on courtship and marriage, Elizabeth refuses to take her at her word:

> ". . . Happiness in marriage is entirely a matter of chance. If the dispositions of the parties are ever so well known to each other, or ever so similar before-hand, it does not advance their felicity in the least. They always continue to grow sufficiently unlike afterwards to have their share of vexation; and it is better to know as little as possible of the defects of the person with whom you are to pass your life."
>
> "You make me laugh, Charlotte; but it is not sound. You know it is not sound, and that you would never act in this way yourself." (pp 23)

It is not that Elizabeth misjudges Charlotte's capabilities, but that she underestimates the strength of the pressures acting upon her. Charlotte is twenty-seven, unmarried, not pretty, not well-to-do, living in a society which treats a penniless old maid less as a joke than as an exasperating burden upon her family. But Elizabeth is inexperienced enough, at the beginning, to judge in terms of personality only. She recognizes Mr. Collins' total foolishness and Charlotte's intelligence, and would never have dreamed that any pressure could overcome so natural an opposition. Complex and simple, aware and unaware, do not belong together—except that in marriages made by economics they often unite, however obvious the mismatching. The trick, as Charlotte decides upon accepting Mr. Collins' proposal, is to have as little as possible to do with the personal accessory to her material well-being:

> The stupidity with which he was favoured by nature, must guard his courtship from any charm that could make a woman wish for its continuance; and Miss Lucas, who accepted him solely from the pure and disinterested desire of an establishment, cared not how soon that establishment were gained. (PP 122)

Living under a pall of economic anxiety has, in fact, withered every desire in Charlotte except the desire for security:

> ". . . I am not romantic. . . . I never was. I ask only a comfortable home; and considering Mr. Collins's character, connections, and situation in life, I am convinced that my chance of happiness with him is as fair, as most people can boast on entering the marriage state." (PP 125)

What Charlotte has resolved, finally, is to grow progessively unaware, to reduce herself to simplicity; and, in the meantime, while that is not yet possible, to close her eyes and ears. Her decision is clear when Elizabeth visits Hunsford:

> When Mr. Collins said any thing of which his wife might reasonably be ashamed, which certainly was not unseldom, she involuntarily turned her eye on Charlotte. Once or twice she could discern a faint blush; but in general Charlotte wisely did not hear. . . . To work in his garden was one of his most respectable pleasures; and Elizabeth admired the command of countenance with which Charlotte talked of the healthfulness of the exercise, and owned she encouraged it as much as possible. (PP 156)

So the natural antithesis which separates simple from complex, and which should separate one from the other absolutely in the closest human relationship, can be upset and annulled by economic pressure.

Elizabeth's continual mistake is to ignore, or to set aside as uninfluential, the social context. It is a question not merely of individuals and marriage, but of individuals and marriage in an acquisitive society. Elizabeth expects nothing except comfort or amusement from simplicity; but she likes to believe that complexity means a categorically free will, without social distortion or qualification.

When complexity and a pleasing manner combine, as they

do in Wickham, Elizabeth is at her least cautious. Wickham is clever and charming, a smooth social being, and for these qualities Elizabeth is ready to believe his long, unsolicited tale of being wronged and even to imagine herself falling in love with him. What she never allows, until much later, to cast a doubt upon his testimony is the fact that he is a dispossessed man in an acquisitive society. It is true that Wickham is very persuasive, and that Elizabeth's prejudice against Darcy (which has grown out of her failure to take into account *his* social context) has prepared her to accept Wickham's accusation. Still, she has reason to reconsider when Wickham turns his attentions to a Miss King, concerning whom the "sudden acquisition of ten thousand pounds was the most remarkable charm." (PP 149) If, instead, she refuses to begrudge him his change of heart, his "wish of independence," (PP 150) and acknowledges to her aunt that she is "open to the mortifying conviction that handsome young men must have something to live on, as well as the plain," (PP 150) she remains quite in character, less perceptive than usual out of her appreciation of Wickham's cleverness and manner, ready to believe that an unknown Miss King can scarcely be as bad as Charlotte's too well known Mr. Collins, that at any rate so charming a man cannot be altogether wrong.

It is with Wickham, nevertheless, that Jane Austen's directing and organizing irony—which functions doubly, at the same time through and upon Elizabeth—begins to fail; and the area of failure, as with Willoughby, is the sexual experience outside marriage.

The first flattening of tone occurs in Darcy's letter, (PP 195ff.), in which Wickham's infamy is revealed. Wickham has attempted to seduce Darcy's sister, Georgiana; and it is this specific attempt, beyond any other evidence of profligacy, that automatically makes him a villain from Darcy's point of view, and from Elizabeth's also as soon as she can accept the truth of the letter. The curious fact is, not that Elizabeth and, here at least, Jane Austen regard seduction as infamous, but that, into an ironic atmosphere elaborated and intensified out of the difficulty of interpreting motive, Jane Austen pushes a

standard black-and-white seduction-scene, with all the ap-
purtenances of an ingenuous young girl, a scheming profli-
gate, a wicked governess, and an outraged brother, and with
no trace of doubt, shading, or irony. It is hardly enough to
say, with Miss Lascelles,[2] that Jane Austen clings to this
novelistic convention through almost all her work as to a usable
climax, which she met in Richardson and for which she could
find no adequate substitute. *Why* she retained this threadbare revelation when, as early as *Pride and Prejudice*, she
could demonstrate the most subtle and resourceful skill in
representing every other particular of the action, remains a
question.

The answer seems to be that, though the nature of her subject makes an approach to the sexual experience inevitable,
Jane Austen will not allow herself (as she did in "Love and
Freindship" and continues to do in her letters[3]) to assimilate
extra-marital sex to her characteristic unifying irony, and
that her only other possible response is conventional. She must
truncate, flatten, falsify, disapprove, all in the interests of an
external morality; and the process in *Pride and Prejudice* is so
out of key with its surroundings as to be immediately jarring.

Lydia is the outstanding victim. Not that Lydia is not
throughout a wholly consistent and living character. On the
solid and simple foundations of her personality she works up
to her triumphant end in marriage to Wickham. If she acts
from her sensual nature, it is Elizabeth and the author themselves who have proved to us that Lydia, being among the
simple spirits who are never really aware and who act only
upon their single potentiality, cannot do otherwise. She is fulfilling herself, as Mr. Collins fulfills himself in marriage and
at Rosings, as Jane and Bingley fulfill themselves. The irony
is, or should be, in her unawareness, in her powerlessness to

---

[2] M. Lascelles, *Jane Austen and Her Art*, Oxford, 1939, 72f.

[3] She quite freely exercised her irony on sex, not only in her *juvenilia*,
but as an adult in her letters also (for a few examples in her letters, see
p. 2, this study). Publication—and the anticipation of social pressure—
inhibited the response entirely; and she had no other defense against the
potential involvement of sex except the conventional response of disapproval
or silence.

change, in the incongruity between her conviction of vitality and her lack of choice. This irony, though, Jane Austen quite cuts off. She is herself silent, but it is clear that she allows Elizabeth to define the proper attitude toward Lydia. Elizabeth can feel, at first, no sympathy for Lydia at all—only shame and self-pity however altruistically phrased:

> Lydia—the humiliation, the misery, she was bringing on them all, soon swallowed up every private care; and covering her face with her handkerchief, Elizabeth was soon lost to everything else. . . . (PP 278)

It is true that this occurs in Darcy's presence, and in her growing consciousness of Darcy's worth. Later, however, when the moment of shame is long past, her attitude has not changed except to harden into sarcastic resentment. Lydia, back at Longbourn, suggests to her mother that the family visit her and Wickham at their new home:

> ". . . when you go away, you may leave one or two of my sisters behind you; and I dare say I shall get husbands for them before the winter is over."
>
> "I thank you for my share of the favour," said Elizabeth; "but I do not particularly like your way of getting husbands." (PP 317)

And when Lydia offers to give Elizabeth an account of the wedding,

> "No really," replied Elizabeth; "I think there cannot be too little said on the subject." (PP 318)

Elizabeth's ill-tempered efforts to shame Lydia are fruitless, as Elizabeth should have known they would be while Lydia is Lydia still. What they amount to is a kind of floating moral judgment. It seems that both Jane Austen and her heroine feel uneasily that a moral lesson must be taught, though they have already proved that Lydia is incapable of learning it:

> . . . how little of permanent happiness could belong to a couple who were only brought together because their passions were stronger than their virtue, she could easily conjecture. (PP 312)

So Jane Austen suspends her irony, suspends her imagination altogether, while Wickham is engaged in seducing Georgiana or Lydia. Yet, apart from this temporary suspension, Wickham fits admirably into the large pattern of Elizabeth's social education. Not only is he, like Charlotte, an example of the complex personality discarding scruples, discarding candor, making the wrong choice under economic pressure; he is also an evil agent, quite willing to corrupt others as well, to involve them in public disgrace if he can thereby assure his own security. What he uses deliberately is what Mrs. Bennet used, much less deliberately, in her conquest of her husband: sexual attractiveness. It is, then, Wickham who by exploiting sex sets off that other intricate character who passively succumbed to it—Mr. Bennet.

It is, in fact, easy to imagine that when Mr. Bennet calls Wickham his favorite son-in-law (PP 379) he is not merely indulging in habitual paradox, but ironically recognizing the painful contrast between Wickham's awareness, however directed, and his own self-delusion, in the same emotional circumstance. Mr. Bennet made his mistake many years before, and must now stand by it because his class recognizes no respectable way out:

> . . . captivated by youth and beauty, and that appearance of good humour, which youth and beauty generally give, he had married a woman whose weak understanding and illiberal mind, had very early in their marriage put an end to all real affection for her. Respect, esteem, and confidence, had vanished for ever; and all his views of domestic happiness were overthrown. But Mr. Bennet was not of a disposition to seek comfort for the disappointment which his own imprudence had brought on, in any of those pleasures which too often console the unfortunate for their folly or their vice. He was fond of the country and of books; and from these tastes had arisen his principal enjoyments. To his wife he was very little otherwise indebted, than as her ignorance and folly had contributed to his amusement. This is not the sort of happiness which a man would in general wish to owe to his wife; but where other powers of entertainment are wanting, the true philosopher will derive benefit from such as are given. (PP 236)

Mr. Bennet has become an ironic spectator almost totally self-enclosed, his irony rigidly defensive, a carapace against the plain recognition of his own irrevocable folly. He observes, he stands apart "in silence . . . enjoying the scene," (PP 103) he likes to make blunt comments on the silliness of his daughters, especially of Lydia and Kitty:

> "From all that I can collect by your manner of talking, you must be two of the silliest girls in the country. I have suspected it some time, but I am now convinced." (PP 29)

and, equally, when Charlotte accepts Mr. Collins:

> . . . it gratified him, he said, to discover that Charlotte Lucas, whom he had been used to think tolerably sensible, was as foolish as his wife, and more foolish than his daughter! (PP 127)

He likes to upset, in small ways, the social decorum which has overwhelmed him in its massive and permanent way, he enjoys pointing the contrast between what he ought to think and what he does think. It is a very minor social victory, but the only one now possible for him. His most dependable source of amusement is, of course, his wife; and he exploits her comic potentialities with a ruthlessness proportional to her unawareness of his purpose.

At the very beginning he is baiting her about Bingley. He baits her continually on the subject of Mr. Collins and the entail, as she raises her continued uncomprehending objection:

> "I cannot bear to think that they should have all this estate. If it was not for the entail I should not mind it."
> "What should you not mind?"
> "I should not mind any thing at all."
> "Let us be thankful that you are preserved from a state of such insensibility." (PP 130)

He even baits her about her death (PP 130), and so finds the only effective way to sidetrack her—the reason, perhaps, why he never tries it again, since her uninterrupted nonsense is more diverting than her fear.

It is true that Lydia's elopement shocks him into exposing himself for as long as it takes him to transact the unpleasant business. When he returns from his futile search in London, in acknowledgment of Elizabeth's

> . . . briefly expressing her sorrow for what he must have endured, he replied, "Say nothing of that. Who should suffer but myself? It has been my own doing, and I ought to feel it."
> "You must not be too severe upon yourself," replied Elizabeth.
> "You may well warn me against such an evil. Human nature

114

is so prone to fall into it! No, Lizzy, let me once in my life feel
how much I have been to blame. I am not afraid of being overpowered by the impression. It will pass away soon enough."
(PP 299)

It does soon enough, or at least the impulse to articulate it.
With Lydia and Wickham safely married, Mr. Bennet re-
stores himself to what he has been—rather, to what he has
seemed. He needs only another letter from Mr. Collins to reaffirm all his amused detachment, to make explicit the only
code by which he can tolerate the vacuity, the hopeless failure
of sympathy, in his life.

".. . For what do we live, but to make sport for our neighbours,
and laugh at them in our turn?" (PP 364)

If Elizabeth cannot answer, it is because she recognizes
that there is nothing else left for her father, that his choice
was made long ago, that he cannot withdraw or alter it, that
he must live by it in the only way endurable for him. Of
course his mistake and his despair might be decently masked;
things would be better, for his children at least, if he could
put up a front of quiet respectability concerning his relations
with his wife:

Elizabeth . . . had never been blind to the impropriety of her
father's behaviour as a husband. She had always seen it with
pain; but respecting his abilities, and grateful for his affectionate treatment of herself, she endeavoured to forget what she
could not overlook, and to banish from her thoughts that continual breach of conjugal obligation and decorum which, in
exposing his wife to the contempt of her children, was so highly
reprehensible. (PP 236)

But the damage to himself is done and cannot be remedied.
Elizabeth knows her father: of the complex characters in the
story, he is the only one whom she has known long and well
enough to judge accurately from the outset. She has learned
from his example that a complex personality may yield to the
pressure of sensuality; that marriages made by sex—as well
as those made by economics—represent, for the free individual,
an abdication of choice, an irremediable self-degradation and
defeat.

In his social context, in his status as a gentleman of independent means, Mr. Bennet was lulled into believing that choice was easy, a matter of simple and unexamined inclination; and in the same society Mrs. Bennet could not believe otherwise than that any gentleman of means must make a desirable husband. This much Elizabeth recognizes about the pressures of an acquisitive society, even upon a free individual like her father. The shock of Charlotte's marriage to a fool makes Elizabeth recognize that these pressures act decisively upon other free individuals as well. In spite of examples, however, it takes a long series of vexations and misunderstandings before she can be convinced that the imposed pride of rank and wealth, perhaps the strongest pressure in an acquisitive society, may act, not yet decisively—for the area of decision is marriage—but conditionally upon a free individual like Darcy, to make him behave with an overconfident and unsympathetic obstinacy, to make him seem far different from what he is capable of being behind the façade of pride.

It is the social façade of the complex person that deceives Elizabeth. She can penetrate her father's, out of sympathetic familiarity and concern; but Charlotte's has deceived her. Wickham's takes her in altogether; and by contrast with Wickham's, by the contrast which Wickham himself takes care to emphasize in his own support, Darcy's façade seems disagreeable indeed, or rather a clear window on a disagreeable spirit.

Darcy's function as the character most difficult for the heroine to interpret, and yet most necessary for her to interpret if *she* is to make a proper decision in the only area of choice her society leaves open, his simultaneous role as the heroine's puzzle and her only possible hero, is clearly marked out during the action. From Elizabeth's point of view, in fact, the process of the interpretation of Darcy's personality from disdain through doubt to admiration is represented with an extraordinarily vivid and convincing minuteness.[4] Never-

---

[4] "In *Pride and Prejudice*, particularly in the presentation of Darcy's character, Jane Austen shows an almost Jamesian awareness of the multiple ways of reading a man's behaviour. She conveys her sense of the possibility of very different interpretations of the 'same' action, as James often does, through dialogues which look trivial and which are extremely ambigu-

theless, Darcy himself remains unachieved: we recognize his effects upon Elizabeth, without recognizing that he exists independently of them.

Mrs. Leavis has persuasively documented her belief that *Pride and Prejudice* is an effort to "rewrite the story of *Cecilia* in realistic terms";[5] and she observes, more particularly, that Darcy fails because he does not transcend his derivation: he is a character out of a book, not one whom Jane Austen created or reorganized for her own purpose. But why Darcy alone: why is he, among the major figures in *Pride and Prejudice*, the only one disturbingly derived and wooden?

The reason seems to be the same as that which compelled Jane Austen to falsify her tone and commentary concerning Wickham's seductions and to supply Elinor and Marianne Dashwood with such nonentities for husbands. The socially unmanageable, the personally involving aspects of sex, Jane Austen can no longer treat with irony, nor can she as yet treat them straightforwardly. Darcy is the hero, he is the potential lover of a complex young woman much like the author herself; and as such Jane Austen cannot animate him with emotion, or with her characteristic informing irony. She borrows him from a book; and, though she alters and illuminates everything else, she can do nothing more with him than fit him functionally into the plot.

Even here the author is so uncharacteristically clumsy as to rely on inconsistencies of personality to move her story along. However difficult Elizabeth's task of interpreting Darcy, it is clear from the beginning that, in his consistent functional impact upon the story, he is a proud man with a strong sense of at least external propriety and dignity, and with no taste whatever for his aunt's vulgar condescension or the kind of

---

ous. At the same time they are not merely confusing because Jane Austen defines so precisely the ironic implications of what is said and because she gradually limits the possibilities with which the reader is to be most concerned." R. A. Brower, "The Controlling Hand: Jane Austen and 'Pride and Prejudice,'" *Scrutiny*, XIII (September, 1945), 99. This essay brilliantly analyzes the process by means of which Elizabeth comes to an understanding of Darcy.

[5] Q. D. Leavis, "A Critical Theory of Jane Austen's Writings," *Scrutiny*, x (June, 1941), 71ff.

sarcasm dispensed by Mr. Bennet. Yet on his first appearance he initiates Elizabeth's prejudice by speaking with a simple vulgarity indistinguishable from his aunt's, and in a voice loud enough to be overheard by the object of his contempt:

> . . . turning round, he looked for a moment at Elizabeth, till catching her eye, he withdrew his own and coldly said, "She is tolerable; but not handsome enough to tempt *me*; and I am in no humour at present to give consequence to young ladies who are slighted by other men. . . ." (pp 11f.)

In spite of his rigid and principled reserve, in spite of Elizabeth's having just turned down his arrogant proposal, he makes his explanation to Elizabeth in a thoroughly frank and unreserved letter, which—more appropriate to a Richardsonian correspondent than to Darcy as he has been presented—seems an author's gesture of desperation to weight the scales in favor of her predetermined hero. Later, Miss Bingley is allowed to sink herself entirely by spitefully recalling to Darcy a remark he made about Elizabeth:

> ". . . I particularly recollect your saying one night, after they had been dining at Netherfield, '*She* a beauty!—I should as soon call her mother a wit.'. . ." (pp 271)

This sounds like something left over from Mr. Bennet's stock; at any rate, we have no cause to believe that Darcy, in his dignified and self-conscious pride, would even have thought it, much less ever expressed it to a woman eager for the indulgence of her spite.

Out of inconsistency, Darcy emerges into flatness. Only in his sparring with Elizabeth, and then only occasionally, does he establish himself with a degree of solidity, of independent reference, as when Elizabeth tries to tease him into communicativeness while they are dancing:

> ". . . One must speak a little, you know. It would look odd to be entirely silent for half an hour together, and yet for the advantage of *some*, conversation ought to be so arranged as that they may have the trouble of saying as little as possible."
>
> "Are you consulting your own feelings in the present case, or do you imagine that you are gratifying mine?"
>
> "Both," replied Elizabeth archly, "for I have always seen a great similarity in the turn of our minds.—We are each of an unsocial, taciturn disposition, unwilling to speak, unless we ex-

pect to say something that will amaze the whole room, and be handed down to posterity with all the éclat of a proverb."

"This is no very striking resemblance of your own character, I am sure," said he. "How near it may be to *mine*, I cannot pretend to say.—*You* think it a faithful portrait undoubtedly." (PP 91)

In dialogue, at least when Elizabeth is an enlivening participant, Jane Austen seems able now and then to overcome her awkwardness in handling Darcy. Otherwise, however, she can only make him serve: he interests us chiefly because he is the center of Elizabeth's interest; and because, in a book in which the individual must choose and in which marriage is the single area of choice, Darcy represents Elizabeth's only plausible, or almost plausible, mate. But Elizabeth's catalogue of his admirable qualities resembles an author's anxious trick to underscore this plausibility:

> She began now to comprehend that he was exactly the man who, in disposition and talents, would most suit her. His understanding and temper, though unlike her own, would have answered all her wishes. It was an union that must have been to the advantage of both; by her ease and liveliness, his mind might have been softened, his manners improved, and from his judgment, information, and knowledge of the world, she must have received benefit of greater importance. (PP 312)

And when Darcy is ironed out into the conventionally generous and altruistic hero, making devoted efforts to shackle Wickham to Lydia, expending thousands of pounds to restore peace of mind to Elizabeth's family, and all for the love of Elizabeth —when he does all this, with no more of personal depth than Jane Austen allows of moral depth in the whole Lydia-Wickham episode, he comes very close to forfeiting even the functional plausibility that Elizabeth's interest lends him.

The last third of the book, as R. A. Brower has pointed out,[6] does in fact diminish suddenly in density and originality: that is, beginning with Lydia's elopement. We get a conventional chase by an outraged father, a friendly uncle, and a now impeccable hero; we get outbursts of irrelevantly directed moral judgment, and a general simplification of the problems of motive and will down to the level of the Burneyan novel. Jane

[6] R. A. Brower, *op.cit.*, 108ff.

Austen herself, routed by the sexual question she has raised, is concealed behind a fogbank of bourgeois morality; and the characters, most conspicuously Darcy, must shift for themselves, or, rather, they fall automatically into the grooves prepared for them by hundreds of novels of sentiment and sensibility.

Only Elizabeth does not. She may yield temporarily to a kind of homeless moralizing on Lydia's disgrace, she may be rather obvious and stiff in acquainting herself with Darcy's virtues at last; but the lapses are minor, and they never seriously dim her luminous vigor, her wit, curiosity, discrimination, and independence. If the novel does not collapse in the predictabilities of the denouement, it is because Elizabeth has from the outset been presented in a depth specific and vital enough to resist flattening, because she remains what she has been—a complex person in search of conclusions about people in society, and on the way to her unique and crucial choice.

She observes, and her shield and instrument together is irony. Like Mary Crawford later, Elizabeth is a recognizable and striking aspect of her author; but, unlike Mary's, her sins are all quite venial, her irony unclouded by the author's disapproval and—after a few detours—grandly vindicated in its effect. Jane Austen has not yet made her first unqualified capitulation to the suspicious sobriety of her class, and surrendered her values in exchange for its own. She can, in fact, embody her personal values in her heroine and be delighted with the result; so she writes to her sister about Elizabeth: "I must confess that I think her as delightful a creature as ever appeared in print, and how I shall be able to tolerate those who do not like *her* at least I do not know." (L II 297, 29 Jan. 1813)

Elizabeth's third dimension is irony; and it is her irony that fills out and sustains the action. Her slightest perception of incongruity reverberates through the scene, and from it out into the atmosphere of the book. When Lydia, having informed Elizabeth that Wickham's wealthy catch has got away, adds:

". . . he never cared three straws about her. Who *could* about such a nasty little freckled thing?"

Elizabeth was shocked to think that, however incapable of such coarseness of *expression* herself, the coarseness of the *sentiment* was little other than her own breast had formerly harboured and fancied liberal! (PP 220)

At Pemberley, she listens as the housekeeper eulogizes Darcy, until her uncle asks:

"Is your master much at Pemberley in the course of the year?"

"Not so much as I could wish, sir; but I dare say he may spend half his time here; and Miss Darcy is always down for the summer months."

"Except," thought Elizabeth, "when she goes to Ramsgate." (PP 248)

recalling by this most astonishing economy of means—like a flashback in intent but with none of its deadening machinery— the whole charged atmosphere of Wickham's earlier attempt at seduction (more successfully than Darcy's letter, our original source of information, had created it at first), recalling the tension of Darcy's insulting and rejected proposal, the excitement of his letter and the depression and change of heart it inevitably brought: and all this richness and clarity of reference out of a single and immediately irrelevant ironic thought.

There is, above all, the perpetual exuberant yet directed irony of her conversation, especially as she uses it to sound Darcy. When Miss Bingley assures her that Darcy cannot be laughed at, Elizabeth exclaims:

"That is an uncommon advantage, and uncommon I hope it will continue, for it would be a great loss to *me* to have many such acquaintance. I dearly love a laugh."

"Miss Bingley," said he, "has given me credit for more than can be. The wisest and the best of men, nay, the wisest and best of their actions, may be rendered ridiculous by a person whose first object in life is a joke."

"Certainly," replied Elizabeth—"there are such people, but I hope I am not one of them. I hope I never ridicule what is wise or good. Follies and nonsense, whims and inconsistencies *do* divert me, I own, and I laugh at them when I can.—But these, I suppose, are precisely what you are without." (PP 57)

Darcy protests that his failings are, not of understanding, but of temper:

> "... My temper would perhaps be called resentful.—My good opinion once lost is lost for ever."
>
> "*That* is a failing indeed!" cried Elizabeth. "Implacable resentment *is* a shade in a character. You have chosen your fault well.—I really cannot *laugh* at it. You are safe from me."
>
> "There is, I believe, in every disposition a tendency to some particular evil, a natural defect, which not even the best education can overcome."
>
> "And *your* defect is a propensity to hate every body." (PP 58)

Whether Elizabeth is teasing him about his silence at dancing (PP 271), or, in Lady Catherine's drawing room, explaining her lack of skill at the piano to refute Darcy's claim of having no talent for sociability:

> "My fingers," said Elizabeth, "do not move over this instrument in the masterly manner which I see so many women's do. They have not the same force or rapidity, and do not produce the same expression. But then I have always supposed it to be my own fault—because I would not take the trouble of practising. . ." (PP 175)

she draws him out in the only ways in which he can be drawn out at all, by a challenging indirection just short of impudence, by the appeal of an intelligence as free and aware as that on which he prides himself, by the penetration of a wit which makes its own rules without breaking any significant ones, which even establishes its priority over simple truth:

> "You mean to frighten me, Mr. Darcy, by coming in all this state to hear me? But I will not be alarmed. . . ."
>
> "I shall not say that you are mistaken," he replied, "because you could not really believe me to entertain any design of alarming you; and I have had the pleasure of your acquaintance long enough to know that you find great enjoyment in occasionally professing opinions which in fact are not your own." (PP 174)

If Darcy, finally sounded and known, hardly differs from the stiff-jointed Burneyan aristocratic hero, except as Darcy is provided with a somewhat more explicit personality, the fault is not Elizabeth's, but her author's. Elizabeth has learned what can be learned about him; she has even learned, with Miss

Bingley, that Darcy is *not* to be laughed at—not, at least, in the matter of his influence over Bingley:

> Elizabeth longed to observe that Mr. Bingley had been a most delightful friend; so easily guided that his worth was invaluable; but she checked herself. She remembered that he had yet to learn to be laught at, and it was rather too early to begin. (PP 371)

In the process of interpretation, moreover—with its deflections, its spurious evidence, its shocks of awareness and repentance—she has brought to a focus at last all the scattered principles which her overconfidence and lack of experience continually obliged her to underestimate, forget or abandon.

She never gives up her first principle: to separate the simple personality from the complex, and to concentrate her attention and interest on the latter. Her point of reference is always the complex individual, the individual aware and capable of choice. Her own pride is in her freedom, to observe, to analyze, to choose; her continual mistake is to forget that, even for her, there is only one area of choice—marriage—and that this choice is subject to all the powerful and numbing pressures of an acquisitive society.

Under pressure, Charlotte denies her choice while making it, degrades herself to the level of a fool in marrying one. Under pressure, Wickham squanders his choice in any opportunity, however unscrupulous and desperate, to make his fortune. Under pressure, Mr. Bennet was led to believe that choice was easy, and to marry a woman who made no demands upon his awareness. And under pressure, Darcy jeopardizes his freedom by believing that, for the man of breeding, choice is not individual but ancestral, narrowly predetermined by rank and family. The simple people—Mrs. Bennet, Lydia, Mr. Collins, Lady Catherine, Jane, Bingley—do not choose at all; they are led, largely unaware; we cannot even submit them to a moral judgment: and the irony, as Elizabeth recognizes about all of them except Jane, is in their illusion of choice, their assumption of will. The complex do, on the other hand, choose; yet it takes a long time for Elizabeth to recognize that choice is never unalloyed, and may indeed be nullified altogether.

The central fact for Elizabeth remains the power of choice. In spite of social pressures, in spite of the misunderstandings and the obstacles to awareness that cut off and confuse the individual, in spite of the individual's repeated failures, the power of choice is all that distinguishes him as a being who acts and who may be judged. There are, certainly, limitations upon his choice, the limitations of an imposed prudence, of living within a social frame in which material comfort is an article of prestige and a sign of moral well-being: since even Elizabeth, though an acute and critical observer, is no rebel, she cannot contemplate the possibility of happiness outside her given social frame. The author is, likewise, pointedly ironic in contrasting Elizabeth's charitable allowances, first for Wickham, and then for Colonel Fitzwilliam, an "Earl's younger son," (PP 184) when her relative poverty obliges them to regard her as ineligible. Yet the irony does not go so far as to invalidate choice or distinctions in choice. Fitzwilliam, no rebel, is prudent in the hope that both prudence and inclination may be satisfied together in the future; but Wickham's "prudence," rather than merely limiting his choice, has deprived him of it entirely. In Elizabeth's feeling, upon touring Darcy's estate, "that to be mistress of Pemberley might be something!" (PP 245) the irony is circumscribed with an equal clarity: Darcy gains by being a rich man with a magnificent estate; but Pemberley is an expression of Darcy's taste as well as of his wealth and rank, and the image of Pemberley cannot divert Elizabeth from her primary concern with Darcy's motives and the meaning of his façade. Pemberley with Mr. Collins, or even with Bingley, would not do at all.

The focus is upon the complex individual; the only quality that distinguishes him from his setting, from the forms of courtship and marriage in an acquisitive society, which otherwise standardize and absorb him, is also his unique function—choice. What Elizabeth must choose, within the bounds set by prudence, is an individual equally complex, and undefeated by his social role. The complex individual is, after all, isolated by his freedom, and must be seen so at the end; for even if pressures from without, from the social system and the social class, deflect or overwhelm him, they demonstrate not that he is indistinguishable from his social role, but that he is vulnerable to it. The fact of choice makes him stand, finally, alone, to judge or be judged.

In *Pride and Prejudice*, Jane Austen's irony has developed into an instrument of discrimination between the people who are simple reproductions of their social type and the people with individuality and will, between the unaware and the aware. The defensive—and destructive—weapon of *Northanger Abbey* and *Sense and Sensibility* has here been adapted directly to the theme through the personality of Elizabeth Bennet, who reflects and illustrates her author's vision without ever becoming (except in her malice toward Lydia) merely her author's advocate. The irony is internal, it does not take disturbing tangents toward the author's need for self-vindication: even self-defensive, it is internal and consistent— Mr. Bennet's shying from the consequences of his disastrous mistake, Elizabeth's provocative parrying of Darcy. And if this new control over her irony permits Jane Austen only to be more clever (and not particularly more persuasive) in avoiding a commitment, by Elizabeth in love, for example:

". . . Will you tell me how long you have loved him?"
"It has been coming on so gradually, that I hardly know when it began. But I believe it must date from my first seeing his beautiful grounds at Pemberley."
Another intreaty that she would be serious, however, produced the desired effect; and she soon satisfied Jane by her solemn assurances of attachment. (PP 373)

the characteristic block of Jane Austen's against direct emotional expression has occasion only very rarely to operate in *Pride and Prejudice*: above all, in the talk and atmosphere of Darcy's proposals, and in his letter—passages which most nearly reproduce the flat or melodramatic textures of *Cecilia*, without any lift of emotion or of irony either. The moment is soon over; and irony is not only back, but back at its proper task of discrimination.

In *Pride and Prejudice*, the flaw of an irrelevant defensiveness has almost vanished; and the flaw of a too obvious personal withdrawal before a moral or emotional issue, as with Lydia and Darcy, is not obtrusive enough, to annul or seriously damage the sustained and organizing power of Jane Austen's irony. Irony here rejects chiefly to discover and illuminate; and, though its setting is the same stratified, materialistic, and severely regulated society, its new text and discovery—its new character, in fact, whom Jane Austen has hitherto allowed only herself to impersonate—is the free individual.

CHAPTER V

GENTILITY: IRONIC VISION AND
CONVENTIONAL REVISION

LADY SUSAN AND *THE WATSONS*

LADY SUSAN is uniquely characteristic of its author. It holds in steady focus, for the only time in Jane Austen's work, her essential subject, that complex of hard, avoidable social facts which is always at the center of her awareness, but which elsewhere—except in her letters—propriety compels her to represent obliquely, piecemeal, in the literary disguise of burlesque, or, at her limit of social uneasiness, not at all.

The facts are in Lady Susan herself. The author, for once, refuses to disguise or mitigate them. Still, they are the facts of a personality which, however purposeful and direct, is never simple, never realizable from a single point of view; and this problem of expression the author solves through the most tactful exploitation of a form so liable to repetitiveness and clumsy indirection, so amenable (she has shown) to parody, as the novel in letters.

The course of Lady Susan is not repetitive, but cumulative and contrapuntal; its indirection, far from clumsily diffusing the facts, is the medium that collects and relates them. The facts are multiple: we receive them, therefore, from no one source, but from the victims of Lady Susan—enemies and dupes—and from that expert at self-analysis, Lady Susan herself; implicitly and perhaps most unimpeachably, from the supervising irony which organizes and measures the world of both.

The first two sources are explicit in the letters: the moral indignation of Mrs. Vernon counterpointing the aptitude of Lady Susan for magnificent wide-eyed hypocrisy with her victims and total candor with her confidante. So, in the first letter, Lady Susan writes from the Manwarings' to her brother-in-law, Mr. Vernon:

> I can no longer refuse myself the pleasure of profitting by your kind invitation when we last parted, of spending some weeks with you at Churchill. . . . My kind friends here are most affectionately urgent with me to prolong my stay, but their hospitable & chearful dispositions lead them too much into society for my present situation. . . . (LS 1f.)

that is, as in the second letter she remarks to her confidante, Mrs. Johnson, "my being only four months a widow," which has permitted her to accept "no one's attentions but Manwaring's," and to notice "no creature besides . . . except Sir James Martin." (LS 4) She has, in plainer language, been so indiscreet as to carry on an affair with a married man before his wife (Mrs. Manwaring is on the premises) and to flirt with his sister's suitor (Sir James's intention, until Lady Susan diverted him, was to court Miss Manwaring); and it is the present furious hostility of the Manwaring women which obliges her to leave for "that insupportable spot, a Country Village, for I am really going to Churchill." (LS 7)

In her first candid letter, even before she moves on to Churchill and finds such unexpected opportunities there, we learn that she is no ordinary flirt or adventuress. She is not promiscuous: motivating her notice of Sir James, when she had already captured Manwaring, was

> . . . the sacred impulse of maternal affection . . . the advantage of my Daughter . . . and if that Daughter were not the greatest simpleton on Earth, I might have been rewarded for my Exertions as I ought. (LS 5)

Nor, when Frederica refuses Sir James, does Lady Susan show herself to be narrowly mercenary:

> I have more than once repented that I did not marry him myself, & were he but one degree less contemptibly weak I certainly should, but I must own myself rather romantic in that respect, & that Riches only, will not satisfy me. (LS 5)

She is not vindictive, and she respects respectability: knowing that her confidante's husband detests her, she comments only that

> . . . as Mr Johnson with all his faults is a Man to whom that

great word "Respectable" is always given, & I am known to be
so intimate with his wife, his slighting me has an awkward
Look. (LS 6f.)

Lady Susan recognizes the advantages of education: she intends to place Frederica at a good school in London

> . . . till she becomes a little more reasonable. She will make
> good connections there, as the Girls are all of the best Fam-
> ilies. The price is immense, & much beyond what I can ever
> attempt to pay. (LS 7)

for cost, in so important a venture, can be no object.

It is true that, writing to her confidante at least, Lady Susan
dispenses with most of the formal attitudes of her sex in her
social class. Her attitude toward the uses of deceit, for example, is real and typical rather than formal, as she remarks
about Mr. Johnson that "it is undoubtedly better to deceive
him entirely; since he will be stubborn, he must be tricked."
(LS 15) Her attitude toward love is equally typical: Reginald
De Courcy, she observes, has

> . . . a sort of ridiculous delicacy about him which requires the
> fullest explanation of whatever he may have heard to my dis-
> advantage, & is never satisfied till he thinks he has ascertained
> the beginning & end of everything.
> This is *one* sort of Love—but I confess it does not particu-
> larly recommend itself to me. I infinitely prefer the tender &
> liberal spirit of Manwaring, which impressed with the deepest
> conviction of my merit, is satisfied that whatever I do must be
> right; & look with a degree of contempt on the inquisitive &
> doubting Fancies of that Heart which seems always debating
> on the reasonableness of it's Emotions. (LS 63f.)

and her attitudes toward propinquity and jealousy are natural
consequences:

> Manwaring is indeed beyond compare superior to Reginald—
> superior in everything but the power of being with me. Poor
> fellow! he is quite distracted by Jealousy, which I am not
> sorry for, as I know no better support of Love. (LS 64)

Lady Susan's objective is double: complete self-indulgence
and complete social approval. At times, one (only very rarely
the former) must yield to the other; but at no time does her
firmness in pursuing both yield to the social compulsion toward cant and self-deceit. Lady Susan always reserves the

right of honest comment when there is no one else to be deceived, when only her alter ego, Mrs. Johnson, is listening: she is not only aware of her objective, but the admiring and analytical spectator of her efforts to achieve it. Self-deceit, sentimentality—even about a potential lover—is wasteful, it blunts the spectator's enjoyment. So, speaking of Reginald's susceptibility, she remarks:

> There is something agreable in feelings so easily worked on. Not that I envy him their possession, nor would for the world have such myself, but they are very convenient when one wishes to influence the passions of another. (LS 123)

She states in simple terms that her acceptance of Reginald depends on his inheriting the wealth and title of his father:

> I am still doubtful at times, as to Marriage. If the old Man would die, I might not hesitate; but a state of dependance on the caprice of Sir Reginald, will not suit the freedom of my spirit; & if I resolve to wait for that event, I shall have excuse enough at present, in having been scarcely ten months a Widow. (LS 137f.)

Yet, whatever her intentions and impulses toward Reginald, she can regulate her behavior and postpone her gratification with the nicest regard for social approval:

> It has been delightful to me to watch his advances towards intimacy, especially to observe his altered manner in consequence of my repressing by the calm dignity of my deportment, his insolent approach to direct familiarity. (LS 36)

for, in such a society, to use conventions instead of being used by them, to control one's own reputation and divorce it from one's character, becomes itself a kind of sensual gratification.

Lady Susan is never sentimental, even where sentimentality is the rule. She sees the mother-daughter relationship at all times clearly, without fussiness or veiling, in its class perspective: the proper aim of the female is a marriage of rank and wealth, and a mother's proper aim is to secure a respectable husband for her daughter. Thus, when Lady Susan tries to persuade Frederica to marry Sir James Martin, who may be fatuous but who has the two social requisites of money and rank, she is not so blinded toward fact by irrelevant emotion as to consider compelling her daughter's acquiescence:

Some Mothers would have insisted on their daughter's accepting so great an offer on the first overture, but I could not answer it to myself to force Frederica into a marriage from which her heart revolted; & instead of adopting so harsh a measure, merely propose to make it her own choice by rendering her thoroughly uncomfortable till she does accept him. But enough of this tiresome girl. (LS 26)

The end, not the means, is the great fact; and, more versatile than the sentimentalist, Lady Susan knows of means often more effective than rigor and authority.

If, of course, the mother happens to be a widow and still young, her own interest is paramount. Lady Susan, taking no personal interest in Sir James, may approve of him for her daughter; but, since Reginald De Courcy is her own game, Frederica's desperate appeal to Reginald—for help, it appears, and not, as her mother believes, for love also—very properly outrages Lady Susan as an intrusion into maternal privilege, and inspires her to a moral disquisition on unsolicited love:

I have not a doubt but that the girl took this opportunity of making downright Love to him; I am convinced of it, from the manner in which he spoke of her. Much good, may such Love do him! I shall ever despise the Man who can be gratified by the Passion, which he never wished to inspire, nor solicited the avowal of. I shall always detest them both. (LS 95)

For Lady Susan has her moments of pique: she is not perfect, and can resent being thwarted or put upon. Here, though, as elsewhere, her reaction is always direct, impatient of formal scruples. Frederica, who "seemed to have all the Vernon milkiness," (LS 61) is a "horrid girl . . . a little Devil" (LS 61) when she attempts to escape from the school where she has been imprisoned until she agrees to marry Sir James. Sir James himself, arriving inopportunely at Churchill, Lady Susan "could have poisoned" (LS 91) for complicating her problems there. Because Mr. Johnson's illness requires his wife's attendance and deprives Lady Susan of her confidante, Lady Susan exclaims in judgment:

My dear Alicia, of what a mistake were you guilty in marrying a Man of his age!—just old enough to be formal, ungovernable & to have the Gout—too old to be agreable, & too young to die. (LS 136)

As for Reginald, who dared to listen to Frederica's story and be troubled by it,

> Where was his reliance on my Sense or Goodness then; where the resentment which true Love would have dictated against the person defaming me, that person, too, a Chit, a Child, without Talent or Education, whom he had been always taught to despise? (LS 96)

The present chosen victims of Lady Susan are Mrs. Vernon, the enemy, who knows her well but who can do very little to balk her, and Reginald De Courcy, the target and dupe, who barely and only luckily escapes without having to know her still better; and perhaps the most interesting fact about them is that they altogether corroborate what Lady Susan tells us about herself.

Reginald, of course, is a prejudiced witness; but his prejudice is indispensable, for it gives us our only lover's view of Lady Susan's formidableness, of her magnitude. As a smug young gallant, eager to meet her and confident that he can amuse himself without being caught, he incidentally reminds us of the fresh and seemingly durable ill-repute against which Lady Susan will have to contend:

> What a Woman she must be! I long to see her, & shall certainly accept your kind invitation, that I may form some idea of those bewitching powers which can do so much—engaging at the same time & in the same house the affections of two Men who were neither of them at liberty to bestow them—& all this, without the charm of Youth. (LS 13)

The next time we hear from him, in a letter to his worried father, he is entirely taken in, accepting her present decorum (and persistent charm) against all the infamy imputed to her, appealing to the show of things in his concluding eulogy:

> Her prudence & economy are exemplary, her regard for Mr Vernon equal even to *his* deserts, & her wish of obtaining my sister's good opinion merits a better return than it has received. As a Mother she is unexceptionable. Her solid affection for her Child is shewn by placing her in hands, where her Education will be properly attended to; but because she has not the blind & weak partiality of most Mothers, she is accused of wanting Maternal Tenderness. (LS 55)

It is remarkable that, if this letter were next in order to the

132

previous one, it would nevertheless be credible, because the implication, the scent almost, of Lady Susan's cleverest maneuvering is so strong; but we have had meanwhile enough of Lady Susan's confidences and Mrs. Vernon's anxieties to allow us even to anticipate Reginald's reversal of feeling.

Reginald is, after all, chiefly an instrument by which we may confirm the direction and urgency of Lady Susan's power. It is, indeed, clear that Reginald never controls and is always himself controlled. He falls in love with Lady Susan because she intends him to. She allows him to provoke her into frankness simply because his uneasy curiosity about Frederica dispels the glancing amorous interest she has taken in him:

> I was quite cool, but he gave way to the most violent indignation. I may therefore expect it will the sooner subside; & perhaps his may be vanished for ever, while mine will be found still fresh & implacable. (LS 96f.)

Expediency and her professional pride oblige her to bring him to heel again:

> It would have been trifling with my reputation, to allow of his departing with such an impression in my disfavour; in this light, condescension was necessary. (LS 120)

Her removal to London only inflames him to recklessness; and even her shy prohibitory letters, occasioned by her preference for Manwaring's bed and her fear that Sir Reginald will not die soon enough to make his booty worth waiting for, cannot keep the lover from blundering ardently into Mr. Johnson's house and the truth:

> I write only to bid you Farewell. The spell is removed. I see you as you are. Since we parted yesterday, I have received from indisputable authority, such an history of you as must bring the most mortifying conviction of the Imposition I have been under, & the absolute necessity of an immediate & eternal separation from you. (LS 148f.)

With all the evidence incontrovertibly before him, it is still uncertain whether Reginald may not yield again, when Lady Susan makes her reply of bewildered innocence, her last reflex of virtuosity; and perhaps, finally, he escapes, not because in his angry disillusion her tentative plea finds him unpersuadable, but because after his outraged retort Lady Susan no longer feels inclined to divert her energy into persuading a man whom she cares nothing about, for whom she has no further present use, and whom she can deliver over to what she is sure will be the bitterest pain for him, the knowledge of her total indifference:

> I am satisfied—& will trouble you no more when these few Lines are dismissed. The Engagement which you were eager to form a fortnight ago, is no longer compatible with your veiws, & I rejoice to find that the prudent advice of your Parents has not been given in vain. Your restoration to Peace will, I doubt not, speedily follow this act of filial Obedience, & I flatter myself with the hope of surviving *my* share in this disappointment. (LS 154f.)

Mrs. Vernon works hard at being a force for good: she warns her brother, deplores with her mother, tries to gain Frederica's confidence—even confronts the enchantress herself, if not with the appropriate disenchanting formula, at least with an unmistakable coldness and disapproval. As the single conscious representative at Churchill of embattled gentility (her husband is too kind or too shallow to recognize the threat, Reginald is already defeated), she feels, apparently, that she ought to be Lady Susan's nemesis. Yet she is as powerless as her brother, and the primary service of her personality is the same passive one: to define under attack the power of Lady Susan.

It is from Mrs. Vernon that we get our most detailed impression of Lady Susan's demeanor:

> . . . she possesses an uncommon union of Symmetry, Brilliancy and Grace. Her address to me was so gentle, frank & even affectionate, that if I had not known how much she has always disliked me for marrying Mr Vernon, & that we had never met before, I should have imagined her an attached friend. One is apt I beleive to connect assurance of manner with coquetry, & to expect that an impudent address will necessarily attend an impudent mind; at least I was myself prepared for an improper degree of confidence in Lady Susan; but her Countenance is absolutely sweet, & her voice & manner winningly mild. (LS 20)

Mrs. Vernon does not anticipate her brother's surrender; but when, in spite of the catalogue of scandal against Lady Susan and the appetite for conquest he himself brings to Churchill,

Reginald abruptly submits almost at sight, his watchful sister
is not too exasperated to acknowledge that there are reasons
more positive than masculine susceptibility alone:

> His opinion of her I am sure, was as low as of any Woman in
> England, & when he first came it was evident that he consid-
> ered her as one entitled neither to Delicacy nor respect. . . .
> Her behaviour I confess has been calculated to do away such
> an idea, I have not detected the smallest impropriety in it,—
> nothing of vanity, of pretension, of Levity—& she is altogether
> so attractive, that I should not wonder at his being delighted
> with her, had he known nothing of her previous to this per-
> sonal acquaintance; but against reason, against conviction, to
> be so well pleased with her as I am sure he is, does really
> astonish me. (LS 30f.)

For Mrs. Vernon has, besides, enough class and family pride
to be astonished—exasperated, rather—that a brother of hers
can reject clear evidence against immorality and evil, however seductive their mask of decorum: beforehand, she "could
not imagine that my Brother would be in the smallest danger
of being captivated by a Woman with whose principles he
was so well acquainted, & whose character he so heartily de-
spised." (LS 41) Her astonishment has no more effect on the
situation, however, than her remonstrances to Reginald or her
letters to Lady De Courcy. She, too, must remain acted upon:
she can only observe and relate, while Lady Susan, secure in
her ascendancy, acts.

Mrs. Vernon is, then, another useful reporter on Lady
Susan's conduct and power; but her conscious role as the
representative of a dominant social class makes her specially
significant. Why, as Lady Susan's antagonist, does she fail,
in spite of her position and her perceptiveness, and fail without even being able to make a fight?

> I could not help asking Reginald if he intended being in
> Town this winter, as soon as I found that her Ladyship's steps
> would be bent thither; and tho' he professed himself quite unde-
> termined, there was a something in his Look and voice as he
> spoke, which contradicted his words. I have done with Lamen-
> tation. I look upon the Event as so far decided, that I resign
> myself to it in despair. (LS 133)

The answer lies not merely in Lady Susan's beauty and

guile—her weapons—but in the social advantage which she shares with Mrs. Vernon, and without which the weapons could never be so powerfully loaded. The social fact is that Lady Susan is a woman of rank, of standing, the widow of Sir Frederic Vernon; a woman of breeding, aware of the responsibilities of reputation, as when Manwaring begs to visit her:

> He has been teizing me to allow of his coming into this country, & lodging somewhere near me *incog.*—but I forbid everything of the kind. Those women are inexcusable who forget what is due to themselves & the opinion of the World. (LS 64)

She is, in short, like Mrs. Vernon, a lady. The requirements are simple: to be born, or marry, into rank; to observe propriety; to make public one's feelings only according to formal, preëstablished patterns. Lady Susan fulfills them, for the most part, meticulously. It is a question, not of character or conscience, but of reputation; Lady Susan has no time for the sentimental superfluity of character. She is a lady because she chose the right husband and because, except for an occasional scandal easily enough scotched under the influence of her charm, her public life is a lady's. She is a titled widow. She is, publicly, a most proper and decorous person, even in her seductions:

> I have subdued . . . [Reginald] entirely by sentiment & serious conversation, & made him I may venture to say at least *half* in Love with me, without the semblance of the most commonplace flirtation. (LS 37)

And she so cleverly exploits the socially approved methods and circumstances of feeling that even the hostile Mrs. Vernon is almost convinced on occasion:

> She speaks of . . . [Frederica] with so much tenderness & anxiety, lamenting so bitterly the neglect of her education, which she represents however as wholly unavoidable, that I am forced to recollect how many successive Springs her Ladyship spent in Town, while her daughter was left in Staffordshire to the care of servants or a Governess very little better, to prevent my beleiving whatever she says. (LS 21)

The author's primary irony focuses on, it defines, Mrs. Vernon the genteel representative; and its agent is Lady

Susan. Mrs. Vernon never recognizes the reasons for her impotence, never understands, or allows herself to understand, that Lady Susan succeeds because their world is negative and anti-personal, because the veneer of gentility over the materialist base reflects manners but not motives, sentiment (in Lady Susan's usage) but not feeling, propriety but not character, because in such a society, inevitably, the individual exists to use and be used, not to know and be known. All these social facts are in Lady Susan's favor, and she profits brilliantly by them. Her motives are wicked but her manners are impeccable, sentiment masks her feeling and propriety her character; and, recognizing the peculiar vulnerability of the individual, she is skilled and active enough to be the user and not the used. She is energetic, full of schemes, successful, even triumphant. Certainly, she takes a high, almost objective delight in the evidences of her virtuosity and in her sense of power, as when she prepares herself to overcome Reginald:

> There is exquisite pleasure in subduing an insolent spirit, in making a person pre-determined to dislike, acknowledge one's superiority. I have disconcerted him already by my calm reserve; & it shall be my endeavour to humble the Pride of these self-important De Courcies still lower, to convince Mrs Vernon that her sisterly cautions have been bestowed in vain, & to persuade Reginald that she has scandalously belied me. (LS 27)

and when she seduces him into remaining at Churchill (and being reconciled with her) after their disagreement over Sir James:

> "... I make it my particular request that I may not in any way be instrumental in separating a family so affectionately attached to each other. Where *I* go is of no consequence to anyone; of very little to myself; but *you* are of importance to all your connections." Here I concluded, & I hope you will be satisfied with my speech. It's effect on Reginald justifies some portion of vanity, for it was no less favourable than instantaneous. (LS 122)

It is clear that Lady Susan triumphs over Mrs. Vernon whenever she wishes to, over Reginald, over everyone else. For Lady Susan is the legitimate beneficiary of the society which moral, sentimental Mrs. Vernon indignantly and desperately defends, but which makes no provision for moral or emotional values, for any values at all except those attaching to birth, money, and show—the society which gives Lady Susan her reason, her constant encouragement for being what she is and succeeding as she does.

Still, the supervising irony of the book is not single, its target is not Mrs. Vernon only; it finds at least one other, and a far more imposing, mark: Lady Susan herself. The virtuoso's delight with which Lady Susan achieves and recollects her victories is insufficient, after all, to sustain her. The victories are, in fact, hollow, as victories must be over a world so hollow. She loses Reginald, finally, as much because he is too pithless to interest her as because he finds out the indelicate "truth" about her. She gives up Frederica because the fun of maneuvering a life palls when the life remains backward and unpromising. She is the only person with passion and will in a milieu of circumscribed and will-less formality; and, alone in such a milieu, the passionate and wilful person must wither, or dissipate his power in cold unfruitful strategies—in, for example, simultaneously maintaining reputation and destroying people of reputation, themselves too worthless to be considered and known. The ultimate, tragic victim is Lady Susan, the beautiful woman who must waste her art in pretense, her passion in passing seductions, her will on invertebrates like her daughter and Reginald; who—in a moment of sardonic self-revelation—drops everyone else and the gratifying efforts of virtuosity to marry Sir James Martin, the greatest booby of all, yet as usable as, and so little different from, the rest. Energy, in her immobile bounded conventional world, turns upon and devours itself. The world defeats Lady Susan, not because it recognizes her vices, but because her virtues have no room in it.

There are, then, two large facts about *Lady Susan*: it is a quintessence of Jane Austen's most characteristic qualities and interests; and it is her first completed masterpiece. Both facts have been generally ignored, perhaps because the latter depends on the former, which itself tends to dispel the sentimental domestic haze through which Jane Austen's admirers prefer to observe her. R. W. Chapman, superb as her editor, but less satisfying as her critic in his polite impatience with those who find her irony neither warm nor simple (". . . the novels are, in fact, radiant with the sunshine of unselfishness," he states categorically[1]), goes so far as to make an inconsistent and shrewd, if qualified, judgment of *Lady Susan*:

> The story is in a manner which the author did not repeat, but which here she handles very unlike a novice. It is as brilliant as its central figure. Its manner is no doubt superior to its matter. The tale is not, as a tale, too convincing, and the characters are not very well individualized. But the hard polish of the style creates a vivid illusion.[2]

Yet by everyone else it has been treated, if at all, as a piece of inconsequential *juvenilia* or as a rough sketch for a later work.[3]

The book is in many ways a culmination of Jane Austen's early period. It compresses and sums up the glittering, analytic, detached, but rather rambling and literary irony of the *juvenilia* and *Northanger Abbey*; it cuts to the social foundations which *Pride and Prejudice* implies; it bypasses the forced priggishness in *Sense and Sensibility* and belongs with those spontaneous creations the John Dashwoods: and if it matches neither of the latter two novels in diversity of characters and complexity of development, it almost certainly did not receive the extensive and frequent revisions to which the author submitted both of the others until their publication half a dozen years or more after *Lady Susan* was laid aside in its enigmatic fair copy.

All we know about the composition of *Lady Susan* is that the fair—and only extant—copy was written on paper some of which bears the watermark 1805.[4] The date is midway through the period during which Jane Austen had apparently lost her impulse for initiating large-scale work: from 1801

---

[1] *Jane Austen: Facts and Problems*, Oxford, 1948, 173.
[2] *Ibid.*, 52.
[3] Mrs. Leavis thinks it later emerges as *Mansfield Park*. "A Critical Theory of Jane Austen's Writings: II 'Lady Susan' into 'Mansfield Park,' " *Scrutiny*, X (October, 1941; January, 1942), 114-142, 272-294.
[4] Chapman, *op.cit.*, 49ff.

until 1809, between the family's departure from her beloved Steventon and their establishment at Chawton. These were critical transitional years for her, and it is not surprising that of the six full-length novels the first three were begun before the former date and the last three after the latter.[5] Her family was unsettled, often separated (unhappy enough for so clannish a family), moving from place to place; in 1803, the novel published posthumously as *Northanger Abbey* was bought by a publisher, but it must have been a blow to the author's pride that he did not, finally, think it worth publishing; in 1805, her father died; and all the while she was growing out of the years of marriageableness into confirmed spinsterhood.[6] It is, therefore, tempting to conclude that a work as ruthlessly and exuberantly sardonic as *Lady Susan* was written in the main before, at least no later than the very beginning of, this period; that it is a consummation of the same hard unapologetic attitudes so individually embodied in the *juvenilia* and, probably, in *Elinor and Marianne* and *First Impressions*; and that the fair copy represents only a cursory revision or expansion (the hasty ending, for example) or mere putting to paper of something with which the author, at the time, had no artistic sympathy. This conclusion is doubly tempting when we consider the single work known to have been begun during this period: *The Watsons*.

As the companion, from any viewpoint, of *Lady Susan*, the most striking quality of *The Watsons* is its lack of a quality:

[5] According to Mrs. Leavis's hypothesis (for a discussion and fuller criticism of it, see Appendix II), Jane Austen was revising continually through this middle period, and all of the later novels are revisions of earlier work: *Mansfield Park* of *Lady Susan*, *Emma* of *The Watsons*, *Persuasion* of an earlier, now lost original. Even if Mrs. Leavis is correct, however, *Mansfield Park* and *Emma* are so different from and so much longer than their presumed prototypes as to embody fresh large-scale impulses (Mrs. Leavis does postulate also an *ur-Mansfield Park* in letters, written 1808-9, though if her evidence, flimsy in any case, may be accepted, the fact remains that this middle version was written at the very end of the period in question; and as for the *ur-Persuasion*, she merely assumes its existence without her usual confident assignment of a date).

[6] Chapman, *op.cit.*, 61ff.: where one may find the cautious family accounts of her single authenticated love affair and of her hasty agitated morning flight from a friend whose proposal of marriage she had accepted the night before.

exuberance—or, in a strictly novelistic sense, impetus. The fragment—and it is, true, a first draft—has no momentum, no lift that carries the reader beyond the necessarily limited setting. It is an unworked reminiscence or anticipation of incidents and characters out of context—at its center a solemn distortion of originally ironic intuitions. Nowhere else is Jane Austen so little the controlling artist.

Not that she avoids irony altogether. The characters tend, in fact, for the author, to separate into two groups: those she treats with total solemnity, and those she treats ironically. Of the latter, she achieves a unique if mild success with two. Charles Blake, in his brief appearance, is the only child to whom Jane Austen ever gives a share in a conversation; and he is a pleasantly credible child, as the eager worshipper to whom Miss Osborne breaks her promise at the ball:

> . . . he stood the picture of disappointment, with crimson'd cheeks, quivering lips, & eyes bent on the floor. His mother, stifling her own mortification, tried to sooth his, with the prospect of Miss Osborne's second promise;—but tho' he contrived to utter with an effort of Boyish Bravery "Oh! I do not mind it"—it was very evident by the unceasing agitation of his features that he minded it as much as ever. (w 41)

and as Emma's grateful, talkative dancing partner:

> "Oh! Uncle, do look at my partner. She is so pretty!" (w 45)

The other success, much less compassionately handled, is Tom Musgrave, Jane Austen's only venture in the character of the conscious courtier. Tom is Lord Osborne's harbinger, apologist, procurer, jester, servant, and parasite. He does the talking for his master in company, makes the advances for him to new, pretty girls at the assembly—Emma Watson, for example—carries all the gossip to him, attends the Osborne ladies out of and back into their carriage, contrives the appropriate jokes and good humor at the expense of provincial womanhood—Emma's too pressing sisters, for example—bears the fame of Lord Osborne's house and entertainment like a torch among the unenlightened:

> ". . . Vingt-un is the game at Osborne Castle: I have played nothing but Vingt-un of late. You would be astonished to hear the noise we make there.—The fine old, lofty Drawing-room

rings again. Ly. Osborne sometimes declares she cannot hear herself speak. . . ." (w 109f.)

He comes before the Osbornes only in order to announce their imminence, and declines to outstay them, all in a spirit of what he, and his numerous female admirers, doubtless regard as unaffected geniality:

> ". . . I shall not shew myself here again when I have had the honour of attending Ly. Osborne to her Carriage. I shall retreat in as much secrecy as possible to the most remote corner of the House, where I shall order a Barrel of Oysters, & be famously snug." (w 53f.)

For himself, Tom is a lady's man, if Emma's family is typical —Elizabeth, Penelope, and Margaret are all in love with him —and if in Elizabeth's account of him her statistics may be trusted against her feelings:

> "A young Man of very good fortune, quite independent, & remarkably agreable, an universal favourite wherever he goes. Most of the girls hereabouts are in love with him, or have been. . . ." (w 4)

Certainly, his social behavior shines with the complacency of the eligible young man; and, even if he receives such a rebuff as Emma's coldness, it is of a sort infrequent enough in his experience not to take the bounce out of him for more than a moment, not to allow the exultant sense to forsake him that he is young, handsome, and well-to-do, and that, with the lent splendor which he magnifies to find protection under it, he uses his lord more often and more valuably than his lord can ever use him.

As for the other characters treated ironically, all of them seem scarcely roughed out: they are thin and, through their thinness, often reminiscent. The feeblest of these is Lord Osborne. The author seems almost on the defensive, almost deferential toward his rank, about making him the second-rate person he must be, with the result that he usually appears no person at all, but just a shadow that Tom Musgrave makes use of in order to keep out of the sun. In the only scene in which Lord Osborne speaks at any length, he recalls to us the early (and inconsistent) Darcy, the Darcy of the Meryton assembly, another arrogant man of rank—though Emma, hearing him command Tom, hears pleasanter things about herself, at least, than Elizabeth Bennet did when playing the eavesdropper:

> "Why do not you dance with that beautiful Emma Watson?—I want you to dance with her—& I will come & stand by you."— "I was determining on it this very moment my Lord, I'll be introduced & dance with her directly."—"Aye do—& if you find she does not want much Talking to, you may introduce me by & bye."—"Very well my Lord—. If she is like her Sisters, she will only want to be listened to.—I will go this moment. . . ." (w 48)

Later, when he and Tom pay their formal visit to Emma, he shows signs of developing individually, once she has lectured him on the evils of poverty, into a gentleman of feeling:

> . . . when he addressed her again, it was with a degree of considerate propriety, totally unlike the half-awkward, half-fearless stile of his former remarks.—It was a new thing with him to wish to please a woman; it was the first time that he had ever felt what was due to a woman, in Emma's situation.—But as he wanted neither Sense nor a good disposition, he did not feel it without effect.—"You have not been long in this Country I understand, said he in the tone of a Gentle^n. I hope you are pleased with it." (w 79f.)

But the sense, the good disposition, and the feeling are evident nowhere else, and this is the last we see or hear of him; the promise remains unfulfilled. Our surviving impression—if we have any at all—is, then, of a person not merely humanly, but artistically, inert.

It is not that Jane Austen fails to provide fresh circumstances, even occasional fresh qualities. Robert Watson, for example, is noteworthy as her only treatment of that newcomer into the circle of gentility, the prosperous plain-speaking commercial man, the man who likes to think of himself as self-made (Robert being "self-made," that is, by his wife's six thousand pounds). Yet, because he is presented in the flat, with a pat introduction by the author and a few too straightforwardly characteristic remarks by the character, he succeeds chiefly in reminding us that Jane Austen has done a figure similar in function, if different in circumstance, much better. Robert is too close to John Dashwood, and without the latter's complication of feeling: the novelty of circumstance gives him no novelty of impetus. As against John's position among the country gentry, Robert is a step down in the social ladder, and, perhaps for that reason, the author makes his social manner more aggressive: so he is less in tune with his wife (the two being not so perfect a match, socially, as the John Dashwoods); and, deploring Aunt Turner's belated rejection of Emma, he can be more brutal with his sister than John would ever dream of being with Elinor or Marianne:

> ". . . After keeping you at a distance from your family for such a length of time as must do away all natural affection among us & breeding you up (I suppose) in a superior stile, you are returned upon their hands without a sixpence." (w 95f.)

Otherwise, however, he duplicates John's motives, his moral atmosphere, his sense of duty, with none of their preparation and development. He too takes seriously his social responsibility as financial adviser and matrimonial assistant to his sisters. Woman's goal in life being a respectable marriage, which she customarily buys, with money or rank or both, or has her family buy for her, the sin of Emma's guardian-aunt is the mortal middle-class sin (as it is the mortal genteel sin): that, as parent *pro tem*, she provided Emma with neither marriage nor the customary means to it. Moreover, Robert, like John, is never one to confuse the issue with irrelevant Christian charity:

> ". . . What a blow it must have been upon you!—To find yourself, instead of Heiress of 8 or 9000£, sent back a weight upon your family, without a sixpence.—I hope the old woman will smart for it." (w 94)

and, also, he will do what he can, in John's brotherly fashion, within reason:

> ". . . Pity you can none of you get married!—You must come to Croydon as well as the rest, & see what you can do there.—I beleive if Marg^t had had a thousand or fifteen hundred pounds, there was a young man who w^d have thought of her." (w 96f.)

These self-revelations are authentic Austen ironies; but they proceed from a character who has nothing else to say, who is a mouthpiece, all function without depth, and would seem so even if he were to remind us of nobody at all.

His wife is still more plainly an unembodied function. Appropriately, she recollects Mrs. John Dashwood; but if the latter is an illustration, Mrs. Watson is only a hasty summation, of smug vulgarity. The author makes an effort, however, for Mrs. Watson is provided with a trait distinguishing her from the rest of Jane Austen's vulgar wives: her position and her smugness concerning it (unlike Mrs. Dashwood's or Mrs. Elton's) are apparently so secure as to have no need of a supporting malice. Yet her distinction is as summary and unacted as her resemblance. If we remember her at all, it is in her closest approach to Mrs. Dashwood, as the patroness who has found her gratifying spiritual complement in a protégée, Emma's sister Margaret, very like Lucy Steele—like Lucy, for example, gratifyingly fond of her patroness's child:

> "Sweet little Darling!—cried Marg^t—It quite broke my heart to leave her.—" "Then why was you in such a hurry to run away from her? cried Mrs R.—You are a sad shabby girl.—I have been quarrelling with you all the way we came, have not I?—Such a visit as this, I never heard of! . . ." (w 89f.)

If *The Watsons* had little but this perfunctory and reminiscent sort of irony and such reminiscent, unrealized characters, it would be reasonable to conclude that the book's lack of inner impulsion is a necessary consequence of the author's failure of interest in, perhaps her boredom with, the material. In the material, however, there is something she treats with a thoroughness so detailed, so nearly obsessive, as to compel an altogether different set of conclusions: that the irony is perfunctory because it has been allowed to decline almost to the status of a reflex, that her attention is turned with an unanalytic gravity upon a subject she has till now compressed and shaped with irony; that, finally, the book fails to move, not because she puts no interest or impulse into it, but because her interest and impulse are moral rather than artistic.

The engrossing subject is husband-hunting; it is of course in some respects always Jane Austen's engrossing subject: but in *The Watsons*, alone, she confronts it directly and with a determined solemnity, effectively shields it, at every crucial point, from irony.

Now it is dangerous to speak, without some qualification, of a lapse of irony in Jane Austen: for no character or subject in her novels does it lapse altogether. So, in *The Watsons*, husband-hunting is a cruel irony as filtered through Robert Watson; it resumes its place as the author's favorite social joke in the remainder of the coy exchange between Mrs. Watson and Margaret (for Margaret had gone to Croydon, unsuccessfully, after a man):

> "... I am sorry, (with a witty smile) we have not been able to make Croydon agreable this autumn."—"My dearest Jane—do not overpower me with your Raillery.—You know what inducements I had to bring me home,—spare me, I entreat you—. I am no match for your arch sallies.—" (w 90)

and so, in the very first conversation of the book, the author throws her customary comic light on the subject as Elizabeth Watson, having just described how Mr. Purvis was won away from her by her sister Penelope, warns Emma to be on guard herself:

> "You do not know Penelope.—There is nothing she w^d not do to get married—she would as good as tell you so herself.—Do not trust her with any secrets of your own, take warning by me, do not trust her; she has her good qualities, but she has no Faith, no Honour, no Scruples, if she can promote her own advantage. ...." (w 6f.)

There is even, between the shaping ironic and the shapeless solemn, a quite new, if here short-lived, shaping tone for Jane Austen, the tone of pathos, as Elizabeth—a younger and more explicit Miss Bates—unveils the social horror of spinsterhood:

> "... I could do very well single for my own part—A little Company, & a pleasant Ball now and then, would be enough for me, if one could be young for ever, but my Father cannot provide for us, & it is very bad to grow old & be poor & laughed at. ...." (w 7)

Yet, beginning as promisingly as she does (if with the same nagging second-hand resemblance to characters—Miss Bates and the elder Miss Steele, for example—in other Austen novels), Elizabeth must nevertheless, even before she has the chance to fade quickly into the good-natured dull gossip of the rest of the book, be expressly corrected, set down with the *right* view, according to Emma, of husband-hunting:

". . . To be so bent on Marriage—to pursue a Man merely for the sake of situation—is a sort of thing that shocks me; I cannot understand it. Poverty is a great Evil, but to a woman of Education & feeling it ought not, it cannot be the greatest. . . ." (w 9f.)

The fact is that the prevailing tone in which the subject is treated, the prevailing tone of *The Watsons*, is solemn and severely moral. The characters and incidents handled ironically, if they are related to this tone at all, exist only to set it off. Husband-hunting has become an unironic evil opposed by an equally unironic morality, a morality, that is, embodied in an inner circle of characters untouched by irony: Emma and her father, Mr. Howard and his sister, Mrs. Blake.

Mrs. Blake, the barest suggestion of a character, little more than her description as "a lively pleasant-looking little Woman of 5 or 6 & 30," (w 39) still comes through enough to make her place in the moral context clear. From her unassuming manner and her pleased absorption in her son, we may infer that she has accepted her widowhood as a final condition, that her spirits have not been dampened by what may have been either a choice or a necessity to ignore the social pressures— upon young widows also—toward husband-hunting and the marriage of convenience, that a woman may be happy giving up the idea of marriage altogether and devoting herself to a more altruistic pursuit, such as Mrs. Blake's rearing of her son—particularly, one might add, if, like Mrs. Blake, she is fortunate enough to have a brother who takes her ungrudgingly (Mr. Howard would not act otherwise) into his house.

Mr. Watson is the only figure in this explicitly simple contest between good people and evil convention who aspires, in outline at least, toward the tragic. An invalid and—by genteel standards—penniless, he is further burdened with four marriageable and unmarried daughters, for whom in life he can do nothing materially except provide them with a home together, and in death perhaps even less, as his self-important, alien son implies:

"I am just come from my Father's room, he seems very indifferent. It will be a sad break-up when he dies. . . ." (w 96)

He is, then, in the world's eye, a failure, he has not been the
provider of respectable marriages that a man, especially a
widower, with daughters should be, he has not even been
respectably well-to-do; and his awareness of the world's judgment is plain in his irritable bewilderment at Lord Osborne's
unprecedented visit to his house:

". . . I have lived here 14 years without being noticed by any
of the family. It is some foolery of that idle fellow T. Musgrave. I cannot return the visit.—*I* would not if I could." (w 84)

Yet, if he has no value discernible to a materialistic society,
he is intended, at any rate, to have value for those who make
a personal rather than a social judgment; he is, for Emma, a
refuge against the noisy and vulgar remainder of her family,
as she takes Elizabeth's place at his bedside:

To Emma, the exchange was most acceptable, & delightful.
Her father, if ill, required little more than gentleness & silence;
&, being a Man of Sense & Education, was if able to converse,
a welcome companion.— (w 117)

And the author clinches his moral position in the story by
making him a churchgoer in spite of his invalidism, and by
choosing him to give us our ultimate indispensable view of
Mr. Howard in the pulpit. But Mr. Watson's *personal* position in the story is never clinched; like Mrs. Blake, he is a
character uncomplicated by substance. These two are, in fact,
swallowed up in their portentous mutual function: to illuminate the periphery of the moral problem—their light is hardly
visible—and to prepare us, by implication and report, for the
authoritative moral nobility of Mr. Howard.

Mr. Howard, whom the author meant to become her
heroine's husband (w121), is, appropriately, a clergyman. He
is, moreover, Jane Austen's first clerical clergyman; and for an
author whose only previous representatives of the profession
have been a bumptious young man of the world, Henry Tilney,
and a perfect ass, Mr. Collins, the distinction is a critical one.
Jane Austen has not till now been disposed to treat her clergymen with deference; one often suspects, indeed, that she takes

a particular delight in treating them as markedly fallible and even foolish human beings, certainly never as spiritual shepherds or considerable men. Mr. Howard, however, is designed to bring this irreverence to a halt.

He is, first of all, personable enough to marry a heroine, being "an agreable-looking Man, a little more than Thirty," (w 39) but—more important—he has not, as Henry Tilney had, an unseemly ebullience: what pleases Emma most about him from the outset is his "quietly-chearful, gentlemanlike air." (w 48) He is a socially accepted man: he spends much time with the Osbornes, with no suggestion of the dependence or mean profiting of Tom Musgrave, not to mention the ecstatic crawling subservience of Mr. Collins in *his* aristocratic household. He was formerly Lord Osborne's tutor, and now, as clergyman of the parish, he is a frequent guest of the Osbornes, sharing their grandeur, perhaps even contributing some of his own, in the eyes of the neighborhood; when Emma mentions having danced with him at the ball, Elizabeth exclaims:

"... Good Heavens! You don't say so! Why—he is quite one of the great & Grand ones;—Did not you find him very high?" (w 69)

(to which Emma, showing herself worthy of him, replies: " 'His manners are of a kind to give *me* much more Ease & confidence than Tom Musgrave's.' ").

Most interesting and central of all is the fact that Mr. Howard is presented, with much approval, as Jane Austen's first *practicing* clergyman. Mr. Watson has heard him preach, and offers his opinion while Emma

... could not help listening with a quicker Ear.—"I do not know when I have heard a Discourse more to my mind—continued Mr W. or one better delivered.—He reads extremely well, with great propriety & in a very impressive manner; & at the same time without any Theatrical grimace or violence.—I own, I do not like much action in the pulpit—I do not like the studied air & artificial inflexions of voice, which your very popular & most admired Preachers generally have.—A simple delivery is much better calculated to inspire Devotion, & shews a much better Taste.— Mr H. reads like a scholar & a gentleman." (w 73f.)

149

Mr. Howard is, then, presented at the beginning as a social man, a man of manners and independence; but it is becoming obvious, by the time the fragment ceases, that these qualities serve primarily as a recognizable hero's frame for his chief value, which, to Emma and the story, will be as the worthy clergyman, the dignified professional moralist, to whom Emma may turn after grandly rejecting the immoral social pressures toward a marriage of convenience. It is also obvious that, in her anxiety to create a serious good man, Jane Austen creates nothing so far except the wordless phantom at the ball and the straw man in the pulpit—a sufficient symbol for the solemn moments of the eighteenth-century parsonage in which she was brought up, and of rational, tidy, secular eighteenth-century gentility in general.[7] The symbol was to reappear more expertly in *Mansfield Park*, as Edmund Bertram, sharpened with detail and allowed the temporary humanity of an infatuation—however indignantly thrust off at the end—with a vivacious, worldly woman. Mr. Howard, though, does not achieve even Edmund's final dullness and priggishness, he achieves no adequate reality at all; and the reason seems to be that in *The Watsons* the author is occupied, never with the artistic problem (as she often is in *Mansfield Park*), which requires individuals for its solution, but with the moral problem—with a moral problem, besides, reduced to its easiest and most conventional terms and requiring therefore only easy conventional symbols.

The center of perception in the book is, as in all the full-length novels, the heroine. Yet while in *Northanger Abbey*, *Pride and Prejudice*, and *Emma* this central position is (and in *Persuasion* was, during the heroine's youth) a deluding one, ironically undermined by the heroine's disposition to simplify or to ignore the multiple and complex, in *The Watsons* it is only strategic and enlightening, like Elinor Dashwood's and Fanny Price's; it is also, like Elinor's, solemnly coincident with

---

[7] G. K. Chesterton, whose religious bias led him to some unbiased truths about Jane Austen, remarked that she is "supremely irreligious," that "her very virtues glitter with the cold sunlight of the great secular epoch between mediaeval and modern mysticism." "The Evolution of Emma," *Living Age*, CCXCIV (August 25, 1917), 503.

the author's. Emma Watson serves, then, as chief agent in the author's resolute unironic simplification of the moral problem. For Emma, perception is always straight and simple, of persons and things. She knows her father in spite of the world's prejudice. From her brisk retort to Elizabeth, we discover that as early as the ball she had penetrated Mr. Howard's "high" manner and accurately—according to the author's view of him—judged the man. Her accuracy is granted, moreover, a freedom of expression without penalty that Jane Austen grants to no other heroine, not even to Elizabeth Bennet. Of Lord Osborne, Emma asserts to Tom Musgrave

> "That he would be handsome even, tho' he were *not* a Lord—& perhaps—better bred; More desirous of pleasing, & shewing himself pleased in a right place.—" (w 65f.)

and she even allows herself to reply with impertinent candor to Tom's impertinent question:

> ". . . Miss Osborne is a charming girl, is not she?"
> "I do not think her handsome." (w 65)

To Elizabeth she offers the obviously definitive judgment of Tom Musgrave:

> "I do *not* like him, Eliz:—. I allow his person & air to be good— & that his manners to a certain point—his address rather—is pleasing.—But I see nothing else to admire in him.—On the contrary, he seems very vain, very conceited, absurdly anxious for Distinction, & absolutely contemptible in some of the measures he takes for becoming so.—There is a ridiculousness about him that entertains me—but his company gives me no other agreable Emotion." (w 70)

She is acutely conscious of the shortcomings of her family— of Robert and his wife, of Margaret—as she makes plain in the temporary respite of her father's company:

> In *his* chamber, Emma was at peace from the dreadful mortifications of unequal Society, & family Discord—from the immediate endurance of Hard-hearted prosperity, low-minded Conceit, & wrong-headed folly, engrafted on an untoward Disposition. (w 117)

Emma's uncomplicated individual perceptions of people are, ultimately, all referred to her large perception of the thing that is the enemy. And her perception of husband-hunt-

151

ing and the marriage of convenience, the evil social require-
ment and its end, is large without complexity—large, in fact,
only because its object is magnified to the easy conventional
symbol of, made directly accountable for, all the evil in her
world. It accounts for ill-bred Lord Osborne and the coxcomb
Tom Musgrave; for her mean-spirited brother and sister-in-
law, who triumphantly condescend to her and her father; for
her posturing, bad-tempered sister Margaret; for poor lonely
Elizabeth.

The trouble is that Emma—from the patent identity of
their points of view, Jane Austen also for the time being—
has no notion of the tragic power and complexity of the opposition. Against evil social pressures it is necessary only to set
up a determined frankness and a Sunday-school morality: so
Emma supposes. Elizabeth Bennet had to learn through hard
experience—this is, indeed, one way of stating the theme of
Pride and Prejudice—that the anti-personal pressures of a
materialistic society are strong and varied enough to overcome, not only those, like Mr. Collins, who have no personality to lose, but forceful, intelligent men like her father and
sensible girls like Charlotte Lucas. Emma, on the other hand,
remains totally unaware of any difficulty. The human will
itself she finds quite uncomplicated: those who have the power
of choice—and it is in striking contradiction to her ostensibly
Christian outlook that Emma finds them very few—choose the
right almost as a matter of course.

At the outset, while she has perhaps not yet excluded Elizabeth from this group, she can scarcely accept as a fact her
sister's pathetic desire to be married *just* to be properly placed,
just to evade loneliness and the social odium of spinsterhood.
" 'To be so bent on Marriage . . . is a sort of thing that shocks
me. I cannot understand it. . . .' " (w 9f.) Otherwise the
problem is simple, the solution unequivocal; and Emma is
too sure of things to be surprised by anything. In the most unfavorable circumstances, she is supported by her "naturally
chearful" temperament:

> . . . from being the Life & Spirit of a House, where all had
> been comfort & Elegance, & the expected Heiress of an easy

Independance, she was become of importance to no one, a
burden on those, whose affection she c^d not expect, an addition
in an House, already overstocked, surrounded by inferior minds
with little chance of domestic comfort, & as little hope of
future support.—It was well for her that she was naturally
chearful;—for the Change had been such as might have plunged
weak spirits in Despondence.—(w 118f.)

And there is never any question about her resistance to temptation, even about her ability to distinguish at once between
good and bad, between truth and pretense. We may be certain that, for her and Mr. Howard at least, no person or thing
is inaccessible—as some crucially were for the very astute
Elizabeth Bennet—to an immediate accurate judgment; that
for both of them choice is automatic (and therefore, perhaps,
inhuman and uninteresting).

As for the "inferior minds," Emma recognizes that they get
in the way sometimes of the choosers, may even make these
unhappy in the mere contemplation of benighted stupidity; but
she never recognizes that people like Margaret and Elizabeth
may themselves be made unhappy in contemplation of themselves, that their plight in the face of pressures beyond their
understanding, not to speak of their control, may be uncomfortable and disconcerting, and that the unhappiness of a person of good but feeble will like Elizabeth Watson is far more
poignant and affecting—even in its glimmer of treatment—
than her self-righteous and uncompromising sister's.

In *The Watsons*, Jane Austen has for the first time im-
mersed herself wholly in the grim business of vindicating
genteel morality against the very society it is organized to up-
hold. She is, in fact, so pledged to her moral issue that she has
lost any sustained shaping interest—which for her has always
been ironic—in the characters and relationships she cannot,
as a novelist, keep from suggesting, she has failed to direct
and fortify our sympathies with anything more conjuring than
an admonitory index finger. The stiff protesting moralist who
first appeared, disquietingly, in Elinor Dashwood's self-justi-
fications is here in full control. And though *The Watsons* remained unfinished—one assumes that Jane Austen recognized

153

in the midst of it the impossible black-and-white pattern that was working out—the accumulating genteel imperatives that obliged her to produce it were by no means finished with her. Their grand—and, as it turned out, final—triumph was to occur later, in her next completed work: *Mansfield Park*.

CHAPTER VI

THE TRIUMPH OF GENTILITY

MANSFIELD PARK

IN Jane Austen's early novels, place and group are strongly present and influential, but each of these holds a variety of moral and emotional climates. The individual moves from one place or group to another, with no implied reorientation or involvement. The problem of action is personal; choice, or the illusion of choice, is personal. It is not Longbourn and Rosings, but Elizabeth and Lady Catherine, who stand opposed: the individual makes his own climate, and does not have to locate himself in any other.

In *Mansfield Park*, Jane Austen abridges this freedom for the first time. The individual can no longer act without locating himself. Place and group have, indeed, become central: the individual faces, not a choice of action, but a choice of allegiance; and the action of the novel is a collision of worlds.

The thesis of *Mansfield Park* is severely moral: that one world, representing the genteel orthodoxy of Jane Austen's time, is categorically superior to any other. Nowhere else does Jane Austen take such pains to make up the mind of her reader. Even the structure of *Mansfield Park*—necessarily larger to encompass its several social atmospheres—is always visible and perfectly distinct, sharp with her preconceived sympathies, hardly touched by her characteristic complicating irony. To the thesis, everything else gives way: in the end, it subordinates or destroys every character; the function of the heroine is to ensure its full acceptance. Fanny Price is not simply the author's heroine, but the example and proof of her thesis.

Fanny's schematic value is clear enough. She is our only point of contact with all the worlds of the novel: proletarian Portsmouth, fashionable London, and Mansfield Park. The child Fanny leaves Portsmouth to be adopted as a semi-menial poor relation at Mansfield Park. Grown into young womanhood, she meets the Crawfords at the Grants' Parsonage, that extension of lively London life and perils, where she first learns to disapprove. When we return with her for a disillusioning visit with her family in Portsmouth, the circle is complete. The author never lets us doubt that Fanny's only freedom is to choose among worlds.

Just as clearly, the author tells us what kind of person Fanny is. By force of circumstance, at least, she is naïve. Exposed half her life to the indifference or scorn of her adopted family, she has learned self-effacement and fear; her mind "had seldom known a pause in its alarms or embarrassments." (MP 35) Only Edmund has been kind to her:

> She regarded her cousin as an example of every thing good and great, as possessing worth, which no one but herself could ever appreciate, and as entitled to such gratitude from her as no feelings could be strong enough to pay. (MP 37)

and from him she has adoringly accepted a love of nature, a taste for didactic poetry, and the principles of the Established Church. She is firm in the Christian virtues, uncorrupted by selfishness, a stranger to ambition. Yet if Fanny is naïve by accident, she is also proper by intuition. She has an insight into the moral premises of everyone she meets; and we must infer that naïveté, far from limiting her vision, serves her as an open window to conscience, her own and everyone else's. So equipped, Fanny—ingenuous moralist—makes her judgments of character and group.

Fanny is seldom happy at Mansfield Park; but Fanny dares not aspire to happiness. If she fears Sir Thomas Bertram, she also recognizes his moral integrity and the authority of his world. Tom is a waster, Maria and Julia are thoughtless and vain, Lady Bertram dozes through a vegetable existence; but they are Sir Thomas's family besides, and about them Fanny never poses a question. Even the ferocious nagging of Mrs. Norris cannot shake her faith. And Edmund can make her happy with a word.

When the Crawfords pay a visit to the Grants' Parsonage and are received into Mansfield Park, Fanny is the first to suspect them. In spite of his courtesy and assurance, Henry does not deceive her for a moment, even before he gives himself away by his flagrant double flirtation with Maria and Julia. Mary is clever, candid, charming; but she is also frivolous and worldly, she speaks with disrespect of authority and the Church, and she regards Edmund with dismay upon learning that he is to be ordained. Fanny has every reason to reject the world of the Crawfords.

Fanny wishes to return to Portsmouth because she cannot endure the prospect of Edmund's marriage to Mary. But in the scrambling noise and disorder of her parents' home, she quickly renews her faith in Mansfield Park. Her father is a drunken idler, her mother a drudge, their children rowdies. Only William and Susan have managed to sustain their self-respect: William, the sailor, presumably through naval discipline; Susan, by good luck alone, which will desert her soon enough without a more favorable setting.

Fanny's naïveté and her moral steadfastness serve, then, to reduce the conflict to its simplest and least ambiguous terms. It is always clear to her that Sir Thomas and Edmund—the guardian spirits of Mansfield Park—are godly and just; and that all who fall away from them are either apostates, like Maria irrecoverably, like Tom and Julia for a time, or unpersuadable heathen, like the Crawfords: all to be pitied, surely, but never forgiven without a full and timely surrender to grace. Her own family is doomed by poverty, the blind enemy: only William, Susan, and Fanny herself escape; and—symbolically—all of these come under the protection of Sir Thomas.

Fanny's judgments may not be the author's: they are, of course, in youthful black and white; but of themselves they reflect the action as a conflict of worlds, and of themselves they prefigure its catastrophe. Even more strikingly, the author vindicates them in every particular, and from the beginning.

The first test of Fanny's judgment is the first crisis of the story, the first conscious taking of sides. Sir Thomas has been called away from England on business. Maria and Julia, freed from the shadow of their father's authority, and warmed by Henry Crawford's attentions, are eager for some positive diversion. The Crawfords have prolonged their visit: Henry, to trifle with the Bertram girls; Mary, to make her decision about Edmund; but their vivacity is cramped by the formal, unvaried atmosphere of Mansfield Park, and they too welcome a change. Tom is home from travel, and restless again. When Tom's friend Yates bursts in upon the company with enthusiastic talk about his venture in amateur theatricals, the disposition of forces becomes inevitable.

Edmund and Fanny rigidly disapprove of such entertainment (although Fanny, of course, dares offer her opinion to no one but Edmund). As plainly as they represent the rocklike Sir Thomas in his absence, they do not surprise us by transforming custom into absolute morality. Their opposition is the traditional moral one: plays themselves may or may not be innocent, but players, by the very requirements of illusion, must be vulgar and immoral counterfeits; in respectable society, to play someone else is to degrade oneself.[1] As Edmund says, with an uncharitable edge, he would go far

> ". . . to see real acting, good hardened real acting; but I would hardly walk from this room to the next to look at the raw efforts of those who have not been bred to the trade,—a set of gentlemen and ladies, who have all the disadvantages of education and decorum to struggle through." (MP 124)

Yet no one agrees with Edmund and Fanny: the old values are already changing. Lady Bertram, who has no principles, good or bad, cannot be induced to adopt Edmund's; Mrs. Norris believes devoutly in self-indulgence, for herself and her favorites; and everyone else, relaxed by sophistication, has no scruple whatever. Even the Reverend Doctor Grant proposes no objection. There is room, then, for a difference of opinion; and Edmund's vehemence—as well as Fanny's—must reflect the strictest view of orthodox genteel morality.

If Sir Thomas were at home, the performance would be unthinkable. Tom, however, is lord of the manor in his father's absence, and Edmund's arguments cannot move him. The play is chosen, the parts distributed, rehearsals begun. Fanny observes everything with growing dread, until at last Ed-

---

[1] But not in Jane Austen's own home, where it was a frequent amusement during her youth. J. E. Austen-Leigh, *A Memoir of Jane Austen*, Oxford, 1926, 26f.

mund, weakened by his infatuation for Mary, accepts the part of her theatrical lover and persuades poor Fanny to play the cottager's wife. At this moment, on the point of disaster, Sir Thomas returns:

> They *did* begin—and being too much engaged in their own noise, to be struck by unusual noise in the other part of the house, had proceeded some way, when the door of the room was thrown open, and Julia appearing at it, with a face all aghast, exclaimed, "My father is come! He is in the hall at this moment." (MP 172)

In the design of the story, the episode stands appropriately as a frontal attack on the integrity of Mansfield Park, a thrust that may bring down the whole formidable structure; and Edmund and Fanny, having chosen their world, can hardly do otherwise than defend it. Even the desperate coincidence of Sir Thomas's arrival clarifies the issue at a stroke: Fanny is justified, Edmund shamed by his yielding, the renegade children reclaimed for a time, the enemy discomfited and driven back to the Parsonage in temporary defeat.

But the novelist who treats a direct moral issue has another and more immediate problem: the problem of sympathy. *Mansfield Park* has nothing of the equivocal tone of *Sense and Sensibility* or the sustained shaping irony of *Pride and Prejudice*: its prevailing tone is grave, its issue unequivocal. Fanny —center of the action—is no heroine indulged, at an ironic distance, by the author; she demands our earnest sympathy, and on her own terms. We approach her primarily through her judgments: they form, in fact, the whole moral framework of the novel; and, although we need not accept them as our own, we must be persuaded of their unifying power in the story, and of their success in establishing her as an active and living presence.

In this light, Fanny looks rather less simple and less convincing. She is shocked by the mere idea of a private theater, and we expect that. At the first opportunity she hastens to read the play, and is shocked again:

> Her curiosity was all awake, and she ran through it with an eagerness which was suspended only by intervals of astonishment, that it could be chosen in the present instance. . . .

Agatha and Amelia appeared to her in their different ways so totally improper for home representation—the situation of the one, and the language of the other, so unfit to be expressed by any woman of modesty, that she could hardly suppose her cousins could be aware of what they were engaging in. . . . (MP 137)

These are supposed to represent the thoughts of a naïve and humbly religious young girl; they sound, however, like Fielding putting words into the mouth of Pamela Andrews. The author, in her zeal to make naïveté expressive, succeeds only in making it smug and even a little prurient.

Lovers' Vows,[2] the play in question, is a threadbare melodrama involving Agatha, an abandoned mother; her illegitimate son, Frederick; the remorseful father, Baron Wildenhaim; his daughter, Amelia; and her tutor, Mr. Anhalt. As Fanny observes, Agatha's very situation is objectionable; and Amelia loses face in her passionate courtship of Anhalt. Fanny knows that modesty forbids a girl to bear a child out of wedlock, or to propose marriage, though she may forget that it also forbids her to assume omniscience about worlds she can hardly have heard of.

The play offends Fanny for other reasons as well. Maria Bertram is engaged to the rich dolt Rushworth, but already charmed by Henry Crawford. Maria takes the part of Agatha; Henry plays Frederick; and to the effusive stage reunion of mother and son they add an obvious personal ardor. This is bad enough; but nothing could make Fanny more miserable than to watch the bemused Edmund, all thought of remonstrance gone, play Anhalt in the love scene to Mary's Amelia. Fanny is left alone with only her scruples to warm her.

It is strange that throughout this episode we feel no sympathy, or even pity, for Fanny. She is always so careful, so exact in points of conscience, that our sympathy has no object. The author arms her with righteousness, and she must prevail. We begin to think with nostalgia of bewildered Catherine Morland; of Marianne Dashwood, that deluded romantic; of Elizabeth and her prejudices: and we look forward gratefully

[2] Mr. Chapman has very helpfully reprinted the entire play as an appendix to his edition of *Mansfield Park*. (MP 481ff.)

to the Olympian self-deception of Emma Woodhouse. Fanny is not of their company, and for more reasons than this.

We never take the author's word for Fanny. The surface is there: humility, shyness, unfailing moral vision; but behind them we feel something persistently unpleasant—complacency and envy, perhaps; certainly an odd lackluster self-pity:

> Every body around her was gay and busy, prosperous and important, each had their object of interest, their part, their dress, their favourite scene, their friends and confederates, all were finding employment in consultations and comparisons, or diversion in the playful conceits they suggested. She alone was sad and insignificant; she had no share in anything; she might go or stay, she might be in the midst of their noise, or retreat from it to the solitude of the East room, without being seen or missed. (MP 159f.)

In this passage, we are struck less by the author's invitation to sympathy than by the perfect, unintentional justice of her remarks. If Fanny would not be seen or missed by the gay company, it is because their vividness almost cancels her out; because even elsewhere in the story, as we watch her "creep into the theatre," (MP 165) or sit silent and unobserved evening after evening at Mansfield Park, we find her image alarmingly dim. We remember what she thinks, not what she is; and we begin to wonder whether she exists at all among the bright presences in Jane Austen's work.

How well, for example, does Fanny stand comparison with Mary Crawford? Mary is Fanny's natural counterweight in the story: gay world and austere world, religious indifference and piety, woman against woman for the same ostensibly worthy young man. If Fanny is to demonstrate her personal value, she must surely do so here, and at the expense of her rival.

On the level of charm, there is, of course, no contest. Mary is poised, witty, a woman of the urban world, at ease among men and women, free to introduce her own liveliness into any company. Fanny, on the other hand, appears most often as a frozen block of timidity. Yet this distinction is irrelevant to the issue, or rather an inescapable handicap for Fanny:

brought up as she was, she could hardly have acquired the virtues of sophistication.

The author underscores Fanny's sensibility. Fanny loves nature: she cries, looking out at the autumn night:

> "Here's harmony! . . . Here's repose! Here's what may leave all painting and all music behind, and what poetry only can attempt to describe. Here's what may tranquillize every care, and lift the heart to rapture!" (MP 113)

But Mary

> had none of Fanny's delicacy of taste, of mind, of feeling; she saw nature, inanimate nature, with little observation; her attention was all for men and women, her talents for the light and lively. (MP 81)

Unfortunately, this is not very convincing. In the first place, Fanny's little rhapsody—even her entire predictable communion with nature—sounds like a tedious echo of her beloved Cowper. Its tone is so flat and false as to cry out for irony, the irony of, say, the *juvenilia*; but Jane Austen sees fit, not only to let it pass as serious, but to mark it with approval in contrast to the indifference of Mary Crawford. Mary prefers people and society, and the author disapproves. But why? Interest in nature hardly implies a grandeur of spirit: it may spring from a strong visual imagination, from childhood associations, it may be enforced by loneliness. Mary has had no such stimuli: her life has been convivial and leisured, among people with whom she has felt at least an equal; and what is unusual or limiting about her preference?

The fact is that Mary has a powerful interest in her human environment: not a shallow or false interest, but detailed, immediate, impatient with generalities. To Fanny's large, solemn, uncomfortable thoughts about nature and morality, Mary counterposes her own cool yet not unkind curiosity about everyone she meets.

On one subject only—authority—is Mary cynical and unkind, does she permit herself to generalize. Having been brought up by her uncle the Admiral, she has heard enough of officer politics and rivalry to mock at the whole fabric of uniformed authority.

". . . Of various admirals, I could tell you a great deal; of them and their flags, and the gradations of their pay, and their bickerings and jealousies. But in general, I can assure you that they are all passed over, and all very ill used. . . ." (MP 60)

And she shocks Edmund with her pun: " 'Of *Rears*, and *Vices*, I saw enough.' " (MP 60)

Laughing at the fearful anticipation of Sir Thomas's homecoming, which bears ponderously upon the atmosphere of *Mansfield Park*, she remarks:

"Sir Thomas is to achieve mighty things when he comes home. . . . Do you remember Hawkins Browne's 'Address to Tobacco,' in imitation of Pope? . . . I will parody them:
     Blest Knight! whose dictatorial looks dispense
     To Children affluence, to Rushworth sense. . . ." (MP 161)

Religion attracts her sharpest arrows, though never directly: she attacks its outward form of authority always. At Sotherton she rails pleasantly at the old rigorous customs of church service (making Fanny "too angry for speech"). (MP 87) Later, having learned that Edmund is to take orders, she tries to dissuade him:

". . . Indolence and love of ease . . . make men clergymen. A clergyman has nothing to do but to be slovenly and selfish—read the newspaper, watch the weather, and quarrel with his wife. His curate does all the work, and the business of his own life is to dine." (MP 110)

And she declines to think of marriage to Edmund unless he gives up his ordination. This attitude may signify an invincible distaste for established religion (as Jane Austen of course means it to); but it signifies also a more immediate contempt for the vulgar, ill-tempered, incongruous secularity to which a genteel priesthood is liable:

". . . though Dr. Grant is most kind and obliging to me, and though he is really a gentleman, and I dare say a good scholar and clever, and often preaches good sermons, and is very respectable, *I* see him to be an indolent selfish bon vivant, who must have his palate consulted in every thing, who will not stir a finger for the convenience of any one, and who, moreover, if the cook makes a blunder is out of humour with his excellent wife. . . ." (MP 111)

The author insists upon the physical contrast between the

two girls: Fanny's frailness, Mary's health and energy. Fanny overtaxes her strength by cutting roses for an hour in the garden, (MP 72) she becomes faint from walking and has headaches easily (like any sentimental heroine), while Mary mounts a horse for the first time and rides tirelessly: her

> . . . enjoyment of riding was such, that she did not know how to leave off. Active and fearless, and though rather small, strongly made, she seemed formed for a horsewoman. . . . (MP 66)

So Edmund in his fatuous remark to Fanny, " '*She* rides only for pleasure, you for health.' " (MP 70); as if Edmund is unconsciously cruel so that we may be consciously kind, as if the author panders to our sense of inadequacy and its charitable mask, in order to make us at once resentful of pure vigor and sentimental toward weakness for its own sake.

The contrast between Fanny and Mary has a sexual ground, which the author herself recognizes and brings forward. Mary appears throughout as a high-spirited girl with a free tongue and a free mind, and one plain implication is that she has her own free, high-spirited ideas about sex. She tends to excuse Henry's flirtations because " 'very few young ladies have any affections worth caring for.' " (MP 363) She casually defends marriage for money and convenience; but falls in love with Edmund, apparently for his personal qualities alone, since he has no money, and since she is deprived even of the satisfaction of sharing his principles. Uninflammable Fanny, of course, will fall in love only when principles invest her lover with a sanctity as dull and secular as her own.

The issue becomes public in Edmund's talk with Fanny after Henry Crawford has proposed to her. Edmund recalls fondly:

> ". . . Miss Crawford made us laugh by her plans of encouragement for her brother. She meant to urge him to persevere in the hope of being loved in time, and of having his addresses most kindly received at the end of about ten years' happy marriage." (MP 354)

The author is still doing her partisan best to keep the issue impartial with a joke: womanly warmth against maidenly frigidity. But her sympathy lies with the immaculate Fanny, and her pose of distance collapses altogether in the scene of Edmund's enlightenment.

Edmund is telling Fanny about his last interview with Mary in London. He has lectured Mary on the wickedness of her brother; she retorts defiantly; and he turns to leave the house.

". . . I had gone a few steps, Fanny, when I heard the door open behind me. 'Mr. Bertram,' said she. I looked back. 'Mr. Bertram,' said she, with a smile—but it was a smile ill-suited to the conversation that had passed, a saucy playful smile, seeming to invite, in order to subdue me; at least, it appeared so to me. I resisted; it was the impulse of the moment to resist, and still walked on. I have since—sometimes—for a moment—regretted that I did not go back; but I know I was right. . . ." (MP 459)

Mary has suddenly become Satan: poor, noble, overheated Edmund smells the brimstone, and beats an ecclesiastical retreat.

Why does Jane Austen resort to such grotesque makeshift to tidy up her plot? On a very aware and proper level, she dislikes Mary Crawford; on an aesthetic level, she fears her vitality; as a working novelist with a plan, she must subdue Mary to the boundaries of that plan.

In *Mansfield Park* Jane Austen proposes a conflict of worlds, and restricts the will of the individual to a choice among worlds. This is her plan, and Fanny fits it smoothly; but Mary keeps escaping. By mere force of personality, in fact, Mary Crawford threatens to overthrow the plan. Skepticism, sexual freedom, abundant personal vitality—all of these qualities laugh at system; while a cold, questionless obedience props up a dying world. This is what the contrast between Mary and Fanny begins to look like; yet Fanny must triumph, and Mary —temptress becoming heroine—be driven out. Lacking other means, the author betrays Mary, as an author must always betray a character outgrowing the canvas, eluding the moral situation.

We observe Mary as impatient with dullness, evil, and pomposity, but good-tempered, affectionate, intelligent, kind. After fixing upon a future baronet, she is capable of falling in love with a man whose possible fortune is very modest. She is far more alert than Edmund to the insults offered Fanny by the Bertram household, and generous and sympathetic to her beyond courtesy, as when Mrs. Norris bursts out characteristically:

". . . I shall think her a very obstinate, ungrateful girl, if she does not do what her aunts and cousins wish her—very ungrateful indeed, considering who and what she is."

Edmund was too angry to speak; but Miss Crawford looking for a moment with astonished eyes at Mrs. Norris, and then at Fanny, whose tears were beginning to show themselves . . . moved away her chair . . . close to Fanny, saying to her in a kind low whisper as she placed herself, "Never mind, my dear Miss Price—this is a cross evening,—everybody is cross and teasing—but do not let us mind them;" and with pointed attention continued to talk to her and endeavour to raise her spirits, in spite of being out of spirits herself. (MP 147)

She carries every conversation by her wit, yet without malice or hypocrisy. Her sisterly affection for Henry is gracious and unproprietary. Moreover, she values her brother's welfare and Fanny's conventional goodness so highly as to rejoice in their prospective marriage, and to remain uninfluenced by snobbery or condescension:

". . . Fanny Price—Wonderful—quite wonderful!—That Mansfield should have done so much for—that *you* should have found your fate in Mansfield! But you are quite right, you could not have chosen better. . . ." (MP 293)

But Fanny can hardly endure her presence: she maliciously interprets every gesture and remark, savagely blackens every motive that Mary exposes or implies. If Mary is generous, Fanny knows that she is really shallow; if witty, light-minded; if in love, basely—"she might love, but she did not deserve Edmund by any other sentiment" (MP 367); if skeptical, irreligious and probably immoral—" 'Her friends leading her astray for years! She is quite as likely to have led *them* astray. They have all, perhaps, been corrupting one another. . . .' "
(MP 424) So reasons the gentle, amiable Fanny, whom the author enforces as the heroine and final victor; and, wanting evidence to support Fanny's judgment, we must assume that she has powers of observation beyond, and indifferent to, our own.

Fanny's intuition is, then, the chief instrument of betrayal;

but the author provides her with a few practical weapons as well. We are reminded often of the "vicious" (MP 41) Admiral Crawford, who brought up his niece and nephew, and who presumably taught them to emulate him; though even this is not clear, since Mary repudiates her uncle's authority and alludes with contempt to his character. Still, the author recognizes the feebleness of the evidence; and she makes two last great efforts to fortify it.

Tom has become ill, and Fanny concludes at once that Mary will wish him dead so that Edmund may succeed to the baronetcy:

> . . . Miss Crawford gave her the idea of being the child of good luck, and to her selfishness and vanity it would be good luck to have Edmund the only son. (MP 430)

Her suspicion is confirmed when Mary writes promptly:

> ". . . I put it to your conscience, whether 'Sir Edmund' would not do more good with all the Bertram property, than any other possible 'Sir.' . . ." (MP 434)

We are asked to believe, therefore, that a worldly, intelligent girl—even if excited by the not uncommon selfishness that comes with the anticipation of a windfall—would confide her feelings unreservedly to a stiff moral object, an obsessed partisan of the Bertram code, like Fanny.

The author's climactic maneuver does not work at all. When, in Mary's last encounter with Edmund, we watch her leering feverishly from her doorway, the unholy nimbus falls, not upon the character, but upon the author. The illusion of consistency falls to pieces, and we are ready to believe that Jane Austen's wit has yielded altogether to her will.

The male images of light and darkness in the novel are Edmund Bertram and Henry Crawford. Edmund is to be a clergyman, and—except for his uneasy adventure with Mary —he never strays from the center of the High-Church path. Even while in love, he deplores Mary's frivolity and independence. He seems more forgiving than Fanny, less liable to inflexible judgment; though in the end we discover that this was just another mistake of his infatuation, that he can condemn almost as thoroughly as Fanny:

". . . Her's are not faults of temper. . . . Her's are faults of principle, Fanny, of blunted delicacy and a corrupted, vitiated mind. Perhaps it is best for me—since it leaves me so little to regret. Not so, however. Gladly would I submit to all the increased pain of losing her, rather than have to think of her as I do. I told her so." (MP 456)

His conversation and conduct are predictably rhetorical and dull. As a hero, he might have made an adequate foil to a sparkling heroine—someone, say, like Mary Crawford.

Henry Crawford is less agreeable than his sister. He seems closer to the conception Jane Austen intends, that of a charming rake; and his calculated trifling with Maria and Julia is credible and unpleasant. From the first, however, we have no evidence to support the author's prissily tendentious remark (in which Jane Austen *becomes* Fanny) about his enthusiasm for the theatrical project, that "in all the riot of his gratifications, it was yet an untasted pleasure" (MP 123); and after he falls in love with Fanny, no one—not even the author—doubts his sincerity. He shows no anxiety or condescension about Fanny's lack of position or fortune. He declares his love to her and to his sister, in the most unmistakably fixed and generous terms:

. . . he had . . . nothing to relate but his own sensations, nothing to dwell on but Fanny's charms.—Fanny's beauty of face and figure, Fanny's graces of manner and goodness of heart were the exhaustless theme. (MP 294)

Fanny, cherishing her hopeless love of Edmund, rejects him time after time; but he persists with delicacy and fervor. He makes use of his uncle's influence to secure the promotion of her sailor brother. He gravely discusses the art of the sermon with Edmund. He visits Fanny at her parents' home in Portsmouth; and, though she herself feels shame and embarrassment regarding her family, Henry acts with perfect tact, dignity, and friendliness toward all of them. Fanny learns that he has even begun to take a hand in the affairs of his estate and to befriend and assist his tenants. Henry leaves Portsmouth after certainly the most encouraging series of talks of his persevering courtship; and the next news we have of him is that he has run off with Maria Rushworth! We are asked to believe that, in spite of love, convenience, and good sense—to all of which he has shown a general affinity—Henry Crawford is essentially wicked; and that, directly after observing signs of hope in his courtship, he must prove his wickedness by running away to live in sin with an empty-headed married woman. Incidentally, this remarkable deed clears the way for Fanny's union with Edmund.

Why are the Crawfords so brutally sacrificed? Henry's resemblance to Willoughby and Wickham is close enough to minimize the shock of his fall from grace: Jane Austen as author has always distrusted the charming young man. But Mary bears only troubling resemblances. " 'I do not pretend,' " says Mary, " 'to set people right, but I often see them wrong.' " (MP 50) She sees, in fact, too much that is wrong. This is Mary as we know her in the novel, unmasking cant in others, free of it herself, driven to no false system: very like Elizabeth Bennet; most like Jane Austen herself, as we know her in her letters.

Mary laughs at the punctilio of convention. Jane writes to a friend: "You are very good in wishing to see me . . . so soon, & I am equally good in wishing to come to you; I beleive our Merit in that respect is much upon a par, our Self-denial mutually strong." (L I 87, 12 Nov. 1800) Mary dislikes religious cant. Jane writes to her sister: "We do not much like Mr. Cooper's new Sermons;—they are fuller of Regeneration and Conversion than ever—with the addition of his zeal in the cause of the Bible Society." (L II 467, 8 Sept. 1816) A hundred instances of quick, amoral wit—like Mary's—punctuate the letters: "We plan having a steady Cook, & a young giddy Housemaid, with a sedate, middle aged Man who is to undertake the double office of Husband to the former and sweetheart to the latter. No children of course to be allowed on either side." (L I 99f., 3 Jan. 1801) What dreadful conclusions about her author might Fanny not have drawn from such a joke! Mary thrives on detail and humor. Jane's letters are a bustle of news-bits, with irony gleaming like a knife-blade among them: a certain friend, she remarks, is "very unreserved and very fond of talking of her deceased brother &

sister, whose memories she cherishes with an enthusiasm which tho' perhaps a little affected, is not unpleasing." (L I 135, 26 May 1801) Jane too adopts the anti-romantic stance: "I have had a most affectionate letter from Buller; I was afraid he would oppress me by his felicity & his love for his wife, but this is not the case; he calls her simply Anna . . . for which I respect and wish him happy. . . ." (L I 85, 8 Nov. 1800) Jane Austen as author invidiously sets Mary's preference for people against Fanny's love of nature and poetry; but Jane herself writes of going "to the Liverpool Museum, & the British Gallery, & I had some amusement at each, tho' my preference for Men and Women always inclines me to attend more to the company than the sight." (L II 267, 18 Apr. 1811) Neither Mary nor Jane would ever be caught thinking broad, solemn thoughts; neither is sentimental about poetry, landscapes, or death. Jane announces to her sister, "I treat you with a dead Baronet in almost every letter" (L II 465, 8 Sept. 1816); and one of her titbits is that ". . . Mrs. Coulthard and Anne, late of Manydown, are both dead, and both died in childbed. We have not regaled Mary with the news." (L I 29, 17 Nov. 1798) Mary is self-confident and worldly enough to allow herself to be attracted by a man for charm or presence alone, regardless of differences in principle. Jane writes of an acquaintance: "I am sure he is clever & a Man of Taste. . . . I am rather in love with him.—I dare say he is ambitious and Insincere." (L II 353, 14 Oct. 1813) And we come finally to be convinced that both Mary and Jane make such continual demands upon their wit in order to protect a certain depth of privacy, to avoid a full commitment.

However deliberately, Jane Austen is attacking much of herself in the image of Mary Crawford: the attack is on the most earnest ethical grounds, and fixes the tone of the novel; and the consequence of the attack is an aesthetic failure. We return, then, to the system, the enclave of conformity, which triumphs over Mary in the novel, but which Mary triumphantly survives as a living figure; just as Jane Austen survives the wreck and oblivion of her closed society.

Whatever Jane Austen was like, she passed her entire life

within a deeply conformist and self-complacent society. She was the daughter of a genteel country clergyman, in a time when religious orthodoxy was a social grace, and its body of doctrine unquestioned by a most comfortable majority of the people. Even in the midst of the Napoleonic wars, the façade of genteel serenity remained so impregnable that Jane Austen mentions war perhaps half a dozen times throughout her novels and letters, and never as a serious matter.

This astonishing insularity was part of her world: it penetrated her genius, and influenced her in setting, in subject, in purpose. Her primary audience was a small circle of family and friends, oriented in the same world. Her *juvenilia* were addressed to them; and if later her audience widened greatly, she was still involved with the same persons for whom her earliest work had been composed, and still affected by their opinions of her work.[3]

Submission to doctrine is the key virtue of such an enclave; and it is not surprising that in memoirs by her family Jane Austen assumes a posture of dutiful piety. Her nephew writes: "She was a humble, believing Christian. Her life had been passed in the performance of home duties, and the cultivation of domestic affections, without any self-seeking or craving after applause."[4] And Jane's brother Henry—himself later a clergyman—writes in his Biographical Notice, prefixed to her posthumous novels: "Faultless herself, as nearly as human nature can be, she always sought, in the faults of others, something to excuse, to forgive or forget" (NA 6); and he concludes: "One trait remains to be touched on. It makes all others unimportant. She was thoroughly religious and devout; fearful of giving offence to God, and incapable of feeling it towards any fellow creature. On serious subjects she was well-instructed . . . and her opinions accorded strictly with those of our Established Church." (NA 8)

These descriptions are as extravagant as Mr. Collins's fancies about himself; and they have the added disadvantage of

---

[3] She carefully transcribed these opinions. J. Austen, *Plan of a Novel and Other Notes* (ed. R. W. Chapman), Oxford, 1926, 13ff.
[4] J. E. Austen-Leigh, *A Memoir of Jane Austen*, Oxford, 1926, 175.

being seriously intended. From every piece of evidence—novels, letters, uncolored recollections—we know that Jane Austen was not the saint her family wished to enshrine; and that her genius, at least, was something quite different.

Yet no artist, not even a genius, can wholly resist the aspirations of his world. If Jane Austen was not what her family regarded as the type of Christian womanhood, still she could hardly have helped being influenced by an ideal that was constantly suggested by the very conditions of her life—by the religion and the social structure that she accepted as true and enduring, by the people she lived with and wrote for. Under such social and personal pressures, which must have become more insistent as she saw herself year after year less likely ever to disavow them, it is easy to believe that Jane Austen felt obliged to produce a work of uncompromising moral purpose, whatever the bent of her taste and imagination.

From her childhood, she had written almost nothing but burlesques and parodies on the Gothic and sentimental novels of the eighteenth century. *Northanger Abbey* was itself an extended variation on the same theme. *Sense and Sensibility* and *Pride and Prejudice* differed in a sharpening of intention, in a growth of power and individuality; but morally they did not differ at all. In all of them there was no court of appeal beyond human reason and reasonableness, no character in them was judged outside his earthly setting, and their dominant tone—with an exception in the figure of Elinor Dashwood—was one of uninvolved amusement, very like the tone of Mary Crawford. All of these novels were finished in first draft before Jane Austen was twenty-three years old. (ss xiii)

Jane Austen began to write *Mansfield Park* in 1811, the year in which *Sense and Sensibility*, her first published work, was issued. She was thirty-five, and had not persevered in a new novel for more than a dozen years. In the interim, her father had died, and her family had moved from Steventon, her childhood home, to the village of Chawton; yet she kept the same friends, and her numerous relatives continued to visit and to write. She had passed through at least one unhappy love affair some years before,[5] and had presumably reconciled herself to spinsterhood and a perpetuation of the same relationships she had known all her life. She was, moreover, about to become a responsible author; her first novel was ready for the public, her second would be issued before *Mansfield Park* was completed; and meanwhile her family and friends read them eagerly and commented in detail. She was now not only oriented in her world, but trapped there, willingly or not; and her resolution to conform followed as a matter of course.

Working on *Mansfield Park*, Jane Austen wrote to her sister that she was attempting "a complete change of subject—ordination." (L II 298, 29 Jan. 1813) She herself recognized what a radical shift in grouping and attitude her new novel would require, and her word for it is a confession. Clearly, she intended to symbolize the conflict in terms of religion and morality, in terms of Edmund's ordination, which Mary would try to prevent. *Mansfield Park* was to be a novel vindicating the ethical foundation of Jane Austen's world.

With her aim apparent, we may reëxamine the worlds of the novel. Mansfield Park itself is, of course, the fortress, the repository of the solid virtues of the Established Church. It is the symbol of stability, discipline, order: universal catchwords of theology. It is the strength of rural conservatism against the encroaching sophistication of the city. Logically, its defenders are the hard, wealthy, rank-conscious core of the landed gentry, because the system is their social embodiment and the text of their privileges. Hemmed in by the forces of change, Sir Thomas and Edmund—and Fanny—know that the integrity of their world must be preserved altogether or not at all. That is why Mansfield Park faces every issue without compromise, why it poses to every character the strict alternative of loyalty or excommunication.

Its active enemy is the world of the Crawfords, the bright, pleasure-seeking atmosphere in which system dissolves; and the Crawfords are especially dangerous because they too have money and position—"advantages," Sir Thomas would say—

[5] R. W. Chapman, *Jane Austen: Facts and Problems*, Oxford, 1948, 61ff.

because they are in fact conscious traitors to the system that makes their comfort possible. It is small wonder that all of Mary's charm cannot save her from judgment.

During most of the novel, Portsmouth exists solely in Fanny's homesick imagination: the author reserves the real Portsmouth as a cold-water shock for Fanny toward the end. To make up for her jealousy of Mary, her stifled love of Edmund, her fear of Henry's attentions, Fanny reconstructs her home as a circle of cozy tranquillity. She is, of course, terribly wrong. Her family is lost, except for the few who by luck and force of purpose have succeeded in tearing themselves away. When Jane Austen deals with poverty, she is not sentimental about it; Fanny's home in Portsmouth

> . . . was . . . in almost every respect, the very reverse of what she could have wished. It was the abode of noise, disorder, and impropriety. Nobody was in their right place, nothing was done as it ought to be. She could not respect her parents, as she had hoped. . . . [Her father] . . . swore and he drank, he was dirty and gross . . . and now he scarcely ever noticed her, but to make her the object of a coarse joke. (MP 388f.)

Poverty is the passive enemy that destroys the will and makes choice impossible. This is the final lesson, the confirmation of Fanny's faith. If in Jane Austen's parable Mansfield Park is Heaven and the Crawfords' London Hell, Portsmouth is the Limbo of the morally unborn.

The author's outline is clear and strong, and never before or after did she attempt one of such symbolic breadth. It remains, nevertheless, an outline and an imposition; it freezes her with its responsibility. Jane Austen is working here, not within her characters, but *at* them, desperately toward them: she keeps misplacing, or misjudging, or fails to define them at all.

In *Mansfield Park*, even the minor figures illustrate and confirm the author's impasse. Elsewhere, Jane Austen takes only a moment to realize and to place her minor but necessary persons; here, they stand out of place or out of focus. Although William Price is intended as the secondary hero, the manly sailor-brother (reminder of Jane Austen's own sailor-brothers) who merits Fanny's joyous confidence, he never comes ashore out of the fog. We learn now and then that he is nearby; we have seen him somewhere before; but we never recall his face, his voice, or his words.

Mrs. Norris, on the other hand, we see and hear without prompting:

> "The nonsense and folly of people's stepping out of their rank and trying to appear above themselves, makes me think it right to give *you* a hint, Fanny, now that you are going into company without any of us; and I do beseech and intreat you not to be putting yourself forward, and talking and giving your opinion as if you were one of your cousins—as if you were dear Mrs. Rushworth or Julia. *That* will never do, believe me. Remember, wherever you are, you must be the lowest and last. . . ." (MP 221)

yet, though fully realized, she has no home. She belongs elsewhere in Jane Austen's work: a fugitive from the sphere of merciless irony, cousin to Mrs. Elton and to Mrs. John Dashwood. It is true that Mrs. Norris plays her part from moment to moment fiercely and vitally, but in the end her envenomed liveness is a liability. She would belong only if all of Sir Thomas's world were on the point of the author's wit; but, impaled alone, she makes us regret that the Bertrams do not join her there. When, to follow her favorite, Maria, into disgrace, Mrs. Norris resigns comfort and avarice and leaves Mansfield Park forever, her exile seems simply a crude dismissal by the author. Since Fanny will not be happy if her aunt remains, her aunt must go; but it is Jane Austen, not Mrs. Norris, who makes this decision. Nor is it accidental that Mrs. Norris goes without a word; for if she were allowed to speak in character, she might give the lie to her forced and unprepared departure.

The character most nearly consistent with his role in the novel is Sir Thomas Bertram. He is always a commanding figure, his weight of manner is genuine and effective. We grant the sincerity and firmness of his motives, and never question his position as first defender of Mansfield Park.

In Jane Austen's design, however, Sir Thomas must be more than this. She has made the issue squarely moral, without a trace of irony or detachment. She has, in fact, conditioned the entire course of the narrative upon our acceptance of Sir Thomas's code; for if that is not acceptable with all its implications, if wit, worldliness, and skepticism are not evil in themselves or at least symptomatic of evil, then we have no reason to accept the final ruin of the Crawfords. The catastrophe of the novel depends upon our moral sympathy with Sir Thomas.

Apart from condemning the Crawfords, what do Sir Thomas's principles deny or affirm? Sir Thomas believes in the imposed distinction of rank. Speaking of Fanny, he is concerned

> ". . . how to preserve in the minds of my *daughters* the consciousness of what they are, without making them think too lowly of their cousin; and how, without depressing her spirits too far, to make her remember that she is not a Miss Bertram. . . ." (MP 10)

This occurs early in the story, and the author allows an echo of irony to persist; but Sir Thomas never sees fit to alter the implied generality. If later he receives Fanny as his daughter-in-law it is because in defense of his principles she has shown herself worthy of elevation—a sort of knighting on the battlefield.

Similarly, age and position must be revered over every claim of personal dignity and sensibility. Thus, having placidly observed the lacerating and inescapable torments inflicted by Mrs. Norris upon Fanny through the years of her childhood and youth, Sir Thomas advises his niece:

> ". . . you will feel that *they* were not least your friends who were educating and preparing you for that mediocrity of condition which *seemed* to be your lot.—Though their caution may prove eventually unnecessary, it was kindly meant. . . . I am sure you will not disappoint my opinion of you, by failing at any time to treat your aunt Norris with the respect and attention that are due to her. . . ." (MP 313)

Sir Thomas believes that marriage is an affair of convenience and material advantage. Wealthy enough to have chosen a wife for her beauty alone, he remains indifferent to her lack of intellect, activity, and emotion. If she displays herself now and then at social assemblies to gratify his vanity and to assert his position, if she perpetuates his name with sons, if she is "faithful" (and it is impossible to imagine Lady Bertram stirring from her trance for the embraces of Don Juan himself), then she has fulfilled all the duties of a wife. On meeting Rushworth, Sir Thomas has some qualms about his unqualified idiocy; but after a conference with Maria, the baronet reassures himself that

> . . . her feelings probably were not acute; he had never supposed them to be so; but her comforts might not be less on that account, and if she could dispense with seeing her husband a leading, shining character, there would certainly be everything else in her favour. (MP 201)

That is, money, rank, security, power over a weak, stupid man; everything, indeed, but love, sympathy, and respect.

Sir Thomas's principles are negative, a code of thou-shalt-nots: the code of a system striving to affirm itself against the as yet unaroused majority of outsiders. The goal becomes, not the happiness or fulfillment of individuals, but the fortification of a privileged world; not accommodation, but war: and, rather than serving as a supernatural support of the Bertram world, religion comes to resemble another apology for the code.

Neither Sir Thomas's world nor his religion has charity, sweetness, compassion, forgiveness. His notion of marriage has encouraged Maria to bind herself to a man she despises. Yet after her escapade with Henry Crawford, Sir Thomas refuses even to consider her return to Mansfield Park. We recall Mr. Collins's letter to Mr. Bennet after Lydia's elopement: " 'You ought certainly to forgive them as a christian, but never to admit them in your sight, or allow their names to be mentioned in your hearing.' " (PP 364) The girl who wrote *Pride and Prejudice* would not have been kind to Sir Thomas Bertram.

Between Mr. Collins and Sir Thomas lies all the distance between the early novels and *Mansfield Park*. So far from accepting Mr. Collins's judgments, we and the author laugh at them; unless, however, we accept the justice of Sir Thomas's severity, the denouement of *Mansfield Park* is annulled, the structure of the novel crumbles into a debris of unrelated characters.

In *Mansfield Park*, the most notable omission is irony; and since, except in the fragment *The Watsons* and in the denouement of *Sense and Sensibility*, irony has been the shaping tone of all of Jane Austen's previous work, the omission is a crucial one. In the *juvenilia*, in *Sense and Sensibility*, in *Pride and Prejudice*, in *Northanger Abbey*, every character (with the single exception of Elinor Dashwood) is either ironic spectator or object of irony, and the author herself maintains an amused detachment that organizes the issue of the novel without forcing it.

As technique, as attitude, irony was peculiarly adapted to Jane Austen's temperament and genius. She was herself a person who, like Mary Crawford, found it difficult to commit herself to anything, and who used her considerable wit as weapon or shield, in any case to guard herself against direct contact. Since irony implies a remoteness, since it requires, not an exposure and analysis of feeling, but suggestion and wit, it did not violate her sense of propriety or make demands upon her emotions which she could not—at least so far—fulfill. Irony was the single life-principle that her art had invoked.

In *Mansfield Park*, however, the very nature of the issue demands commitment. The author intends to justify the ways of her world, and to do that she must discard the relative and uncommitted judgments made by irony—always the opponent of an absolute morality. Moral sympathy must be substituted as the life-principle; but sympathy is first of all a personal involvement. A catalogue of virtues will not do. The author must induce us, finally, to admire or love the Bertrams—at least Fanny and Edmund, their youthful champions—and to reject Mary and Henry, the youthful, unrelenting enemy.

The Crawfords are the only characters in the novel whose source and mode of expression is irony. They exist for the most part as ironic spectators, the role which Jane Austen projects most skillfully, for which as an artist she has the shrewdest sympathy. It must have been clear to her, therefore, that she could sustain Fanny and Edmund against the brilliance of their adversaries only by persuading the reader of their honesty, of their depth of feeling, of the need for their survival in a world corrupted by sophistication.

But the author can never come close enough to them, she cannot supply them with the personal warmth that would enliven their convictions. If Fanny and Edmund had tenderness to offer against the Crawfords' wit and worldly kindness, they might win us over. But Jane Austen was unwilling or unable to project tenderness; she could give them only a mechanical heart.

Whatever life Fanny and Edmund begin with ebbs away in priggishness and self-satisfaction, toward a norm of orthodox nonentity. It is no wonder that their final union seems almost narcissistic, and that the author herself dismisses it with an embarrassed brevity:

> I only intreat every body to believe that exactly at the time when it was quite natural that it should be so, and not a week earlier, Edmund did cease to care about Miss Crawford, and became as anxious to marry Fanny, as Fanny herself could desire. (MP 470)

The author's revulsion from involvement—carefully transmuted in the irony of her early novels—comes here, in the hard light of righteousness, to seem a revulsion physical and particular, unpleasant in itself and destructive of form. In the early novels, for example, if we never hear the private talk of lovers,[6] we tend to assume notwithstanding that they can and do talk of love, but that the tone and resolution of the story do not require our eavesdropping. Only with *Mansfield Park* does it become obvious that their silence represents a confession of inadequacy by the author. We become curious about overt omissions; for the current of irony has failed, and Edmund and Fanny have only hollow phrases and a transparent forgery of feeling to protect their privacy. What imagination will not quail before the thought of a Saturday night at the Edmund Bertrams, after the prayer-books have been put away?

It is no mistake that sex is the great taboo of *Mansfield*

---

[6] *Cf.* M. Lascelles, *Jane Austen and Her Art*, Oxford, 1939, 126.

Park. Maria effects the catastrophe by her surrender to Henry, and her guilt is irreversible. Sir Thomas, Fanny, Edmund are defending custom against personality, obedience against expression, system against energy; and sexual vitality is a rebel, an enemy of system. Frigidity becomes the standard of sexual conduct; marriage, the means of consolidating privilege and passing it on; and the deadly sins are passion and infidelity.

In her early novels, Jane Austen's moral imagination functions chiefly to undermine, by irony, the postulates of gentility. Gentility is there, in fact, the great enemy, the creator and sustainer of uncreative confining forms; and if the author is not yet prepared to assert the positive emotional values it ignores or inhibits, she takes every ironic advantage of its exhaustless supply of unportentous incongruities. The world of *Mansfield Park* fails to convince because Jane Austen is cutting off her only spontaneous response to it, to its inflexible and deadening moral dogma. This dogma was part of her own world, of her life with her family and her friends, but it was no part of her art; and when she tried to introduce it there, she could not even unbar the door: not simply that we disbelieve her dogma and reject the unnatural authoritative tone in which she delivers it, but that we disbelieve the story with which she illustrates it, the characters to whom she entrusts it.

Irony has been Jane Austen's only internal principle, her only method of suggesting impulse and response; and here she gives it up. The frame of reference is violated from without: Fanny and Edmund triumph, not through a development of will or vitality, clearly not with the inner justice of *Pride and Prejudice*, but because they represent a world which the author intrudes into her world of irony, and which she has engaged herself to affirm. The process leaves Fanny and Edmund stripped of feeling and purpose, naked in the cold wind of casuistry. The larger misfortune is that *Mansfield Park* and, for the time being, Jane Austen herself are there beside them.

CHAPTER VII

IRONY AS FORM

EMMA

Emma is a throwing off of chains. The author and her characters move with a freedom and assurance unparalleled in Jane Austen's earlier work, and all the more astonishing by contrast with the uneasy stiffness of *Mansfield Park*. The new impetus is her old familiar one, but—from our first impression of *Emma*—purely assimilated to the medium as, in *Northanger Abbey* or even in *Pride and Prejudice*, it is not: the impetus is irony. In *Emma*, the sense of strain and anxiety is purged altogether. This time the author is in her novel and never out of it, never imposing upon us as in *Northanger Abbey* with her condescension or in *Pride and Prejudice* with her occasional prim moral reminders; and she is there for the comic artist's purpose only—to embody and direct our laughter.

The relaxation of an achieved technique is the very climate of *Emma*. Certainly, no other of Jane Austen's novels offers so pleasant and comfortable an atmosphere, so much the effect of an uncomplex and immediate art: wit, irony, light laughter shining in a triumph of surface. Its surface is, in fact, unmarred by a trace of self-justification, ill humor, or backsliding into morality. The story tells itself, and nothing seems more superfluous than inquiry or deep thought about it.[1]

Emma, like *Pride and Prejudice*, is a story of self-deception, and the problem of each heroine is to undeceive herself. Yet Emma needs, not facts, but people, to help her. If Elizabeth Bennet is self-deceived under a set of special, doubtful circumstances, if she waits mainly for facts, Emma Woodhouse is a girl absolutely self-deceived, who takes and refashions

---

[1] Far from thinking about it, some critics seem to drift out of it into a warm, irrelevant daydream of their own, in which they discover in the book a "good-natured, placid, slightly dispersed and unoccupied quality . . . pleasantly reflected in the character of its heroine" (O. W. Firkins, *Jane Austen*, New York, 1920, 96).

whatever circumstances may arise, who can be checked only by a personality as positive as her own. We follow Emma's comic train of misunderstandings in the happy conviction that she cannot act otherwise until someone with will and intelligence takes her in hand—someone like Mr. Knightley, for example. We sympathize with Emma because she *must* fall in love, and we are relaxed because we know that she will. The love story in *Emma* is, then, predetermined to a degree unimaginable in *Pride and Prejudice*; for all Elizabeth needs in order to see is to have the facts before her, while Emma— in spite of her will and intelligence—cannot even begin to see clearly or steadily until Mr. Knightley tells her what is there.

Everything, it seems, is made as easy for us as for Mr. Woodhouse. Emma is provided from the beginning with a man not only admirable, but indispensable to her education. We need not worry about that. We have no financial anxiety: Emma is an "heiress of thirty thousand pounds." (E 135) Rank is no problem: Emma is herself of an "ancient family," and her potential lover has an ancestry equally antique. Precedence is no problem: for Emma reigns alone at Hartfield and over Highbury, unencumbered by sisters, aunts, tyrannical parents or guardians, or petty nobility. Emma is, of course, habitually self-deceived; yet Mr. Knightley will come to the rescue: and we can read the novel, with no discomfort and only a pleasant minimum of suspense, as the ironic portrait of a girl who falls into mild self-deception and whose trustworthy friend always and finally helps her out.

Emma likes to manage things. Brought up by a doting governess, mistress of her father's house, almost from her childhood obliged to manage her invalid father, Emma—not surprisingly—wishes to dominate elsewhere as well; and the wish to dominate, unimpeded by anxieties over wealth or rank, quickly translates itself into action. It is not surprising that, after her governess leaves to be married, Emma takes on a protégée, especially one so malleable as Harriet Smith, and that in her extension of self-conceit she persuades herself that Harriet can trap into marriage men whose rank and ambition would lead them to aspire even to Emma. It is not surprising that Emma feels confident of her ability to manage Mr. Elton or Frank Churchill—everyone, in fact, except Mr. Knightley. It is Mr. Knightley who sets us at ease. His acute and decisive mind circumscribes Emma always, keeps her from the gravest consequences of her mistakes, enlightens her when she commits a particularly flagrant snobbery or stupidity, as at Box Hill after her brutal insult to Miss Bates:

". . . Her situation should secure your compassion. It was badly done, indeed!—You, whom she had known from an infant, whom she had seen grow up from a period when her notice was an honour, to have you now, in thoughtless spirits, and the pride of the moment, laugh at her, humble her—and before her niece, too—and before others, many of whom (certainly *some*,) would be entirely guided by *your* treatment of her.—This is not pleasant to you, Emma—and it is very far from pleasant to me; but I must, I will—I will tell you truths while I can, satisfied with proving myself your friend by very faithful counsel, and trusting that you will some time or other do me greater justice than you can do now." (e 375)

We know that this will bring Emma up sharply, as it very satisfactorily does. Through all of Emma's self-deceptions, we feel Mr. Knightley's reassuring nearness; and we know that nothing can go crucially wrong.

Nowhere else is Jane Austen so relaxed, so certain, skilled, and exact in her effects. There is no excess; almost no sense of plot in this delicate ordering of a small calm world, the miniature world of the English rural gentry at the start of the nineteenth century. The ease of style and setting predisposes us to an easy response, prepares us for a mellowing, even a softening, of Jane Austen's newly reasserted irony. The characters of *Emma* seem our familiars at once, in what has been called—with a dangerous patness—"the absolute triumph of that reliance on the strictly ordinary which has been indicated as Miss Austen's title to pre-eminence in the history of the novel."[2]

Emma herself seems one of the most attractive of all heroines: beautiful, cultivated, intelligent; solicitous of her father;

[2] G. Saintsbury, *The English Novel*, London, 1919, 198.

inclined to snobbery and to rash judgment, but appealing even in her errors and caprices. There is more, but it does not bear out our preconception. Mr. Knightley is a man of integrity, of force, wit, and high sense, and—we suspect—rather too good for Emma; but this is just a suspicion. Frank Churchill is an elegant and engaging trifler, whose secret courtship of Jane Fairfax, the worthy girl in unworthy circumstances, comes finally to light as his only recommendation. The yielding Mrs. Weston, as Emma's sympathetic confidante, recalls to us the yielding Miss Taylor who could only have given way before her pupil's precocious wilfulness; so that with her we add to our stock of good reasons why Emma is what she is. The author provides us with five varieties of nonentity, will-less comic foils to Emma's wilfulness: Harriet, the obliging; Mr. Woodhouse, the gently querulous; Mr. Weston, the congenial; Isabella, the domestic; and Miss Bates, the interminably talkative. John Knightley sets off his brother's forthrightness by presenting the same quality with a bristly manner and a touch of misanthropy. For villains—harmless enough to be only amusing—the author gives us the Eltons: Mr. Elton, a pillar of meanly aspiring egotism; and his perfectly appropriate wife, Augusta, radiating that field of monomaniac affectation and self-deceit which no sarcasm or earthly judgment can penetrate.

These are Jane Austen's creatures in her new mild climate, and at the end she placidly disposes of them all: nobody left out, no strand left unwoven, nobody unhappy. The plot is fulfilled when the characters are placed where they wish to be: Emma with Mr. Knightley, Frank Churchill with Jane Fairfax, Mr. Elton with his Augusta, motherly Mrs. Weston with her first child; everybody at Hartfield, Donwell, Randalls, and Highbury comfortably settled.

Still, as we follow her attentively, Emma comes to appear less and less an innocuous figure in a novel of simple irony. She begins as a representative young gentlewoman of her age: snobbish, half-educated, wilful, possessive; and, certainly, her consciousness of rank accounts for a good many of her prejudices and cruelties. The fact remains that Emma has unpleasant qualities, which persist in operating and having effect. Whether we try to explain these qualities on the ground of up-bringing or youth or personal impulse, we cannot blind our-selves to them. They are there, embedded in the novel.

Emma is, of course, an inveterate snob. Having defined her attitude toward the yeomanry,

". . . precisely the order of people with whom I feel I can have nothing to do. A degree or two lower, and a creditable appear-ance might interest me; I might hope to be useful to their fam-ilies in some way or other. But a farmer can need none of my help, and is therefore in one sense as much above my notice as in every other he is below it." (E 29)

she advises (or, more accurately, commands) Harriet to de-cline Robert Martin's proposal:

"Dear affectionate creature!—*You* banished to Abbey-Mill Farm!—*You* confined to the society of the illiterate and vulgar all your life! I wonder how the young man would have the assurance to ask it. . . ." (E 54)

Without having seen Mrs. Elton, Emma dismisses her at once upon learning that she

. . . brought no name, no blood, no alliance. Miss Hawkins was the youngest of the two daughters of a Bristol—merchant, of course, he must be called; but, as the whole of the profits of his mercantile life appeared so very moderate, it was not unfair to guess the dignity of his line of trade had been very moderate also. (E 183)

She decides to turn down an invitation from the Coles because, though they

. . . were very respectable in their way . . . they ought to be taught that it was not for them to arrange the terms on which the superior families would visit them. This lesson, she very much feared, they would receive only from herself; she had little hope of Mr. Knightley, none of Mr. Weston. (E 207)

Her first thought is always of rank and family. She regards Mr. Knightley's possible attachment to Jane Fairfax as a "very shameful and degrading connection" (E 225); and although here she has other reasons, yet unknown to herself, for ob-jecting, it is significant that her first target is Jane's family. She thinks with satisfaction of the Knightleys as a "family of . . . true gentility, untainted in blood and understanding." (E

358) When Harriet turns out to be only the daughter of a tradesman, "Such was the blood of gentility," Emma reflects, which she

> . . . had formerly been so ready to vouch for!—It was likely to be as untainted, perhaps, as the blood of many a gentleman: but what a connexion had she been preparing for Mr. Knightley—or for the Churchills—or even for Mr. Elton!—The stain of illegitimacy, unbleached by nobility or wealth, would have been a stain indeed. (E 482)

Nor are we allowed to charge these snobberies wholly to the temper of her class and age, since they draw rebukes for her not only from Mrs. Weston, on the subject of Jane's suitableness for Mr. Knightley (E 224ff.), but, on her attitude toward Robert Martin (E 65) as well as toward Miss Bates (E 375), from the impeccably pure-blooded Mr. Knightley himself.

Emma has neglected the genteel feminine accomplishments, and cannot endure being reminded of her neglect. Shamed by Jane's superior playing on the piano, she detests her more unjustly than ever. (E 168f.) She sketches a fair likeness of Harriet; and the immoderate praise of her subject and Mr. Elton, though it cannot delude her, is enough to flatter her ego into silence:

> She was not much deceived as to her own skill either as an artist or a musician, but she was not unwilling to have others deceived, or sorry to know her reputation for accomplishment often higher than it deserved. (E 44)

Yet Mr. Knightley remarks,

> ". . . I do not think her personally vain. Considering how very handsome she is, she appears to be little occupied with it. . . ." (E 39)

She lacks, that is, the customary vanity that springs from the desire to please a suitor or lover; Mr. Knightley adds:

> ". . . her vanity lies another way. Mrs. Weston, I am not to be talked out of my dislike of her intimacy with Harriet Smith, or my dread of its doing them both harm." (E 39)

It is true that much of Emma's unpleasantness can be attributed to her consciousness of rank. In her class, family is the base, property the outward symbol, and suitable marriage the goal; and family and property are the chief criteria of acceptability for Emma. Marriage, however, she dismisses as a goal for herself:

". . . Were I to fall in love, indeed, it would be a different thing! but I never have been in love; it is not my way, or my nature; and I do not think I ever shall. And, without love, I am sure I should be a fool to change such a situation as mine. Fortune I do not want; employment I do not want; consequence I do not want: I believe few married women are half as much mistress of their husband's house as I am of Hartfield; and never, never could I expect to be so truly beloved and important; so always first and always right in any man's eyes as I am in my father's." (E 84)

Emma deals only in measurable quantities: anything uncertain is to be dismissed, avoided; and marriage, however neatly and by a balance of tangibles she may arrange it for others, seems for her both an uncertainty and an abasement.

Emma is an arranger, a manager of other people's affairs. Accustomed to look after her father's every whim and to forestall his every possible discomfort, she tries to extend this duty over her circle of friends and acquaintances as well. Yet she prophesies only what she wills, and she is always wrong. She will never admit what she herself has not contrived, until the truth strikes her in the face. She is wrong about Mr. Elton's feelings toward Harriet. She quite misconceives her own feelings toward Mr. Knightley. Baffled and angered by Jane Fairfax's reserve, she creates without a shred of evidence the most outrageous slander about an affair she imagines Jane to have had with another woman's husband; and she is even ready to pass her slander on to Churchill:

". . . I do not mean to reflect upon the good intentions of either Mr. Dixon or Miss Fairfax, but I cannot help suspecting either that, after making his proposals to her friend, he had the misfortune to fall in love with *her*, or that he became conscious of a little attachment on her side. One might guess twenty things without guessing exactly the right; but I am sure there must be a particular cause for her chusing to come to Highbury instead of going with the Campbells to Ireland. Here, she must be leading a life of privation and penance; there it would have been all enjoyment. . . ." (E 217)

She is wrong about Harriet's feelings toward Churchill. She complacently fabricates an entire love affair between Churchill and herself—including its decline and dissolution—with no more encouragement than the gentleman's adroit and uncommitting flirtation; yet throughout this imaginary affair she reiterates her "resolution . . . of never marrying" (E 206): for though Emma can imagine everything else, she cannot imagine her own commitment. She is wrong about Mr. Knightley's feelings toward both Harriet and herself. Even when she has recognized her own love for Mr. Knightley and heard his declaration joyfully, she finds the duty of remaining with her father superior to the claim of love:

> . . . a very short parley with her own heart produced the most solemn resolution of never quitting her father. (E 435)

She is ready, then, to alter everyone's life but her father's, which is after all only a shadowy extension of her own.

Emma is occupied in altering, as she sees fit, the lives of others; and to this end any means will do. If, to save Harriet for gentility, Robert Martin must be made unhappy, he is merely another obstacle to be set aside with no more than a moment's uneasiness; so, after Emma's quarrel with Mr. Knightley over her intervention:

> ". . . I only want to know that Mr. Martin is not very, very bitterly disappointed."
> "A man cannot be more so," was his short, full answer.
> "Ah!—Indeed I am very sorry.—Come, shake hands with me." (E 99)

Even death, the death of Mrs. Churchill, is for Emma a means, serving to freshen her wholly fanciful hope for a match between Churchill and Harriet:

> The character of Mrs. Churchill, the grief of her husband— her mind glanced over them both with awe and compassion— and then rested with lightened feelings on how Frank might be affected by the event, how benefited, how freed. She saw in a moment all the possible good. Now, an attachment to Harriet Smith would have nothing to encounter. (E 388)

The personal, as personal, cannot engage Emma for more than a moment: her mind cannot rest upon it without making it over altogether into a means.

Emma claims the role of adviser, but denies its responsibility. She delights in bullying anyone who will yield—poor Harriet most of all:

> ". . . Dear Harriet, I give myself joy of this. It would have grieved me to lose your acquaintance, which must have been the consequence of your marrying Mr. Martin. . . ." (E 53)

yet at the last, unwilling to face Harriet after her own disastrous series of errors in her protégée's affairs, she limits her compunction and their relationship to letters:

> Harriet expressed herself very much as might be supposed, without reproaches, or apparent sense of ill usage; and yet Emma fancied there was a something of resentment, a something bordering on it in her style, which increased the desirableness of their being separate.—It might be only her own consciousness; but it seemed as if an angel only could have been quite without resentment under such a stroke. (E 451)

and Emma is utterly relieved when Harriet falls into the patient arms of Robert Martin:

> She must laugh at such a close! Such an end of the doleful disappointment of five weeks back! Such a heart—such a Harriet! (E 475)

Far from examining the past, Emma absolves herself of it. Even when Harriet's confession of love for Mr. Knightley has roused Emma to the pitch of self-analysis, Emma's outcry sinks easily into the luxury of an acknowledged defeat:

> She was most sorrowfully indignant; ashamed of every sensation but the one revealed to her—her affection for Mr. Knightley.—Every other part of her mind was disgusting. (E 412)

the act of self-abasement that claims sin, in order to avoid the responsibility of self-knowledge.

Emma and Harriet are the most unexpected companions in all of Jane Austen's work. Nor may we pass off their intimacy—at least from Emma's side—as the effect of blind adolescent exuberance. Emma is already a worldly twenty-one; and she is aware enough of Harriet's intellectual limitations to comment ironically on Mr. Elton's charade:

> ". . . Harriet's ready wit! All the better. A man must be very much in love indeed, to describe her so. . . ." (E 72)

Emma has no intellectual ties with the unalterably sheeplike

Harriet, and she can gain no material advantage from her friendship. Of course, Emma likes to manage people, and Harriet is manageable. But why Harriet, of all people; and why so tenaciously Harriet, at least until every trick has failed? Emma observes Harriet's beauty with far more warmth than anyone else:

> She was so busy in admiring those soft blue eyes, in talking and listening, and forming all these schemes in the in-betweens, that the evening flew away at a very unusual rate. . . .
> (E 24)

This is the clever and sophisticated Emma, transported by the presence of the most insipid girl imaginable. Moreover, Emma's attention never falls so warmly upon a man; against this feeling for Harriet, her good words for Mr. Knightley's appearance seem pale indeed. Emma will excuse low birth in no one else, but Harriet's parentless illegitimacy she will talk away with nonsense about gentle lineage:

> ". . . The misfortune of your birth ought to make you particularly careful as to your associates. There can be no doubt of your being a gentleman's daughter, and you must support your claim to that station by every thing within your own power, or there will be plenty of people who would take pleasure in degrading you." (E 30)

To Mr. Knightley, Emma maintains heatedly that since men are attracted by pretty faces Harriet will have all she wants of handsome offers:

> ". . . she is . . . a beautiful girl, and must be thought so by ninety-nine out of a hundred; and till it appears that men are much more philosophic on the subject of beauty than they are generally supposed; till they do fall in love with well-informed minds instead of handsome faces, a girl, with such loveliness as Harriet, has a certainty of being admired and sought after, of having the power of choosing from among many, consequently a claim to be nice. . . ." (E 63)

Nor is she moved, except to discomfort, by Mr. Knightley's natural objection:

> ". . . Miss Harriet Smith may not find offers of marriage flow in so fast, though she is a very pretty girl. Men of sense, whatever you may chuse to say, do not want silly wives. Men of family would not be very fond of connecting themselves with a

girl of such obscurity—and most prudent men would be afraid of the inconvenience and disgrace they might be involved in, when the mystery of her parentage came to be revealed. . . ." (E 64)

Emma merely lies about her hopes for Harriet with Mr. Elton, and keeps her opinion intact. Yet—with the exception of the young farmer, Robert Martin—not one man through the range of the novel ever shows the slightest interest in Harriet. When Emma tries to cool the ardent Mr. Elton in the coach by asserting that his attentions have been directed not toward her but toward Harriet, he rejects the very notion with horror:

"Good heaven! . . . what can be the meaning of this?—Miss Smith!—I never thought of Miss Smith in the whole course of my existence—never paid her any attentions, but as your friend: never cared whether she were dead or alive, but as your friend. . . ." (E 130)

No one, it seems, is attracted by *this* pretty face except Emma.

Harriet draws her unqualified confidence as only one other person does: Mrs. Weston. Mrs. Weston has been her affectionate governess, and continued affection between them is natural enough. But Emma's regard reaches the same noteworthy excess as with Harriet. Emma has imagined herself to be falling in love with Frank Churchill; now he and Mrs. Weston, who is his stepmother, come upon her together:

She was wanting to see him again, and especially to see him in company with Mrs. Weston, upon his behaviour to whom her opinion of him was to depend. If he were deficient there, nothing should make amends for it. (E 196)

One assumes that not even imagining herself in love with him could impel Emma to forgive Churchill's possible coolness toward his stepmother.

Emma's attitude toward young men—when she is not trying to drive them into Harriet's arms—touches now and then upon the thought of a suitable marriage for herself. With Churchill she can sustain the idea of marriage just as long as it remains an idea, a neat, appropriate, socially approved arrangement:

She had frequently thought—especially since his father's marriage with Miss Taylor—that if she *were* to marry, he was the

191

very person to suit her in age, character and condition. He
seemed by this connection between the families, quite to belong
to her. She could not but suppose it to be a match that every
body who knew them must think of. (E 119)

The direct threat of marriage, however, she always thrusts
aside, indignantly with Mr. Elton:

". . . I have no thoughts of matrimony at present." (E 132)

after long deliberation (which has nothing to feed on but
itself), with respect to Churchill:

Her own attachment had really subsided into a mere nothing;
it was not worth thinking of. . . . (E 315)

even, for a time, in answer to Mr. Knightley. Meanwhile, her
involvement with Harriet—until the culminating error—remains steady and strong.

The fact is that Emma prefers the company of women,
more particularly of women whom she can master and direct;
the fact is that this preference is intrinsic to her whole domi-
nating and uncommitting personality. The same tendency has
been recognized by Edmund Wilson; but Mr. Wilson adds
that it is "something outside the picture which is never made
explicit."[3] The tendency is certainly never made explicit; but
is it for that reason external? The myth of Jane Austen's simplicity persists; and its corollary, that in her work the unex-
plicit is an error of tone: for surface must tell all.

Emma needs to dominate, she can of course—in her class
and time—most easily dominate women; and her need is
urgent enough to forego even the pretense of sympathetic understanding. She feels affection only toward Harriet, Mrs.
Weston, and her father: instances, not of tenderness, but
rather of satisfied control. She feels affection only toward those
immediately under her command, and all of them are women.
Mr. Woodhouse is no exception. The effect of decayed gentle-
manliness that he produces is a *tour de force* of Jane Austen's,
nothing else; for Mr. Woodhouse is really an old woman, of
the vacuous, mild-natured, weakly selfish sort very common
to novels and (possibly) to life. He has no single masculine

[3] E. Wilson, "A Long Talk About Jane Austen," *The New Yorker*, xx
(June 24, 1944), 69.

trait, and his only distinction lies in the transfer of sex. He is Mrs. Bates elevated to the dignity of Hartfield.

As she herself admits, Emma has no tenderness:

"There is no charm equal to tenderness of heart. . . . There is nothing to be compared to it. Warmth and tenderness of heart, with an affectionate, open manner, will beat all the clearness of head in the world, for attraction. I am sure it will. It is tenderness of heart which makes my dear father so generally beloved—which gives Isabella all her popularity.—I have it not—but I know how to prize and respect it. . . ." (E 269)

This last is already a misjudgment, for Emma does *not* know how to prize and respect tenderness in anyone who rejects her domination. Still, she recognizes her defect. Emma is a beautiful and clever girl, with every grace but tenderness. Without it, she exhibits the strong need to dominate, the offhand cruelty, the protective playfulness, the malice of Jane Austen, the candid Jane Austen of the letters—in which miscarriage is a joke:

Mrs. Hall, of Sherborne, was brought to bed yesterday of a dead child, some weeks before she expected, owing to a fright. I suppose she happened unawares to look at her husband. (L I 24, 27 Oct. 1798)

and death equally amusing:

Only think of Mrs. Holder's being dead! Poor woman, she has done the only thing in the world she could possibly do to make one cease to abuse her. (L II 350, 14 Oct. 1813)

recalling the more literary echo in *Emma*, on Mrs. Churchill's death:

Goldsmith tells us, that when lovely woman stoops to folly, she has nothing to do but to die; and when she stoops to be disagreeable, it is equally to be recommended as a clearer of ill fame. (E 387)

and marriage also, as—anticipating Emma on Churchill—she shrugs off the fading interest of an eligible young man:

This is rational enough; there is less love and more sense in it than sometimes appeared before, and I am very well satisfied. It will all go on exceedingly well, and decline away in a very reasonable manner. (L I 28, 17 Nov. 1798)

Emma, of course, is only an "imaginist" (E 335) and twenty-one; creating her, Jane Austen is an artist and thirty-nine. In the assurance of mastery—with a quarter-century of writing behind her, a portion of fame, and a congenial subject isolated from moral qualms[4]—Jane Austen could be freely aware of the Emma in herself, she could convert her own personal limitations into the very form of her novel. All she had to discard for the character of Emma was her own overarching artist's awareness, her unresting irony, which even in life, in her letters at least, directed and used her need to dominate, her fear of commitment: which made her coldly right where Emma is coldly wrong.

Emma is moved to play God, but without tenderness or social caution (or the artist's awareness) she falls into every conceivable mistake and misjudgment. She must feel herself to be central and centripetal, the confidante and adviser of all. Without tenderness or caution, she makes the worst of every situation: imagines evil when there is good—because Jane Fairfax is "disgustingly reserved" (E 169) or has an "odious composure" (E 263)—and good where there is nothing but an extension of self.

Mrs. Elton—for all of Emma's heartfelt aversion to her— is Emma's true companion in motive. Both must dominate every situation. Both must have admirers to confirm their position. Both are profoundly wanting in altruism and sympathy. The chief difference is that Mrs. Elton's motive lies bare, without ornament of intelligence, beauty, or rank. Mrs. Elton is "vulgar" (Emma's favorite word for her and her friends):

". . . A little upstart, vulgar being, with her Mr. E., and her *caro sposo*, and her resources, and all her airs of pert pretension and under-bred finery. . . ." (E 279)

and Emma is "refined."[5] Mrs. Elton has no brake of intelli-

---

[4] Anticipating objections to Emma, Jane Austen said: "I am going to take a heroine whom no one but myself will much like." (J. E. Austen-Leigh, *A Memoir of Jane Austen*, Oxford, 1926, 157); the moral finickiness of *Mansfield Park* is put decisively behind.

[5] Emma "is the type in fiction of a whole race of English ladies . . . for whom refinement is religion. Her claim to oversee and order the social things about her consisted in being refined. . . ." G. K. Chesterton, "The Evolution of Emma," *Living Age*, CCXCIV (August 25, 1917), 504.

gence or breeding upon her egocentrism; she can rattle on and give herself away without self-consciousness:

". . . I honestly said that *the world* I could give up—parties, balls, plays—for I had no fear of retirement. Blessed with so many resources within myself, the world was not necessary to *me*. I could do very well without it. To those who had no resources it was a different thing; but my resources made me quite independent. And as to smaller-sized rooms than I had been used to, I really could not give it a thought. I hoped I was perfectly equal to any sacrifice of that description. Certainly I had been accustomed to every luxury of Maple Grove; but I did assure him that two carriages were not necessary to my happiness, nor were spacious apartments. . . ." (E 277)

Since she is happy as long as she is allowed to condescend:

"My dear Jane, what is this I hear?—Going to the post-office in the rain!—This must not be, I assure you.—You sad girl, how could you do such a thing?—It is a sign I was not there to take care of you." (E 295)

Jane Fairfax's mere politeness she can accept as homage. Emma, though, is neither fatuous nor unperceptive. She must play the idol and the confidante, but she requires some evidence of idolatry; and she builds up a vindictive dislike of Jane Fairfax precisely because it is clear that Jane will worship or trust neither her nor anyone else.

Emma can fall back on the nonentities of her world, those vessels of neutral purpose that are always governed from the outside: Harriet, Mr. Woodhouse, Mr. Weston, Isabella, and Miss Bates. Not that they have anything to offer beyond agreeableness: Mr. Weston, happy with his son, ready to be satisfied with everyone, even Mrs. Elton; Isabella, dwindling pleasantly in hypochondria and her husband's shadow; Harriet, with her infinite pliancy; Miss Bates, spreading her obsessive good cheer:

". . . It is such a happiness when good people get together— and they always do. . . ." (E 175)

Mr. Woodhouse has not even this recommendation. He is not agreeable. He is, in fact, an annoyance, with his gruel, his hypochondria, his often quoted friend Perry, his feeble but effective insistence that nothing, nothing at all, be changed in his life or in the lives of the people around him; and we can sympathize with John Knightley when he looses his hot temper against the nagging solicitations of his father-in-law. Mr. Woodhouse—after long years of invalidism, of being coddled by his daughter, of scarcely stirring from his house or seeing a new person—is an idiot. He is quite incapable of thought or judgment. Miss Bates, Jane Fairfax, Mr. Knightley, Frank Churchill—all are agreeable persons, as long as the young ladies dry their stockings after a rain and the young men do not insist on opening windows. Even on Mrs. Elton, "considering we never saw her before," he remarks that

> ". . . she seems a very obliging, pretty-behaved young lady, and no doubt will make him a very good wife. Though I think he had better not have married. . . ." (E 279f.)

When Emma, in a rare mood of almost irritable playfulness with him, tries to point out the contradiction between his respect for brides and his dislike of marriage, she only makes him nervous without making him at all understand. (E 280) Anything is satisfactory as long as it does not require change; and there is no distinction between satisfactory things. As he has no taste for people, so he has no taste for food—except for thin, smooth gruel and soft-boiled eggs—or for Mr. Knightley's objects of art:

> Mrs. Weston had been showing them all to him, and now he would show them all to Emma;—fortunate in having no other resemblance to a child, than in a total want of taste for what he saw, for he was slow, constant, and methodical. (E 362)

He has his habits, his advice, his fears, his small worn-out courtesies—without a touch of discriminating thought or feeling except between what is familiar and what is alien. His tenacious clinging to Emma, to his acquaintances, to the seen boundaries of his world comes to resemble the clinging of a parasitic plant, which must be now or sometime shaken off. Mr. Woodhouse is the living—barely living—excuse for Emma's refusal to commit herself to the human world.

He is also, like the other governable characters and like Mrs. Weston (whom Emma, at least, can govern), the kind of person whom Emma can most easily persuade of her supremacy; and it is significant that she treats them all—except

196

one—with the utmost kindness and solicitude. The exception
is Miss Bates, whom Emma mimics in company and shock-
ingly ridicules to her face:

"Oh! very well," exclaimed Miss Bates, "then I need not be
uneasy. 'Three things very dull indeed.' That will just do for
me, you know. I shall be sure to say three dull things as soon
as ever I open my mouth, shan't I?—(looking round with the
most good-humoured dependence on every body's assent)—
Do not you all think I shall?"
Emma could not resist.
"Ah! ma'am, but there may be a difficulty. Pardon me—but
you will be limited as to number—only three at once." (E 370)

since Miss Bates, unluckily for her, has no greater pleasure
than chattering the praises of her niece, Jane Fairfax.

The only character in the story who sees Emma at all clearly
is Frank Churchill. He is as egoistic and calculating as she,
but he beats her at her own game because he is far less self-
deluded. Emma's prodigious self-deception springs at least
partly from inexperience. With experience, with the especially
valuable experience of pampering a cross and dictatorial old
woman, Churchill has learned to be cautious, to blunt the
edge of his ego with careless charm. He has learned to use
people more successfully than Emma, but he is not less destructive. His playing at love with Emma is required, perhaps, in order to keep the secret of his engagement to Jane;
but he takes cynical delight in tormenting the latter and
mystifying the former. He convinces Emma that he wholly
accepts her slander about Jane and Mr. Dixon, and her view
that it is Mr. Dixon who has sent the piano:

"Indeed you injure me if you suppose me unconvinced . . .
now I can see it in no other light than as an offering of love."
(E 218f.)

Allusion to Mr. Dixon and Ireland becomes, in fact, his fa-
vorite method of simultaneously hurting Jane and amusing
Emma while he laughs at both. He jokes with Emma about
Jane's hair-do:

". . . Those curls!—This must be a fancy of her own. I see nobody else looking like her!—I must go and ask her whether it
is an Irish fashion. Shall I?—Yes, I will—I declare I will—

and you shall see how she takes it;—whether she colours." (E 222)

Concerning the gift piano, he baits Jane openly, over Emma's feeble objection:

> "It is not fair," said Emma in a whisper, "mine was a random guess. Do not distress her."
> He shook his head with a smile, and looked as if he had very little doubt and very little mercy. Soon afterwards he began again,
> "How much your friends in Ireland must be enjoying your pleasure on this occasion, Miss Fairfax. I dare say they often think of you, and wonder which will be the day, the precise day of the instrument's coming to hand. . . ." (E 241)

He persists, though Emma is "half ashamed":

> Emma wished he would be less pointed, yet could not help being amused. . . .
> "You speak too plain. She must understand you."
> "I hope she does. I would have her understand me. I am not in the least ashamed of my meaning."
> "But really, I am half ashamed, and wish I had never taken up the idea."
> "I am very glad you did, and that you communicated it to me. I have now a key to all her odd looks and ways. Leave shame to her. If she does wrong, she ought to feel it." (E 243)

At Hartfield, Mr. Knightley, with considerable suspicion of Churchill's deceit, watches the word-game in progress:

> He saw a short word prepared for Emma, and given to her with a look sly and demure. He saw that Emma had soon made it out, and found it highly entertaining, though it was something which she judged it proper to appear to censure; for she said, "Nonsense! for shame!" He heard Frank Churchill next say, with a glance towards Jane, "I will give it to her—shall I?"—and as clearly heard Emma opposing it with eager laughing warmth. "No, no, you must not; you shall not, indeed."
> It was done, however. This gallant young man, who seemed to love without feeling, and to recommend himself without complaisance, directly . . . handed over the word to Miss Fairfax, and, with a particular degree of sedate civility entreated her to study it. Mr. Knightley's excessive curiosity to know what this word might be, made him seize every possible moment for darting his eye towards it, and it was not long before he saw it to be *Dixon*. (E 348)

In the strained and heavy atmosphere at Box Hill, with the

company separating into small sullen parties, with Jane bitterly jealous (though no one but Churchill knows) of Churchill's attentions to Emma, he flirts defiantly with Emma and directs his scorn at everyone else:

> "Our companions are excessively stupid. What shall we do to rouse them? Any nonsense will serve. They *shall* talk. . . ." (E 369)

Through his unsuspecting dupe, Emma, Churchill recalls to Jane their meeting at a resort and baits her cruelly about her family:

> ". . . as to any real knowledge that Bath, or any public place, can give—it is all nothing; there can be no knowledge. It is only by seeing women in their own homes, among their own set, just as they always are, that you can form any just judgment. Short of that, it is all guess and luck—and will generally be ill-luck. How many a man has committed himself on a short acquaintance, and rued it all the rest of his life." (E 372)

And all the while he makes Jane sick with shame, jealousy, bitterness, and fear: uncertain of his affection, uncertain even whether she desires it, sick with the burden of a clandestine engagement,[6] bitterly resigned to sinking her talent, her taste, her intelligence into the governess-role by which—if Churchill fails her—she must live:

> ". . . There are places in town, offices, where inquiry would soon produce something—Offices for the sale—not quite of human flesh—but of human intellect." (E 300)

Moreover, Churchill does all this consciously and with relish, enjoying his duplicity:

> ". . . I am the wretchedest being in the world at a civil falsehood." (E 234)

He has no scruples, for he needs none: charm and wealth excuse everything. One wonders whether Emma—even under the vigilance of Mr. Knightley—will not be polished into the same engaging ruthlessness after several years of marriage.

Emma accepts Mr. Knightley doubtless because she loves and admires him. She has failed so discouragingly with Harriet as to give up all thought of protégées for the present; and

---

[6] Mr. Chapman documents "the enormity of Jane Fairfax's deviation from right" in her particular social context. (E 512f.)

Mr. Knightley is after all a very impressive and admirable man. He is even the most likable and most heroic of Jane Austen's heroes: unlike Darcy, he is a frank and social man; he is not a prig like Edmund Bertram, or a wary ironist like Henry Tilney. He is intelligent, perceptive, mature—but not so indivertibly as to save his judgment altogether from the effects of love:

> He had found her agitated and low.—Frank Churchill was a villain.—He heard her declare that she had never loved him. Frank Churchill's character was not desperate.—She was his own Emma, by hand and word, when they returned into the house; and if he could have thought of Frank Churchill then, he might have deemed him a very good sort of fellow. (E 433)

That he should continue to love Emma at all, after observing her through all her misdemeanors, is in fact a tribute to the power of love; for Mr. Knightley is quite capable of recognizing and pointing out the implications of her conduct, with Harriet, with Churchill and Jane Fairfax, with Miss Bates— implications he vigorously points out to Emma herself. Success in love, though, overthrows him. As for Emma, she has been defeated. All her dreams of fruitful dominion have been at least temporarily dissipated; and, for the time being, she is willing to be dominated by a man of whom her intelligence and her snobbery can approve (though even now she accepts only on condition that he move into her father's home!). The flood of repentance has not yet subsided. Yet there is no sign that Emma's motives have changed, that there is any difference in her except her relief and temporary awareness. Later on, the story may turn back again: it is hard to think of Emma undominant for any length of time.

Emma plays God because she cannot commit herself humanly. Her compulsion operates in the absence of one quality: a quality which Emma, Frank Churchill, and Mrs. Elton— the only destructive figures in the novel—are all without. The quality is tenderness. For Emma, there is no communication of feeling. She can esteem, loathe, praise, censure, grieve, rejoice—but she cannot feel like anyone else in the world. Her ego will admit nothing but itself. Frank Churchill and Mrs.

Elton fall under the same charge: but Mrs. Elton is too trans-
parently vulgar to be effective; and Churchill, too astute to be
caught playing God, keeps his own counsel, trifles, observes,
and makes use of people by the less imposing and less dangerous tactic of charm. Of the three, only Emma is both foolish
enough to play God and dazzling enough to blind anyone even
for a short time.

The primary large irony of the novel is, then, the deceptive-
ness of surface. Charm is the chief warning-signal of Jane
Austen's world, for it is most often the signal of wit adrift
from feeling. The brilliant façades of Emma and Frank
Churchill have no door. Indeed, the only charming person in
all of Jane Austen's novels whom both she and the reader
fully accept is Elizabeth Bennet, and Elizabeth has obvious
virtues—a clear head and good intentions—to lend depth and
steadiness to her charm. The other heroines—Elinor Dashwood, Catherine Morland, Fanny Price, Anne Elliot—are presented in the quietest colors. And Willoughby, Wickham,
Mary Crawford, Frank Churchill—the charming interlopers—
always betray.

In *Emma*, Jane Austen has given surface the benefit of
every alluring quality in the persons of the heroine and of
Frank Churchill. She has given them beauty, wealth, position,
and immediate circumstances most favorable to the exercise
of their wills. The only results have been confusion and unhappiness, on the reduced scale appropriate to the people and
the society involved.

Of course, the denouement brushes aside confusion and unhappiness, and brings Emma and Churchill into ostensibly
happy marriages. *Emma* can be read as the story of a spoiled
rich girl who is corrected by defeat and love, and who lives
happily ever after. This is a limited vision, but it is not a false
one; for Jane Austen does succeed on her primary levels in
achieving her "ripest and kindliest,"[7] her most perfect love
comedy. On these levels, Emma is "faultless in spite of all her
faults" (E 433), Frank Churchill's frivolity will be tempered

[7] R. Farrer, "Jane Austen, *ob*. July 18, 1817," *Quarterly Review*,
ccxxviii (July 1917), 26.

by the sense and grave sweetness of his wife, even Mrs. Elton can do little harm, and everyone else is comfortably settled—with the exception of poor Mrs. Churchill, who had to die to clear the way for her nephew's marriage. The conditions are almost standard for romantic comedy: two love-affairs, one complicated by self-deception, the other by secrecy, both turning out well; no strong issue, no punishment.

Emma can be read so; but it has more to give, and not easily. Reginald Farrer, one of the few critics of Jane Austen who have taken the trouble to read her carefully, has observed that *Emma* "is not an easy book to read; it should never be the beginner's primer, nor be published without a prefatory synopsis. Only when the story has been thoroughly assimilated, can the infinite delights and subtleties of its workmanship begin to be appreciated, as you realize the manifold complexity of the book's web, and find that every sentence, almost every epithet, has its definite reference to equally unemphasized points before and after in the development of the plot. Thus it is that, while twelve readings of 'Pride and Prejudice' give you twelve periods of pleasure repeated, as many readings of 'Emma' give you that pleasure, not repeated only, but squared and squared again with each perusal, till at every fresh reading you feel anew that you never understood anything like the widening sum of its delights."[8]

It is this multiplicity and sureness of reference that most immediately distinguishes *Emma* from the rest of Jane Austen's work: the total confident control of all her resources, without intrusion of derivativeness or fatigue or morality. The author's vision and instrument is, of course, irony: the widening sum of delights in *Emma* is, first of all, our widening recognition of the decisive pertinence with which every word,

---

[8] *Ibid.*, 23f. The fact that great novels require frequent re-experience to produce their full effect is perhaps less insisted upon than it should be. The same fact is taken for granted with respect to lyric poetry and "absolute" music. In a work of art, one can arrive at form only by apprehending specifically—and in a great work this is always difficult—all the individual relationships, implications, and resolutions that together make up form. In a novel, one is tempted to stop at narrative and plot, and to imagine that these—plus several lively characters—constitute all the form of which a novel is capable. *Novel* and *story* become nearly interchangeable, especially when the technique is superficially as simple and traditional as Jane Austen's.

every action, and every response of Emma's establish her nature, confirm her self-deception, and prepare for her downfall. The ironic reverberations, rather than conflicting with one another or passing out of context—as they do sometimes in *Pride and Prejudice* and often in *Northanger Abbey*—remain internal and interdependent, they reinforce one another in a structure whose apparent lightness is less remarkable only than its compact and powerful density.

When we first observe Emma's maneuverings with Harriet, it is with the consciousness of her urge to dominate. Soon, though, this urge has become inextricable from Emma's own snobbery and her vicarious snobbery for Harriet, which drive it even farther from the possibility of caution or rational direction. Why does Emma want Harriet to marry? Harriet begins to seem a kind of proxy for Emma, a means by which Emma —too reluctant, too fearful of involvement, to consider the attempt herself—may discover what marriage is like. If Harriet is a proxy for Emma, she must serve as a defense also. Emma is outraged by Mr. Elton's proposal, not merely because she has not expected it (the basis of the simple irony here), but because Mr. Elton dares to circumvent the buffer she has so carefully set up. Harriet is to experience for her what she refuses to commit herself to, but cannot help being curious about. Yet Harriet is a very pretty girl, and being infinitely stupid and unperceptive, may be used in other uncommitting ways. Emma's interest in Harriet is not merely mistress-and-pupil, but quite emotional and particular: for a time at least—until Harriet becomes slightly resentful of the yoke after Emma's repeated blunders—Emma is in love with her: a love unphysical and inadmissible, even perhaps undefinable in such a society; and therefore safe. And in all this web of relations, by no means exhausted here, we return always to Emma's overpowering motive: her fear of commitment.

The simple irony of Emma's flirtation with Frank Churchill rises, of course, from the fact that Churchill is in love with someone else and uses Emma as a decoy. More than this, however, Churchill uses Emma so successfully only because he knows her so well. Emma is a perfect decoy for a man in love with someone else. She enjoys and invites admiration, but will draw away from any sign of serious attachment. Churchill does not use Emma merely for want of other dupes: he knows her, and exploits her with a ruthless thoroughness, not making a fool of her but revealing her as she is. " 'But is it possible,' " he asks Emma blandly, later, " 'that you had no suspicion?' " (E 477) He knows that she neither did nor could have had. She took part so eagerly in the flirtation because there she could be at once admired and unengaged, there she could smugly exchange scandal in the guise of wit, and be cynically and most delicately stroked into a pleasant (though wary) submissiveness by flattery without feeling, by assurances of her Olympian superiority.

The one quality which Mr. Knightley may regard as Emma's saving grace is her honesty. It is a very circumscribed honesty, it operates characteristically in the trough of failure and disaster, before the next rise of confidence and self-delusion; and it is another inextricable strand in the complex ironic web. Emma can recognize how badly her matchmaking schemes have turned out, and resolve never to attempt them again—but without recognizing why she attempts them at all and keeps coming back to them. She can set her calculating nature against Harriet's simple and lachrymose one, without understanding the motives behind either, or anticipating the author's charge of sentimentality:

> It was rather too late in the day to set about being simple-minded and ignorant. . . .(E 142)

Most crucially, after the conventional settling of accounts, after Mr. Knightley has secured his Emma and Churchill his Jane, Emma for the first time can judge herself and Churchill as they must have seemed together in their flirtation, as they have been and are now alike:

> . . . Emma could not help saying,
> "I do suspect that in the midst of your perplexities at that time, you had very great amusement in tricking us all.—I am sure you had.—I am sure it was a consolation to you."
> "Oh! no, no, no—how can you suspect me of such a thing?— I was the most miserable wretch!"
> "Not quite so miserable as to be insensible to mirth. I am

sure it was a source of high entertainment to you, to feel that you were taking us all in.—Perhaps I am the readier to suspect, because, to tell you the truth, I think it might have been some amusement to myself in the same situation. I think there is a little likeness between us."

He bowed.

"If not in our dispositions," she presently added, with a look of true sensibility, "there is a likeness in our destiny; the destiny which bids fair to connect us with two characters so much superior to our own." (E 478)

This is honesty, and very acute. In an interlude with the man who most completely understands her, Emma recognizes and gives us the truth; and it is no mistake that Jane Austen places this clarifying exchange so close to the end of her book. Emma has finally—almost—got to know herself; but only because the knowledge is here painless and may be discarded in a little while with Mr. Knightley again, where she may resume, however self-amusedly for the present, her characteristic role:

"Do you dare say this?" cried Mr. Knightley. "Do you dare to suppose me so great a blockhead, as not to know what a man is talking of?—What do you deserve?"

"Oh! I always deserve the best treatment, because I never put up with any other . . ." (E 474)

Emma knows that she is moving toward a happy ending. Emma and Churchill are very lucky in the irony that finds them a Mr. Knightley and a Jane Fairfax to sober and direct them: this much Emma sees. So Mr. Knightley, not yet accepted by Emma, speaks bitterly of Churchill:

". . . Frank Churchill is, indeed, the favourite of fortune. Every thing turns out for his good.—He meets with a young woman at a watering-place, gains her affection, cannot even weary her by negligent treatment—and had he and all his family sought round the world for a perfect wife for him, they could not have found her superior.—His aunt is in the way.—His aunt dies.— He has only to speak.—His friends are eager to promote his happiness.—He has used every body ill—and they are all delighted to forgive him.—He is a fortunate man indeed!" (E 428)

Still, Churchill—as Mr. Knightley knows—and Emma are lucky not by luck (except the luck of an invalid aunt's dying), but because in their social milieu charm conquers, even as it makes every cruel and thoughtless mistake; because, existing apart from and inevitably denying emotion and commitment, it nevertheless finds committed to it even the good and the wise, even when it is known and evaluated. The irony of *Emma* is multiple; and its ultimate aspect is that there is no happy ending, no easy equilibrium, if we care to project confirmed exploiters like Emma and Churchill into the future of their marriages.

Emma's and Frank Churchill's society, which makes so much of surface, guarantees the triumph of surface. Even Mr. Knightley and Jane Fairfax succumb. Jane Austen, however, does not ask us to concern ourselves beyond the happy ending: she merely presents the evidence, noncommittally.

CHAPTER VIII

THE LIBERATION OF FEELING

PERSUASION

JANE AUSTEN has already demanded that we accept some of her characters, not in their own light, but at her word: Elinor Dashwood is not quite what the author tells us she is; nor, certainly, is Fanny Price, nor Edmund, nor either of the Crawfords. This shirking of the novelist's office seems chargeable, however, less to an intrusion of self than to a tactful (if uneasy) surrender to convention. Her tone is personal, only as personality is contained and sheltered in the social mind; and she escapes an unequivocal involvement by persuading society—her own, of course; or, more specifically, her own class—to applaud and reaffirm its prejudices.

In *Persuasion*, Jane Austen's tone has acquired a sharp personal edge. This edge, which she does not vindicate by any claim of aesthetic or social propriety, emerges in the novel as a compulsive exasperation,[1] turned, at unpredictable moments, against any character who fails—for whatever reason—to advance the interests of her heroine. Her chief target is Sir Walter Elliot; but not until Sir Walter has been solidly created. He sustains himself so well, in fact, that his vitality obscures the directness of her assault, and diverts one's attention from the minor figures whom she attacks with far more damage to their integrity: Elizabeth, Mrs. Clay, above all Mrs. Musgrove and the deceased Dick Musgrove. Of these, not only does she tell us what to think; she seems to resent even the creative effort by which she must embody before she can impale them.

Elizabeth Elliot begins promisingly enough. She is con-

---

[1] For the word, though not for the idea, I am indebted to Miss Lascelles, who, speaking of Jane Austen's life at Chawton, sees her "as in the novels . . . translating her critical impressions of individuals into general terms, and so extracting the sting of exasperation. The mood of these last eight years of her life was the mood that Meredith attributes to the true comic artist: 'The laughter of Comedy is impersonal and of unrivalled politeness.' " M. Lascelles, *Jane Austen and Her Art*, Oxford, 1939, 28f.

temptuous of Anne (p 5), but only—it seems at first—as the Bertram girls are contemptuous of Fanny, with the same diffused careless snobbery of smartness and rank; for Elizabeth, since her mother's death thirteen years before, has been the lady of Kellynch Hall (p 5), and, encouraged by a vain and foolish father, she will—not strangely—share and reinforce his opinion of her quiet sister. Besides, Elizabeth bears a private anxiety:

> ... she had the consciousness of being nine-and-twenty, to give her some regrets and apprehensions. She was fully satisfied of being still quite as handsome as ever; but she felt her approach to the years of danger, and would have rejoiced to be certain of being properly solicited by baronet-blood within the next twelvemonth or two. (p 7)

Finally,

> She had had a disappointment. . . . The heir presumptive, the very William Walter Elliot, Esq. whose rights had been so generously supported by her father, had disappointed her. (p 7)

And Jane Austen concludes the first short arc of the story by remarking:

> Such were Elizabeth Elliot's sentiments and sensations; such the cares to alloy, the agitations to vary, the sameness and the elegance, the prosperity and the nothingness, of her scene of life—such the feelings to give interest to a long, uneventful residence in one country circle, to fill the vacancies where there were no habits of utility abroad, no talents or accomplishments for home, to occupy. (p 9)

This peroration—noteworthy as Jane Austen's first admission that life must be narrow and may be very dull for the landed gentry—marks also the end of Elizabeth's development as a character. We hear that, in her father's financial distress, she proposes to retrench by cutting off "some unnecessary charities" (p 9) and taking no gift for Anne back from their yearly visit to London. (p 10) We hear of her friendship with Mrs. Clay (p 15, 34f.) another of those woman-and-protégée affairs which Jane Austen burlesqued in *Northanger Abbey*, balanced on the most tenuous tight-rope of irony in *Emma*, and here merely sketches in order to disapprove:

208

Elizabeth would go her own way . . . in this selection of Mrs. Clay; turning from the society of so deserving a sister to bestow her affection and confidence on one who ought to have been nothing to her but the object of distant civility. (P 16)

Mary, the youngest sister, invites Anne to stay with her family at Uppercross Cottage, when the Elliots are ready to move to Bath; and Elizabeth, compelled less by what we know of her than by what the author wishes us to think, replies too explicitly, " 'Then I am sure Anne had better stay, for nobody will want her in Bath.' " (P 33)

Much later, in one of Elizabeth's rare reappearances, the author's index finger is still more insistent:

> Very, very happy were both Elizabeth and Anne Elliot as they walked in. Elizabeth, arm in arm, with Miss Carteret, and looking on the broad back of the dowager Viscountess Dalrymple before her, had nothing to wish for which did not seem within her reach; and Anne—but it would be an insult to the nature of Anne's felicity, to draw any comparison between it and her sister's; the origin of one all selfish vanity, of the other all generous attachment. (P 185)

And Elizabeth expires in a pale flare of "heartless elegance" (P 226), with one small, doomed flirtatious gesture (P 226)— the author's revenge for Anne?—toward the invulnerably pledged Captain Wentworth.

Mrs. Clay also makes a good beginning. The image of female vulgarity—of what Jane Austen might have called illbreeding[2]—has always been congenial to her talent, and she finds this image at every social level: Isabella Thorpe, Mrs. John Dashwood, Lady Catherine, Mrs. Norris, the incomparable Mrs. Elton (among whom the individual differences are still more remarkable than the identity of species). Mrs. Clay is a lower-class opportunist, determined to rise, like Uriah Heep, by "humbleness," but more limited in her ambition by the fact of her sex, and far more finely conceived.

The daughter of Sir Walter's agent, she has returned "after an unprosperous marriage" (P 15) to her father's house; and

---

[2] She might have been surprised to find this word, which she likes to apply freely to others, applied to her own letters: E. M. Forster characterizes them as "Triviality, varied by touches of ill breeding. . . ." (E. M. Forster, "Jane Austen," *Abinger Harvest*, New York, 1936, 160)

she ingratiates herself with Elizabeth, in order, as Anne suspects, to try for the prize of the baronet himself. Flattery is Sir Walter's daily food, and no one feeds him more eagerly than Mrs. Clay. Sir Walter, obliged to consider renting Kellynch Hall to a retiring admiral,

> . . . observed sarcastically,
> "There are few among the gentlemen of the navy, I imagine, who would not be surprised to find themselves in a house of this description."
> "They would look around them, no doubt, and bless their good fortune," said Mrs. Clay. . . . (p 18)

and the author comments, with not less sarcasm than Sir Walter:

> . . . for Mrs. Clay was present; her father had driven her over, nothing being of so much use to Mrs. Clay's health as a drive to Kellynch. . . . (p 18)

Sir Walter is very handsome, and very severe upon the rapid aging of sailors, whereupon Mrs. Clay remonstrates:

> "Have a little mercy on the poor men. We are not all born to be handsome. The sea is no beautifier, certainly; sailors do grow old betimes; I have often observed it; they soon lose the look of youth. But then, is not it the same with many other professions, perhaps most other? Soldiers, in active service, are not at all better off; and even in the quieter professions, there is a toil and a labour of the mind, if not of the body, which seldom leaves a man's looks to the natural effect of time. The lawyer plods, quite care-worn; the physician is up at all hours, and travelling in all weather; and even the clergyman—" she stopt a moment to consider what might do for the clergyman; —"and even the clergyman, you know, is obliged to go into infected rooms, and expose his health and looks to all the injury of a poisonous atmosphere." (p 20)

It appears to her, in fact, that only the country landowner has the hope of immortal beauty.

Mrs. Clay succeeds, to the disquiet of Anne and Lady Russell, in winning an invitation to Bath; and we look forward in pleased suspense to accompanying her. There is a single scene at Bath, after Anne's arrival, when Mrs. Clay lives up to our expectation, in her cautious playing-off of Anne and Elizabeth (p 213); but that is all. And if we can believe that the insinuating, tenacious softness of her personality might be overcome by Mr. Elliot's own brand of opportunism, we can scarcely accept her fall, in the absence of evidence, as the reckless sexual surrender which the author abruptly summarizes:

Mrs. Clay's affections had overpowered her interest, and she had sacrificed, for the young man's sake, the possibility of scheming longer for Sir Walter. She has abilities, however, as well as affections; and it is now a doubtful point whether his cunning, or hers, may finally carry the day; whether, after preventing her from being the wife of Sir Walter, he may not be wheedled and caressed at last into making her the wife of Sir William. (P 250)

Perhaps: certainly, this is a credible prospect; but we have never learned what came before. The fact remains that Mrs. Clay is not given time to condemn herself by incident, though the author has taken pains to condemn her by assertion. Jane Austen told us long before about this woman "who ought to have been nothing . . . but the object of distant civility." (P 16) In that exasperated sneer, the author dissolves into the impassioned participant.

Why are Mrs. Musgrove and her son so ill-treated? Mrs. Musgrove is a pleasant, hospitable matron, not brilliant, not sensible of Anne's full worth, but otherwise harmless except for one fault: she loves to grieve publicly for the son she lost at sea. Jane Austen—novelist or country spinster—has never shown much tolerance toward the dead;[3] but she shows none at all, nothing indeed but a fierce personal distaste, toward Dick Musgrove.

[3] In her novels before *Persuasion*, this intolerance takes the form of omission or of the briefest possible mention; for, whatever her personal attitude, the tone of these novels would not support a subject which seems susceptible at any length only to grave or tragic treatment, or to that sort of universal irony which contrasts, by the shock of death, the pitifulness of man's schemes with the grandeur and finality of his fate (as in the death of Captain Blifil, in *Tom Jones*). Of either of these alternatives, Jane Austen has been incapable: she has not sufficiently committed herself for the former; nor does she have the comprehensive vision required for the latter. The deaths (except Dick Musgrove's) in *all* her novels often precede the action of the story, and are always out of sight and simply useful to the plot: the elder Dashwoods', the Rev. Dr. Norris's, Mrs. Churchill's, Lady Elliot's, Fanny Harville's, Mrs. Elliot's. For examples of her personal attitude, see following note. One interesting fact about *Persuasion* is that its tone does seem capable of a grave treatment of death; but Jane Austen never attempts it.

211

The real circumstances of this pathetic piece of family history were, that the Musgroves had had the ill fortune of a very troublesome, hopeless son; and the good fortune to lose him before he reached his twentieth year; that he had been sent to sea, because he was stupid and unmanageable on shore; that he had been very little cared for at any time by his family, though quite as much as he deserved; seldom heard of, and scarcely at all regretted, when intelligence of his death abroad had worked its way to Uppercross, two years before.

He had, in fact, though his sisters were now doing all they could for him, by calling him "poor Richard," been nothing better than a thick-headed, unfeeling, unprofitable Dick Musgrove, who had never done anything to entitle himself to more than the abbreviation of his name, living or dead. (p 50f.)

Jane Austen attacked the Crawfords knowing that all the moral weight of the rural gentility was behind her; but Dick Musgrove's posthumous annihilation is her own responsibility. Besides, this savage caricature—without pretext itself—serves as a pretext for abusing Mrs. Musgrove, who, at a time when she is seated, apparently unaware of her reflected glory, between Anne and Wentworth, dares to mourn for such a son:

They were actually on the same sofa, for Mrs. Musgrove had readily made room for him;—they were divided only by Mrs. Musgrove. It was no insignificant barrier indeed. Mrs. Musgrove was of a comfortable substantial size, infinitely more fitted by nature to express good cheer and good humor, than tenderness and sentiment; and while the agitations of Anne's slender form, and pensive face, may be considered as very completely screened, Captain Wentworth should be allowed some credit for the self-command with which he attended to her large fat sighings over a son, whom alive nobody had cared for. (p 68)

This is irrelevant enough, but consider the bland apology which directly follows:

Personal size and mental sorrow have certainly no necessary proportions. A large bulky figure has as good a right to be in deep affliction, as the most graceful set of limbs in the world. But, fair or not fair, there are unbecoming conjunctions, which reason will patronize in vain,—which taste cannot tolerate,—which ridicule will seize. (p 68)

The most obvious response to this generalization is that it is not generally true. A more important fact is that we have

here a bare statement of Jane Austen's personal sense of
humor, as she displays it in her letters again and again.[4] So
Dick Musgrove is exhumed from his undeserved sanctifica-
tion, and Mrs. Musgrove engages Jane Austen's sense of
humor; but neither Mrs. Musgrove nor her son illustrates anything except the author's exasperation with both. Later, Jane
Austen has forgotten, or relented; and Mrs. Musgrove resumes her probable role in Anne's eyes:

> They found Mrs. Musgrove . . . within . . . and Anne had
> the kindest welcome. . . . Mrs. Musgrove's real affection had
> been won by her usefulness when they were in distress. It was
> a heartiness, and a warmth, and a sincerity which Anne de-
> lighted in the more, from the sad want of such blessings at
> home. (P 220)

But it is too late: this is a different Mrs. Musgrove from the
one already demolished.

Sir Walter, alone among these figures, is never vitally im-
paired: perhaps because his necessary prominence in the plot
attracted more of Jane Austen's aesthetic sympathy than she
could, in her present mood, spare the others. From the moment we meet him, in the very first lines of the book, poring
blissfully over the Baronetage, we never doubt his individuality, even when the author helps us a little too pointedly:

> Vanity was the beginning and the end of Sir Walter Elliot's
> character; vanity of person and of situation. He had been re-
> markably handsome in his youth; and, at fifty-four, was still a
> very fine man. Few women could think more of their personal
> appearance than he did; nor could the valet of any new made
> lord be more delighted with the place he held in society. He
> considered the blessing of beauty as inferior only to the bless-
> ing of a baronetcy; and the Sir Walter Elliot, who united these
> gifts, was the constant object of his warmest respect and de-
> votion. (P 4)

Sir Walter illustrated is always unique and inevitable. After

---

[4] She speaks of a "Dr. Hall in such very deep mourning that either his
mother, his wife, or himself must be dead"; and remarks, in the same letter,
that "Mrs. Bromley is a fat woman in mourning, and a little black kitten
runs about the staircase." (L I 60, 17 May 1799) In another letter: "Our
first cousins seem all dropping off very fast. One is incorporated into the
family, another dies, and a third goes into Staffordshire." (L I 18, 21 Jan.
1799) These are quite representative samples: for others, see preceding
chapters, and many other letters to Cassandra.

Lady Elliot's death, he does not marry again; and the author remarks:

> . . . Sir Walter's continuing in singleness requires explanation. —Be it known then, that Sir Walter, like a good father, (having met with one or two private disappointments in very unreasonable applications) prided himself on remaining single for his dear daughter's sake. (p 5)

His preoccupation with physical beauty smugly revolves about himself and his eldest daughter:

> . . . and Sir Walter might be excused . . . in forgetting her age, or, at least, be deemed only half a fool, for thinking himself and Elizabeth as blooming as ever, amidst the wreck of the good looks of every body else; for he could plainly see how old all the rest of his family and acquaintance were growing. Anne haggard, Mary coarse, every face in the neighbourhood worsting; and the rapid increase of the crow's foot about Lady Russell's temples had long been a distress to him. (p 6)

Sir Walter's estate, understandably enough, cannot support the degree of consequence which he demands for his ancient name; and his resulting financial anxieties prepare the major turn of plot which sends the Elliots to Bath and which ultimately reunites Anne and Wentworth at Kellynch. In the meantime, Kellynch Hall must be rented, perhaps to a retiring naval officer; and Sir Walter has an occasion to express his two firm objections to naval life:

> ". . . First, as being the means of bringing persons of obscure birth into undue distinction, and raising men to honours which their fathers and grandfathers never dreamt of; and secondly, as it cuts up a man's youth and vigour most horribly; a sailor grows old sooner than any other man . . ." (p 19)

When we meet him again, in Bath, his opinion of its women tells us enough about his life there:

> ". . . The worst of Bath was, the number of its plain women. He did not mean to say that there were no pretty women, but the number of the plain was out of all proportion. He had frequently observed, as he walked, that one handsome face would be followed by thirty, or five and thirty frights; and once, as he had stood in a shop in Bond-street, he had counted eighty-seven women go by, one after another, without there being a tolerable face among them. . . ." (p 141f.)

Sir Walter survives throughout on these terms, to the point where he graciously accepts Wentworth as a son-in-law in consideration of "his superiority of appearance," (P 248) and his "well-sounding name," (P 248) which may balance Anne's "superiority of rank," (P 248) and which perhaps justify "the insertion of the marriage in the volume of honour." (P 249)

That is all for Sir Walter, whom we leave, appropriately, making the latest entry in his Baronetage. Yet after all, in spite of his survival, he has never been allowed to leave his study, to act rather than merely to be. Jane Austen calls him a "fool" and "not very wise," and we agree; but his potentialities for foolishness—even of a comic sort—are never realized out in the world.

Sir Walter was born to be a dupe, and Mrs. Clay was born to dupe him. Why then, after setting them face to face, idle together at a resort, and chaperoned only by Sir Walter's deluded daughter, does the author never give us a word of their relationship, until (as she arbitrarily informs us) Mr. Elliot steps in to claim his conquest? Miss Lascelles has suggested[5] that this failure reflects again[6] Jane Austen's unfortunate reliance on the seduction-climax conventional to the sentimental novel, and her block against treating such a subject comically. But the failure has also more immediate causes.

Jane Austen's moral uneasiness, her tendency to omit or distort situations artistically sound but ethically abhorrent to her age, is obvious enough here, as it is far more extensively in *Sense and Sensibility* and in *Mansfield Park*. There were, however, conditions which freed her to treat the subject of seduction. She could treat it comically, provided she did not have to regard it as actual and achieved. Not only was Emma permitted to speculate widely and amorally on Jane Fairfax's *supposed* seduction, but she confided her speculations to Frank Churchill—and with no filter for the whole of her malicious daydream except the author's irony. Jane Austen could also treat seduction seriously, provided she might set the tone of

---

[5] M. Lascelles, *op.cit.*, 81, 206f.
[6] As in *Sense and Sensibility*, *Pride and Prejudice*, *Mansfield Park*: see previous chapters of this study.

social disapproval. In the frigid atmosphere of *Mansfield Park*, she did not hesitate to present several distinct stages of the intrigue between Henry Crawford and Maria. Yet Sir Walter and Mrs. Clay—so much more plausible in conjunction than Henry and Maria, and so rich in comic possibility—are ignored.

Jane Austen's difficulty here is, then, not entirely a moral one; nor is it technical. Anne, the eye of the novel, is elsewhere; but Sir Walter and Mrs. Clay might have been seen, at some time, by someone communicating to Anne, during the preliminary maneuvers of a seduction which never comes off anyway. Jane Austen had her precedents. If she *had* allowed us glimpses of Mrs. Clay in action at Bath, she would have been no more explicit than she had been already in the theater scenes in *Mansfield Park*. Instead, we have only Anne's early suspicions and Mrs. Smith's belated gossip. (P 206)

The fact is that Sir Walter *pains* Jane Austen, that Mrs. Musgrove and Dick Musgrove and Elizabeth Elliot and Mrs. Clay pain her by their very existence, that she recoils continually from the touch of them, as if they are too close and too present, not images but flesh; and she can end only by treating them, not with irony, with illustrative incident, with perspective of any sort, but with sarcasm, abuse, or silence. And this exasperation—a quite new quality in the novels of Jane Austen—must be explained before the equally new tone of *Persuasion* becomes explicable in either personal or aesthetic terms.

One thing we do know which distinguishes *Persuasion* from the other novels: it was never thoroughly revised. In March 1817, Jane Austen wrote to her niece Fanny Knight: ". . . I have a something ready for Publication which may perhaps appear about a twelvemonth hence." (L II 484, 13 Mar. 1817) But she was already very ill,[7] and four months later she died. We know that it was her practice to write carefully and to revise intensively:[8] *Sense and Sensibility* and *Pride and*

---

[7] J. E. Austen-Leigh, *A Memoir of Jane Austen*, Oxford, 1926, 171.

[8] See Introductory Notes by R. W. Chapman in his edition of the novels; and her own more general information, about the "little bit (two Inches

Prejudice were rewritten several times; *Mansfield Park* required two and a half years; even *Emma*, written at the peak of her self-confidence and (however limited) recognition and in her most characteristic style, took well over a year. *Persuasion*, on the other hand, occupied her less than a year, its period of composition marked by the bankruptcy of her favorite brother, Henry, and by the beginning of her illness. The first draft was, in fact, the shortest of her full-length novels, until—dissatisfied with the penultimate chapter—she altered and expanded it into two, in the same summer (of 1816) in which she had finished the first draft.

A comparison between the original chapter[9] and its final metamorphosis throws much light on that major part of the novel which she apparently never revised. The advance in smoothness and consistency is of course the most striking change: Jane Austen deletes all the clumsy machinery of Admiral Croft's obtuseness and indirection (in a character whose leading traits have been acuteness and straightforward good humor), and replaces it with the transition scene at Sir Walter's and the climactic, crowdedly and beautifully imagined scene at the White Hart Inn, where Anne grows out of her fear at last. Of more immediate concern to us, however, is the fact that Mrs. Musgrove and Mrs. Clay, who do not appear in the original chapter at all, are treated in the revision with the first touches of aesthetic impartiality which the author has granted them since their introduction. Not until the revision does Jane Austen see Mrs. Musgrove as the muddle-headed but kindly matron (p 220) demanded by the story and hitherto overcome by the author's irrelevant assault; not until now does she suggest that Mrs. Clay is capable of feeling guilt or passion. (p 228)

In the revision, then, art gained notably over exasperation; and one might infer that further revision would have banished this alien quality altogether. Possibly. But exasperation is only a crude evidence of self-commitment, of which we find no

---

wide) of Ivory on which I work with so fine a Brush, as produces little effect after much labour." (L II 469, 16 Dec. 1816)

[9] J. Austen, *Two Chapters of Persuasion*, ed. R. W. Chapman, Oxford, 1926.

trace in any other of the novels, or even in the recovered *juvenilia*, the latter so far from the look of rewriting as to bear the look of impromptu. The point is that never before, at any stage of composition, has Jane Austen been close enough to her material for exasperation. Persistent through all her work has been a sense of distance between author and subject: successfully (as in *Emma*), filled with the cool light of irony; unsuccessfully, when irony fails (as in *Mansfield Park*), obstructed by the flattening mirror of social judgment; always, a distance as much personal as aesthetic. Only in *Persuasion* does the irony coarsen to sarcasm, and the judgment become ardently personal. Reginald Farrer has observed that, as Jane Austen regards the world, "she has no animosity for it; but she has no affection."[10] These words apply profoundly to all her previous work, but they fail to apply to *Persuasion*; and though, in the practice of her art, she might finally have expunged the animosity, which is here the waste energy in the creation of a new image, she could not have expunged the affection without canceling the new image whose very frame it is.

The new element in *Persuasion* is personal feeling. It pervades the characters and settings, it complicates the moral climate. Further revision would—we may surmise—have altered the book for the better, but only by refining and proportioning its novelty. Jane Austen's old need for detachment is gone; and if she is sensitive to the point of vexation and haste in her treatment of villains, she is also, for the first time in her work, sensitive to the point of detailed and sympathetic analysis in her treatment of heroes and heroines. She dismisses Sir Walter only to let Anne come back intensely to herself.

Anne is the heroine, the center of action, and the point of view of *Persuasion*. She must be disposed of in marriage; she must illustrate and resolve, wherever resolvable, whatever conflict surrounds her and cuts her off from a fulfillment; and, finally, she must open her mind to observe and transmit as much as we need to know of the story.

Jane Austen has laid such a responsibility on no other of

[10] R. Farrer, "Jane Austen, *ob.* July 18, 1817," *Quarterly Review*, CCXXVIII (July, 1917), 11.

her heroines. Elinor is more bystander than anything else; Catherine and Fanny are the constant points of reference, but the point of view in *Northanger Abbey* and *Mansfield Park* is the omniscient author's; and Elizabeth Bennet and Emma offer their point of view for the very reason that it may in the end be proved prejudiced, capricious, deluded, or wholly false. Always Jane Austen supervises: with irony toward Catherine, Elizabeth, and Emma; with a predetermined partiality toward Elinor and Fanny which merely exposes their poverty of substance. But Anne needs no supervision. She sees clearly, without caprice; and even the author's obvious partiality toward her serves only to provide space and light for a mind richly responsive to both.[11]

How can this notion of Anne's personality be reconciled with the distorted images of Sir Walter, Elizabeth, Mrs. Clay, and the Musgroves which she, as the point of view, must have given us? The answer is that no reconciliation is possible: we never do believe that Anne sees them so. These figures, at least in the pattern of the whole novel, represent a failure of technique and a misdirection of feeling. They are never assimilated to Anne's story: the abuse that holds them off is so patently the author's, and generally so amusing, that we neither cavil at it for the moment nor ever trace it back to Anne, who seems incapable of it anyway; but it leaves them all, even Sir Walter, external and wasted. The story of *Persuasion* is, ultimately, Anne's story; as it would have been, perhaps, altogether and from the beginning, if we had had the promised revision.

Of the characters whom we do see through Anne's eyes, the most interesting is also, in the end, the most disappointing: Mr. Elliot. Heir presumptive to the baronetcy, Mr. Elliot

---

[11] Treating the myth of artistic "impersonality," Percy Lubbock remarks: ". . . it has been argued that the opinions of a really artistic writer ought not to appear in his story at all. But of course with every touch that he lays on his subject he must show what he thinks of it; his subject, indeed, the book which he finds in his selected fragment of life, is purely the representation of his view, his judgment, his opinion of it. The famous 'impersonality' of Flaubert and his kind lies only in the greater tact with which they express their feelings—dramatizing them, embodying them in living form, instead of stating them directly." P. Lubbock, *The Craft of Fiction*, New York, 1929, 67f.

earns our tentative sympathy when we learn that he has de-
clined Elizabeth's outthrust hand. We are encouraged, besides,
to like the man who foregoes Sir Walter's company, who
makes his first appearance before Anne as the admiring
stranger at Lyme (p 140f.), and of whom Lady Russell—
fallible enough—disapproves. (p 133)

Yet we, like Anne, are puzzled when Mr. Elliot turns up at
Bath back in the circle of grace with Sir Walter and Elizabeth. (p 138ff.) Why should a man of culture and intelligence, as Mr. Elliot seems, resume acquaintance with a pair
of elegant nonentities whom he has neglected for years, and
from whom he can expect no material gain except what will
be his by law anyway? This is the heroine's puzzle in *Persuasion*, as Jane Fairfax was Emma's puzzle.

Emma Woodhouse had time to spin her plausible web about
Jane, and time to watch it being swept cleanly away by facts.
Anne, on the other hand, has little time to think about Mr.
Elliot: she is most consciously in love with another man: that
much reason she has for limiting the space Mr. Elliot occupies
in her thoughts and in the story. But Mr. Elliot needs no more
space than he has; what he needs is more understanding, which
Anne, and Jane Austen, are still unprepared to give.

Is he in love with Anne? He is very attentive; and she, in
turn, accepts his attentions graciously enough, though without emotion. (p 150, 186) When Lady Russell becomes his
unsolicited advocate for Anne's favor (p 159), Anne even
grasps for a moment at the seductive dream of being the next
Lady Elliot (p 160); and then—Anne and Jane Austen, unwilling to wait upon events, pour out their judgment of him:

> Though they had now been acquainted a month, she could
> not be satisfied that she really knew his character. That he was
> a sensible man, an agreeable man,—that he talked well, pro-
> fessed good opinions, seemed to judge properly, and as a man
> of principle,—this was all clear enough. He certainly knew
> what was right, nor could she fix on one article of moral duty
> evidently transgressed; but yet she would have been afraid to
> answer for his conduct. She distrusted the past, if not the pres-
> ent. The names which occasionally dropt of former associates,
> the allusions to former practices and pursuits, suggested sus-

picions not favourable of what he had been. She saw that there had been bad habits; that Sunday-travelling had been a common thing; that there had been a period of his life (and probably not a short one) when he had been, at least, careless on all serious matters; and, though he might now think very differently, who could answer for the true sentiments of a clever, cautious man, grown old enough to appreciate a fair character? How could it ever be ascertained that his mind was truly cleansed? (p 160f.)

To this, Anne subjoins a comparison between Mr. Elliot's polish and Wentworth's "warmth and enthusiasm"—presumably, to redirect this pious digression into the current of her story and of her mind as we know them; but the damage has been done, and of a different sort from that inflicted on Sir Walter—of a sort, indeed, common in her earlier novels. Jane Austen is not exasperated with Mr. Elliot: she simply cannot cope with his type, as she cannot cope with Willoughby or Henry Crawford. Her plots require that all these men be ultimately defined as rakes; but her genius was either inadequate, or too blocked by moral taboos, to develop events (and thoughts are the most signal events in her novels) probable and vivid enough for the purpose. She could picture them ironically as flirts and agreeable triflers; she could respond to what she considered evil in them, however, not by picturing them, but only by giving them up to the annihilating disapproval of her society.[12] Within the novels, the conflict was between her subject, with its frequent undigested chunks of morality,[13]

[12] John Bailey, among others, has observed the fact that ". . . her scoundrels never come alive." (J. Bailey, *Introductions to Jane Austen*, Oxford, 1931, 54.) But this may be because her direct moral intent compels her to regard Willoughby, Crawford, and Mr. Elliot first as scoundrels, not as characters. In an amoral plot like that of *Emma*, Frank Churchill, an implied scoundrel, comes very much alive.

[13] I do not wish to deny Jane Austen her choice of subject, with or without morality. "We must grant the artist his subject . . ." says Henry James: "our criticism is applied only to what he makes of it." ("The Art of Fiction," *Partial Portraits*, London, 1911, 394f.) My criticism applies only to what she makes of her subject: more particularly, that part of her subject containing impersonal and fossilized bits of eighteenth-century theological casuistry. These bits remain just bits, discrete fragments of something else which stick out of the otherwise organic texture of her novels: untransformed material, in short, which (to adopt another of James's celebrated dicta) neither determines incident nor illustrates character. Morality is, of course, a possible subject, like any other interest of mankind; but it must be handled in terms of character and incident, not on its own terms.

and her ironic genius, which could treat morality, if at all, only most obliquely. Nothing but a wholly comic subject, without catastrophe or overt moral challenge (and only *Emma* and —tentatively—*Sanditon* meet these conditions), could free her altogether.

So Mr. Elliot, brilliantly begun as the mysterious heir, and carried on as the prospective rival of Wentworth, is given up under pressure; and, much later, Anne is confirmed in her distrust by the tiresome tale of that most tiresome of Jane Austen's characters, Mrs. Smith. For all her bright and rather cynical gossip and the specious singularity of her illness, Mrs. Smith does nothing but provide the facts of his perfidy. Her presence is too useful, her story too pat in its corroboration of Anne. In the end, nothing remains of Mr. Elliot except Anne's suspicions, Mrs. Smith's disclosure, and the author's curt summary: in this opacity of words, the character has disappeared; and Mrs. Smith, having served, is rewarded with a small fortune (P 251f.) and disappears also.

Anne, then, in certain ethical compartments, can still be flat and unconvincing as Elinor and Fanny were, for Jane Austen was still propitiating the parsonage audience into which she had been born. But Anne is much more than Elinor and Fanny. These three do, indeed, share one distinction which no other major Austen character may claim: they are all unsubjected to the temper of Jane Austen's irony. In *Mansfield Park*, however, as in all her work previous to *Persuasion*, nothing has tempered her protagonists finely and vitally *except* irony; among her "serious" heroines, Elinor is shadowy and blurred, Fanny a model of inappropriate priggish insipidity which cries out for the ironist. Only Anne survives without the dimension of irony. The third dimension of Jane Austen's heroines (except for the embarrassingly live, and finally snuffed out, Marianne) has been the author's irony or nothing at all; but Anne's depth—and her unique quality in the Austen gallery—is the sustained depth of projected and implicit personal emotion.

This emotion is not simply Anne aware of herself: she is discriminatingly aware of feeling, and capable of analyzing it with delicate accuracy; but it is as often the feeling of others (not just their principles or prospects, which the other heroines find far more engrossing) and the emotional atmosphere of groups and of places.

Unlike Emma or Elizabeth Bennet, she never imposes her tone upon others; nor in her shyness does she resemble Fanny, crouched fearfully in a corner and ready always with small, sharp teeth against a breach of propriety; for Anne seems to have withdrawn mainly by choice, and without prejudice to her awareness. Identity of interest is no longer prerequisite, as at Mansfield Park, to godliness: Anne has learned, between Kellynch and Uppercross, to accept the emotional disparateness of groups:

> Anne had not wanted this visit to Uppercross, to learn that a removal from one set of people to another, though at a distance of only three miles, will often include a total change of conversation, opinion, and idea. She had never been staying there before, without being struck by it, or without wishing that other Elliots could have her advantage in seeing how unknown, or unconsidered there, were the affairs which at Kellynch-hall were treated as of such general publicity and pervading interest; yet with all this experience, she believed she must now submit to feel that another lesson, in the art of knowing our own nothingness beyond our own circle, was become necessary for her. . . . (P 42)

Deeply in love herself, she is capable of distinguishing without malice between love and what often passes for love; in the Musgrove sisters' attachment to Wentworth:

> . . . while she considered Louisa to be rather the favourite, she could not but think, as far as she might dare to judge from memory and experience, that Captain Wentworth was not in love with either. They were more in love with him; yet there it was not love. It was a little fever of admiration; but it might, probably must, end in love with some. (P 82)

or in the sentimental Benwick's attachment to any girl available at the moment:

> He had an affectionate heart. He must love somebody. (P 167)

Anne is Jane Austen's first heroine to take a detailed and disinterested pleasure in sensory impressions; in the beauty of autumn:

Her *pleasure* in the walk must arise from the exercise and the day, from the view of the last smiles of the year upon the tawny leaves and withered hedges, and from repeating to herself some few of the thousand poetical descriptions extant of autumn, that season of peculiar and inexhaustible influence on the mind of taste and tenderness, that season which has drawn from every poet, worthy of being read, some attempt at description, or some lines of feeling. (P 84)

in the "romantic" attraction of Lyme (and it is remarkable that *Persuasion* is the first book in which Jane Austen uses the words "romance" and "romantic" without irony and in their favorable sense):

. . . the woody varieties of the cheerful village of Up Lyme, and, above all, Pinny, with its green chasms between romantic rocks, where the scattered forest trees and orchards of luxuriant growth declare that many a generation must have passed away since the first partial falling of the cliff prepared the ground for such a state . . . (P 95f.)

These descriptions are perhaps the more revealing in their awkward and breathless, their almost travel-book style; for Jane Austen is opening compartments of her mind that have been shut till now, and she has not yet achieved the form most expressive of her new material. The fact remains that the world is enlarging—with some loss of hard, sharp contour initially, but with a great potential (and often realized) gain in variety and power.

Anne's devotion to Wentworth is, of course, the sustained emotional impulse of the book; and Anne traces it with unremitting sensitivity. Her feeling is clear enough in her first thought of him:

. . . Anne . . . left the room, to seek the comfort of cool air for her flushed cheeks; and as she walked along a favourite grove, said, with a gentle sigh, "a few months more, and *he*, perhaps, may be walking here." (P 25)

Without bitterness, but with a fixed regret, she recalls her decision, on Lady Russell's advice, to refuse him:

. . . Anne, at seven and twenty, thought very differently from what she had been made to think at nineteen. (P 29)

How eloquent could Anne Elliot have been,—how eloquent, at least, were her wishes on the side of early warm attachment, and a cheerful confidence in futurity, against that over-anxious

caution which seems to insult exertion and distrust Providence!
—She had been forced into prudence in her youth, she learned
romance as she grew older—the natural sequel of an unnatural
beginning. (p 30)

If this last remark sounds to us irresistibly biographical, Jane
Austen has only the tone of her earlier books, and the contrast
of this late one, to blame.

Responding to an apparent reference to Wentworth,

> Anne hoped she had outlived the age of blushing; but the
> age of emotion she certainly had not. (p 49)

Continually she analyzes what she imagines his present
feelings to be, and her hope rises or is depressed as she revolves what little evidence, favorable or unfavorable, she can
gather:

> . . . He must be either indifferent or unwilling. Had he wished
> ever to see her again, he need not have waited till this time . . .
> (p 58)

> He could not forgive her,—but he could not be unfeeling. (p 91)

And, having ascended by imperceptible gradations of hope, she
can at last allow herself to feel that he loves her still. (p 186)

Entering the room in which she meets Wentworth again
for the first time in eight years, she must pass the first, and
most unnerving, test:

> Her eye half met Captain Wentworth's; a bow, a curtsey
> passed; she heard his voice—he talked to Mary, said all that
> was right; said something to the Miss Musgroves, enough to
> mark an easy footing: the room seemed full—full of persons
> and voices—but a few minutes ended it. (p 59)

Events of the smallest scale take on breadth and depth. In
a scene full of perilously balanced tensions and embarrassments, with Wentworth still uncomfortable in Anne's presence, and Charles Hayter sitting petulantly silent and hostile
toward his supposed rival for Henrietta's hand, Anne kneels
in attendance by a sick Musgrove child. His mischievous little
brother persists in climbing upon her back, until suddenly
she feels the child carried off and knows that Wentworth has
done it:

> Her sensations on the discovery made her perfectly speech-

less. She could not even thank him. She could only hang over little Charles, with most disordered feelings. His kindness in stepping forward to her relief—the manner—the silence in which it had passed—the little particulars of the circumstance—with the conviction soon forced on her by the noise he was studiously making with the child, that he meant to avoid hearing her thanks, and rather sought to testify that her conversation was the last of his wants, produced such a confusion of varying, but very painful agitation, as she could not recover from, till enabled by the entrance of Mary and the Miss Musgroves to make over her little patient to their cares, and leave the room. (p 80)

And the effect is neither trivial nor sentimental, but ample and moving, because we have been convinced that it is not Anne's feeling which is limited but the life in which she has been imprisoned since Wentworth left. If she feels so minutely, it is because nothing remains to give her hope of happiness except the memory of Wentworth and such pathetic shreds of a relationship as he may now allow her. Anne comes near losing her hope, but she never loses the strength and dignity of her feeling.

When at last Jane Austen attends Anne on her walk to Mrs. Smith's the morning after the concert, at which Wentworth betrayed his jealousy of Mr. Elliot, we share the author's overt sympathy:

> Prettier musings of high-wrought love and eternal constancy, could never have passed along the streets of Bath, that Anne was sporting with from Camden-place to Westgate-buildings. It was almost enough to spread purification and perfume all the way. (p 192)

This burst of affection is relevant because Anne has already been created to such an ideal; the specific image here is incident, it expresses and illustrates—in a kind of objective valuation of her new joy—the Anne we already know.

It was not till her partial revision of *Persuasion* that Jane Austen permitted Anne to speak of feeling; but when Anne finally does speak, her sudden articulateness is the symbol of the new wide world which her confidence in Wentworth's reawakened love has thrown open to her, even as she looks back on the past and argues passionately with Captain Harville for the superior constancy of women:

> ". . . I should deserve utter contempt if I dared to suppose that true attachment and constancy were known only by woman. No, I believe you capable of every thing great and good in your married lives. I believe you equal to every important exertion, and to every domestic forbearance, so long as—if I may be allowed the expression, so long as you have an object. I mean, while the woman you love lives, and lives for you. All the privilege I claim for my own sex (it is not a very enviable one, you need not covet it) is that of loving longest, when existence or when hope is gone." (P 235)

If the author is still too diffident to let Anne speak aloud her confession of love to Wentworth, their reunion is nevertheless a new thing for Jane Austen:

> There they exchanged again those feelings and those promises which had once before seemed to secure every thing, but which had been followed by so many, many years of division and estrangement. Then they returned again into the past, more exquisitely happy, perhaps, in their reunion, than when it had been first projected; more tender, more tried, more fixed in a knowledge of each other's character, truth, and attachment; more equal to act, more justified in acting. And there, as they slowly paced the gradual ascent, heedless of every group around them, seeing neither sauntering politicians, bustling housekeepers, flirting girls, nor nursery-maids and children, they could indulge in their retrospections and acknowledgments, and especially in those explanations of what had directly preceded the present moment, which were so poignant and so ceaseless in interest. All the little variations of the last week were gone through; and of yesterday and to-day there could scarcely be an end. (P 240f.)

Elizabeth Bennet made a joke about having fallen in love with Pemberley. Emma's love the author summed up in the imperturbable catechism: "What did she say? Just what a lady ought." Fanny and Edmund faded mercifully out of sight before they pledged themselves to each other. And whether we agree that Anne's emotion "proves not merely the biographical fact that Jane Austen had loved, but the aesthetic fact that she was no longer afraid to say so,"[14] we do know that Anne

[14] V. Woolf, "Jane Austen," *The Common Reader*, New York, 1925, 205.

has experienced something which none of Jane Austen's previous heroines, by temperament or incident, even came near.

Persuasion is the story of Anne Elliot: its newness is in her sensitivity; its source and impulse are in her love of Wentworth; its limitations derive chiefly from her inconsistent limitations of vision, as if the author, dealing with a wholly different sort of heroine, was not yet able to exploit or even to recognize all the fresh possibilities arising. Consistent or inconsistent, however, Anne is perpetually at the center of the novel; and any analysis of its theme and effect must explain why.

If we feel that Anne is so different from, say, Elizabeth Bennet and Emma, and that she is at the center of her novel, it seems likely that we shall find *Persuasion* equally different in theme and effect from *Pride and Prejudice* and *Emma*. Yet in the only studies—by Miss Lascelles[15] and Mark Schorer[16] —which treat *Persuasion* in any detail as a work of art (and not simply as an instrument of biography or gossip), neither critic finds it crucially different from the other novels. Miss Lascelles calls it a "delicate comedy,"[17] and suggests that the thematic climax of the novel is the long, eloquent scene between Anne and Captain Harville at the White Hart Inn:

> . . . the strong feelings which she may not express make her sensitive to the force of feeling in others; she penetrates to Captain Harville's undiminished silent grief.[18]

Benwick's false graceful sorrow and Mrs. Musgrove's at least partly real but ungraceful sorrow are implicitly balanced against Anne's silent love and Captain Harville's silent grief:

> If it were not for these two, and all that is implied in the talk between them, one might almost take *Persuasion* for a satire on the frailty of human sorrow and the support it seeks from delusion; it is they who reveal it as a delicate study in shades of distinction between the true and the not quite true.[19]

Such a study is in the book, as it is in every other of Jane Austen's books: but is it the *axis* of *Persuasion*? And already we are approaching that edge of criticism where category is

---

[15] M. Lascelles, *op.cit.*, 78ff., 203ff.

[16] M. Schorer, "Fiction and the 'Matrix of Analogy,' " *Kenyon Review*, XI (Autumn, 1949), 541-560.

[17] M. Lascelles, *op.cit.*, 81.   [18] *Ibid.*, 80.

[19] *Loc.cit.*

no useful guide: *Persuasion* may be a comedy, but it is so close to being something else, and so different from such outright comedies as *Pride and Prejudice* and *Emma*, that we still seem best advised to analyze it without prejudice of category, in its own terms.

Mr. Schorer's argument is of special importance because he documents it at length from the novel, and because he comes closer to the question of comedy itself. *Persuasion* is, as he says, a novel of courtship and marriage: that is, the subject of the novel, the area in which it moves, is courtship and marriage; more particularly, as these proceed under the conventions of bourgeois society.[20] He goes on, then, to illustrate the author's metaphorical focus on material values, and, ultimately, to define what he regards as its comic impact upon the subject.

Persuasion, Mr. Schorer contends, "is a novel about marriage as a market, and about the female as marketable, and . . . [it] makes the observation that to sentimental scruple and moral fastidiousness . . . much property is not necessary but *some* is essential—and this is shown us primarily in the style";[21] and he concludes: "The basis of the comedy lies in the difference between the two orders of value"—moral and material—"which the metaphors, like the characters, are all the while busily equating."[22]

Yet the style, "derived from commerce and property, the counting house and the inherited estate,"[23] is after all the bourgeois dialect: it is comic if its users equate the two opposed orders of value; but if its users discriminate between the two orders, it may be an entirely serious vehicle. Rather than "busily equating" the two orders, Anne and Wentworth are engaged in a serious effort to settle the claim of each.

Marriage may be a market for all bourgeois lovers, and "females" marketable, but only insofar as bourgeois conven-

---

[20] On the use of the word "bourgeois" to denote Jane Austen's hybrid society, see above Chapter I, note 26. But *Persuasion*—as I shall point out later in this chapter—also treats the problems raised by the conflict between feudal and bourgeois values within the same society.

[21] M. Schorer, *op.cit.*, 543. [22] *Loc.cit.*

[23] *Ibid.*, 540.

tions prescribe: the conventions may omit, but they do not prohibit, the personal claim. Both Anne and Wentworth— like other bourgeois lovers—recognize, as one recognizes the rules of a game which one must play, that without money one does not live comfortably in bourgeois society; both, therefore, accept the material conditions which their society imposes upon marriage, but neither feels that these conditions limit or falsify the emotion which marriage formalizes.

A core of delusion or incongruity does seem essential to comedy; and the core of *Emma* may be very well described in such terms as Mr. Schorer uses to describe what he considers the comic essence of *Persuasion*: namely, "the discrepancy between social sentiment"—the professed values of a society, which are moral—"and social fact"—the real values of the society, which are material, and to be found "not so much in the professions of her characters as in the metaphorical texture of her style." This discrepancy, which is of course a condition of existence in bourgeois society, can produce comedy in a novel only if it goes unrecognized by the characters; and Mr. Schorer states that in *Persuasion* it does. The fact is, however, that Anne and Wentworth are quite aware of the discrepancy, and of the obstacles to resolving it. Both distinguish love from economics, though they accept their close relation in bourgeois society. Anne refused, eight years before, to marry Wentworth because he had no money, and because his chances of making his fortune seemed too remote, at least to her cautious adviser, Lady Russell. Wentworth still smarts over Anne's rejection because, loving him, she was too fearful to take the risk—which even he sees as a risk—of marrying him first and hoping for his good luck in time. Yet both, it must be emphasized, are first of all in love, though both see economics as a possible bar to marriage. They disagree on the extent of risk, they have been persuaded into opposing states of mind; but they never confuse love and money, or love and rank: and if someone objects that other characters in the novel do, then he must be reminded that the story of Anne *is* the story of *Persuasion*, not simply its love interest, and that a novel may contain comic characters without being a comedy.

Anne and Wentworth are not deluded into professing one set of values while acting under another: they are aware of both, as internal and external pressures. For them, indeed, "social sentiment" is nothing but personal feeling, since they profess only what they feel; and "social fact" is the economic compulsion to which they must reconcile their feeling in order to secure the advantages of nutrition and social acceptance. (Remember the harsh example of Lieutenant and Mrs. Price, who spurned social fact.) Anne and Wentworth neither overlook nor rebel against the material base of their society: if they overlooked it, they would be deluded, which they are not; if they rebelled, they would be outcasts, which they do not wish to be. Their problem—and they are both wholly aware of it— is to determine just how far the claim of feeling can yield, without effacing itself altogether, to the claim of economics; and this central problem of *Persuasion* is not comic.

This is the problem, a problem of economic anxiety, concerning which an initial disagreement has kept Anne and Wentworth apart for eight years, and which redefines itself now that they are together again: now Wentworth must decide—for the conventions of bourgeois society restrict decisive action to the man, and neither Anne nor Wentworth questions these conventions—whether Anne destroyed his love and forfeited her own by her timidity. Mr. Schorer's study is of the highest interest, not because it bears out his conclusion, but because it illuminates the economic anxiety underlying and largely directing the course of the novel. Yet the central opposition in the novel is not, as both he and Miss Lascelles suggest, between false and true, or hidden and overt (though these are always in Jane Austen's background, and come to the fore in *Pride and Prejudice* and *Emma*); the problem of Anne and Wentworth is only a reflection, in personal terms, of a much more polarized opposition in the novel: a conflict between worlds.

Mansfield Park was the only other novel in which Jane Austen set up separate and irreconcilable worlds in conflict: but there the conception, though on her broadest and most imposing scale till then, was executed with a starched moral caution that introduced her hero and heroine stillborn and smothered her villains ruthlessly when their liveness was about to redirect the story. Jane Austen, in her regular pendulum swing to compunction, had determined to write a serious, a "moral" book, and she recognized that the small, ironically conceived, personal tensions which had kept her earlier novels moving were not suitable to a serious subject; yet irony was still her only organizing impulse. Without irony, she could not organize her story around the figure of her heroine, she could not even make her heroine sympathetic; she could only set up her worlds and dispose of their inhabitants by means of an imported and arbitrary social judgment named Fanny Price. *Mansfield Park* failed as a work of art because its only sustaining impulse was external.

In *Persuasion*, not only is the conflict grander and more dramatic in conception; it is organized and resolved, gravely and unironically, in the feelings of the heroine. The conflict is between the feudal remnant, conscious of its tradition, and the rising middle class, conscious of its vitality, at the turn of the nineteenth century: between Sir Walter and Mr. Elliot, between Lady Russell and Wentworth, between Mary Musgrove and her husband; and always at the center, mediating directly or as an involved onlooker, is Anne Elliot.

In its mildest form, the conflict is observed reluctantly by Anne between Charles and Mary Musgrove. Mary has little energy to spare from her hypochondria, but what she has she devotes to upholding her notions of consequence, small scattered echoes of Sir Walter's grandiose self-congratulation. When her sister-in-law Henrietta seems preferred by Wentworth, Mary exclaims:

> ". . . Dear me! If he should rise to any very great honours! If he should ever be made a Baronet! 'Lady Wentworth' sounds very well. That would be a noble thing, indeed, for Henrietta! She would take place of me then, and Henrietta would not dislike that. Sir Frederick and Lady Wentworth! It would be but a new creation, however, and I never think much of your new creations." (p 75)

She will not consider Charles Hayter as a possible suitor for Henrietta because "she looked down very decidedly upon the

Hayters." (P 75) But her husband, who has no patience with mere mooning over rank, retorts with the hypnotic bourgeois incantation of advancement and property:

> "Now you are talking nonsense, Mary. . . . It would not be a *great* match for Henrietta, but Charles has a very fair chance, through the Spicers, of getting something from the Bishop in the course of a year or two; and you will please to remember, that he is the eldest son; whenever my uncle dies, he steps into very pretty property. . . ." (P 76)

Neither ever convinces the other, and neither ever feels the need to convince: Mary has her ailments to turn to; Charles is too contemptuous of his wife's logic, and too shallow and easy, to require more than an occasional "Now you are talking nonsense, Mary." The contrast is nevertheless basic and symbolic, for Charles can always offer well documented arguments in response to Mary's feeble snobbery: the ascendant middle class, whether freeholding farmer or (like Wentworth) freebooting sailor or adventurer or lawyer, knows where its strength lies, and is already talking down the enemy. This is their contrast; but their agreement signifies still more. Except for Charles's casual remark, buried in his statistics, that Charles Hayter is a "good sort of fellow," (P 76) neither Charles nor Mary makes a single reference to the personal qualities of the prospective suitors. Personality is never an issue.

Sir Walter is, of course, the epitome of blind blood-worship: feudalism in its last, inverted stage. Mr. Elliot, nominally his heir but too impatient to wait for the honor, turns out finally to have been an adventurer seeking wealthy bourgeois respectability by the quickest means, according to Mrs. Smith's revelation:

> "Mr. Elliott . . . at that period of his life, had one object in view—to make his fortune, and by a rather quicker process than the law. He was determined to make it by marriage. . . ." (P 200f.)

Later, having made his fortune by marriage, and having soon after providentially lost his wife, Mr. Elliot returns to the pursuit of respectability by rank. The real opposition is here: Sir Walter, wishing simply to keep what he has, feels no need

233

—indeed, has no talent—for cunning or aggressiveness (in business affairs, even his lawyer, Mr. Shepherd, can lead him without much trouble); while Mr. Elliot, who wished to get what he did not have, had to be both cunning and aggressive.[24] But they also, like Charles and Mary, agree in their indifference to personality. Neither Sir Walter nor Mr. Elliot moves out of the circle of his own possessive ego: Sir Walter sees everyone else as a possible foil, Mr. Elliot sees everyone as a possible tool. And just as neither Mary nor Charles wins Anne over, so neither Sir Walter nor Mr. Elliot gains her sympathy or is allowed any notion of what she feels.

The antagonism which chiefly engages Anne is, of course, that between Lady Russell and Wentworth. Anne loves them both, but to the end they are suspicious of each other. In view of their attitudes, this mutual distrust is not strange. Lady Russell is as much a supporter of title and tradition as Sir Walter:

> She had a cultivated mind, and was, generally speaking, rational and consistent—but she had prejudices on the side of ancestry; she had a value for rank and consequence, which blinded her a little to the faults of those who possessed them. (p 11)

Not only is she incapable of recognizing Sir Walter's fatuity, but she can be taken in by Mr. Elliot's manner as soon as he assumes an outward respect for his uncle. (p 146f.) Finally, she maintains a strong dislike of Wentworth:

> Such confidence, powerful in its own warmth, and bewitching in the wit which often expressed it, must have been enough for Anne; but Lady Russell saw it very differently.—His sanguine

---

[24] Why does Jane Austen not dramatize their differences by bringing Sir Walter and Mr. Elliot into direct collision? And why is Anne so indignant when Mrs. Smith discloses Mr. Elliot's contemptuous disrespect of Sir Walter? (p 203f.) Partly, I think, because, knowing that in any clash Mr. Elliot would make a complete fool of Sir Walter, Jane Austen is not yet ready to relinquish her preference for the man of title and tradition, however wrong and foolish he may be, over the upstart adventurer, who has no stability at all. Anne, and Jane Austen, still believe in certain feudal amenities, among them respect for rank and birth, and scorn of "trade." So, answering Anne's question about Mr. Elliot's wife, " 'But was she not a very low woman?' " Mrs. Smith remarks: " 'Yes. . . . Her father was a grazier, her grandfather had been a butcher. . . .' " (p 202) In her novels, at least, Jane Austen never lost this touch of irrelevant and obtrusive snobbery.

temper, and fearlessness of mind, operated very differently on her. She saw in it but an aggravation of the evil. It only added a dangerous character to himself. He was brilliant, he was headstrong.—Lady Russell had little taste for wit; and of any thing approaching to imprudence a horror. She deprecated the connexion in every light. (p 27)

For Wentworth possesses all the qualities calculated to offend a widow whose only stability is rank and family; all the new bourgeois virtues—confidence, aggressiveness, daring, an eye for money and the main chance. Even as a sailor, loving battle and glory, he is still frankly a businessman:

"Ah! those were pleasant days when I had the Laconia! How fast I made money in her.—A friend of mine, and I, had such a lovely cruise together off the Western Islands.—Poor Harville. . . ! You know how much he wanted money—worse than myself. He had a wife. . . ." (p 67)

Battle and glory have their place and their excitement; but Wentworth and his fellow officers (and Jane Austen's sailor brothers) are far more excited at the prospect of a prize-ship or a promotion. Even kind Admiral Croft can scarcely think past a man's chances:

"I thought Captain Benwick a very pleasing young man," said Anne. . . .

"Oh! yes, yes, there is not a word to be said against James Benwick. He is only a commander, it is true, made last summer, and these are bad times for getting on, but he has not another fault that I know of. . . ." (p 171)

The irony is Jane Austen's; but the economic compulsion, the anxiety, is not only Admiral Croft's (habitually, by now) but Wentworth's. The Admiral loves his wife, Wentworth loves Anne; their problem has been to neutralize this anxiety—their own and that of the women they marry—without damage to their love. They are men of business, but they are men of feeling too; and their feeling survives its burden of middle-class anxiety and middle-class metaphor, just as Lady Russell's affection for Anne survives her immovable feudal prejudice.

Anne, then, can take no side in the conflict. For her, the only issue is feeling, whose survival—possible, though unlikely, on either side—is without bearing on the conflict itself. Lady Russell, Wentworth, and Admiral Croft—these are the persons to whom Anne warmly responds, and they are all persons whose feelings survive the economic battleground: even Lady Russell "was a very good woman, and if her second object was to be sensible and well-judging, her first was to see Anne happy." (P 249) Only Anne observes, from its center, the whole history of the conflict that divides into two camps all the major characters of the book except herself; and her decision—which she made before the story begins—is that both sides are wrong. If it were not for Wentworth's return, however, she would have lived with her feelings unspoken and unfulfilled. Throughout the book, she is caught in the center of a struggle whose issues—precedence, power, money, property—are hateful to her as issues, among people who pursue material goals in a wreckage of personality; and she will remain caught, forever, because she is a woman and unmarried in a society which maintains unmarried women on sufferance, because she has nowhere to go and nothing to say—unless the lover, not suitor but lover, whom she rejected in ignorance of his momentous distinction from the others, comes back to claim her. The worlds of Anne Elliot are not nearly so simple and definable as Fanny Price's, for Fanny could choose Mansfield Park and be sure of heaven. Anne has either no choice at all, or no need of choice: except in extremity, Sir Walter's world is hardly preferable to Mr. Elliot's; and Wentworth, as she loves him and responds to his love, is outside the conflict altogether. Anne has learned that the conflict of her time engages objects and symbols, and that she can deal only with persons.

It is not that Anne escapes finally, but that she grows through and out of her prison. Understanding is prerequisite to growth and release, and understanding comes only within and through the pull of opposed tensions, even if these are pulling away from personality: the conflict must be gone through before it can be evaluated and rejected. Having gone through it in eight years of accumulating observation and judgment, Anne has grown to understand just how rare a lover Wentworth is; but she has learned, even more somberly, how rare love is, and if she has decided, after her ordeal, that

our first duty is—more than to ourselves or to immediate inclination—to *all* who love us, we may accept, in her joyous
present, her charitably strict application of this truth to Lady
Russell's mistake:

> ". . . I must believe that I was right, much as I suffered from
> it, that I was perfectly right in being guided by the friend
> whom you will love better than you do now. To me she was
> in the place of a parent. . . . I am not saying that she did not
> err in her advice. . . . But I mean, that I was right in submitting
> to her, and that if I had done otherwise, I should have
> suffered more in continuing the engagement than I did even
> in giving it up, because I should have suffered in my con-
> science." (p 246)

Consider those characters who are always outside the conflict: the Musgrove sisters, Captain Benwick. Anne treats
them as she treats her sister's children, with a detached and
undiscriminating sympathy. Regarding Wentworth's courtship of Louisa or Henrietta, she feels that "Either of them
would, in all probability, make him an affectionate, good-
humoured wife" (p 77); and Admiral Croft genially adds:
" 'And very nice young ladies they both are; I hardly know
one from the other.' " (p 92) Benwick's misty sentimentality
and his enthusiasm for Scott and Byron evoke nothing more
from Anne than a schoolmistress's advice to an inflammable
adolescent:

> . . . he repeated, with such tremulous feeling, the various lines
> which imaged a broken heart, or a mind destroyed by wretched-
> ness, and looked so entirely as if he meant to be understood,
> that she ventured to hope he did not always read only poetry;
> and to say, that she thought it was the misfortune of poetry,
> to be seldom safely enjoyed by those who enjoyed it com-
> pletely; and that the strong feelings which alone could estimate
> it truly, were the very feelings which ought to taste it but
> sparingly.
> His looks showing him not pained, but pleased with this al-
> lusion to his situation, she was emboldened to go on; and feel-
> ing in herself the right of seniority of mind, she ventured to
> recommend a larger allowance of prose in his daily study . . .
> (p 100f.)

Most significant is the fact that these characters—the only
ones outside the conflict—are also the only ones whom Jane

Austen treats with a relaxed irony. Their place, and their tone, are outside the main current of the story. Where, then, do Louisa and Benwick—who after all occupy considerable space —stand in relation to the story? and why, unlike the major characters, are they tempered by irony? The answers to these questions are embedded in two incidents: Louisa's fall on the Cobb, and her sudden engagement to Benwick. The former is the false climax, and the latter the anticlimax, of the book.

Whatever its defects of execution (and certainly the postures and outcries of Wentworth are awkward and melodramatic enough to annul, almost, our favorable impression of him), the scene on the Cobb is intended ironically:[25]

> By this time the report of the accident had spread among the workmen and boatmen about the Cobb, and many were collected near them, to be useful, if wanted, at any rate, to enjoy the sight of a dead young lady, nay, two dead young ladies, for it proved twice as fine as the first report. (P 111)

As a false climax, the scene brings several values into focus, for Wentworth and for us. It is here that Wentworth is struck by Anne's presence of mind into regarding her personally again, and here that the Musgrove sisters and Benwick suddenly appear in all their undignified triviality, like puppets in an unamusing show, leaping childishly, fainting (Jane Austen has never cared for women who faint), running jerkily off for help, alike in exaggerated and ineffectual response. The subsequent anticlimax is inevitable: that Louisa and Benwick, having securely ascertained their mutual triviality, should forsake their previous attachments—Wentworth and Anne respectively—and go off out of the story together.

They were always intruders in the story, anyway; or, rather foils. The point is that Jane Austen uses these uninvolved characters with a dual aim: to set off, by their lively inconsequence, the seriousness of the conflict; and to make the real climax inescapable by showing, in a false climax, how inadequate and irresponsible they are. If Louisa and Benwick

---

[25] Miss Lascelles points out the irony (*op.cit.*, 77), successfully meets Herbert Read's truculent objection to the scene (*ibid.*, 78), and suggests a convincing explanation of Jane Austen's failure to offer a more credible accident (*ibid.*, 129).

are handled ironically, it is because Jane Austen so informs us
—by treatment, not by prompting—that they are not to be
taken as seriously as the others. In *Persuasion*, irony is no
longer a compulsion, but an index to the uninvolved character
and the indecisive incident.

There are, then, comic scenes and comic characters in *Persuasion*; but its inner orbit and final effect are not comic. "The
comic poet," says George Meredith, "is in the narrow field, or
enclosed square, of the society he depicts; and he addresses
the still narrower enclosure of men's intellects, with reference to the operation of the social world upon their characters."[26] This might well have been written with Jane Austen's
comedies in mind; but it is precisely here that *Persuasion*
diverges, for *Persuasion* is concerned, not focally with the operation of the social world upon men's characters, but with the
emotional resistance that men put up against the perpetual
encroachments of the social world. The whole pattern of the
novel is one, not of delusion and face-saving (as in *Emma* or
The Egoist), but of resistance and tension. Statically, *Persuasion* offers a figure caught between pairs of opposites:
Anne between Sir Walter and Mr. Elliot, between Mary and
Charles, between Lady Russell and Wentworth. The course
of the story shows how she was caught and how she is finally
able to transcend the conflict. The interest of the story is to
illustrate the plight of a sensitive woman in a society which
has a measure for everything except sensitivity. And the climax of the story occurs when Anne—Jane Austen's only
heroine so aware of, and so irrevocably cut off from, her society—is ready to articulate and define her lonely personal
triumph.

So Wentworth is enlightened, and Anne is freed, as the
novel rounds to its authentic climax at the White Hart Inn,
where Anne can speak at last what she is now so sure of, after
eight years. The perfection and emotional resonance of this
scene are unique in Jane Austen's work: nowhere else do we
grasp so much of personality grown and summed up. Unlike

[26] G. Meredith, *An Essay on Comedy and the Uses of the Comic Spirit*,
New York, 1897, 79f.

Elizabeth Bennet and Emma, who did not grow except in our aggregating perception of them, bit by bit, through the perspective of the author's irony; unlike Fanny Price and Elinor, who had not even this ironically simulated growth—Anne has grown altogether and truly, out of the constrictions of her group, out of her timidity, out of the defiant need for wit and self-assertion, out of the author's tight, ironic feminine world. *Persuasion* has a new impulse, feeling; and a new climax, self-fulfillment.

What Jane Austen might have achieved if she had been able to revise the whole book as she revised this scene, is no more than interesting speculation. Here is the book, and as it is we must judge it. Certainly, it marks the most abrupt turn in Jane Austen's work: it shows the author closely attentive to personal feeling and to economic tensions for the first time; and—perhaps most notable—it shows that Jane Austen has at last discarded the shield of irony, as in her sharp and brilliant comedies, and the shield of casuistry, as in her heavy failures. Irony has become a controlled and uncompulsive instrument, casuistry must submit to being examined in the light of personality; and the universe is enlarging to include many things undreamed of—or *just* dreamed of—in her youth. *Persuasion* has its defects of execution, its languors, its relapses into old bad habits: Jane Austen was, after all, on strange ground, after a lifetime of alternation between amusing and edifying her family, that singular family which must have demanded from its most talented member laughter and moral lessons, but never tenderness, or must at least never have felt the lack of it. If *Persuasion*, however, is a partial failure as a work of art, it is an astonishingly new and sure direction in a great novelist, toward a door that Jane Austen lived only long enough to set ajar. She was even apologetic about this new direction to the end. Writing about *Persuasion* to her niece, she remarked: "You will not like it, so you need not be impatient. You may *perhaps* like the Heroine, as she is almost too good for me." (L II 487, 23 Mar. 1817) She could not be confident about Anne or the new direction: it was still too early.

CHAPTER IX

THE LIBERATION OF IRONY

SANDITON

E. M. FORSTER has observed that *Sanditon* "gives the effect of weakness, if only because it is reminiscent from first to last";[1] and the temptation is strong to accompany him in dismissing it, with due respect to the circumstances of its composition and some palliating reference to Jane Austen's new interest in scenery and the Romantic poets, as a retrospective, anticlimactic conclusion to her work. The temptation rests on two facts: that in its tone *Sanditon* reverts from the controlled and moving somberness of *Persuasion* to an irony quite as persistent and deliberately unengaged as the irony of, say, *Northanger Abbey*; and that the author has not yet developed this considerable fragment to a stage at which its leading characters and the relations between them are more than most tentatively, if at all, defined.

Still, the facts need to be investigated before they can provide an adequate basis for judgment. The first is, of course, no positive symptom of retrogression: to resume an earlier tone may, indeed, be to develop and extend it. As for the second, which may seem merely the sad inevitable result of Jane Austen's failing health and powers (the book was written within the last half-year of her life, when she was already very ill), Miss Lascelles has pointed out how startlingly it distinguishes *Sanditon* from Jane Austen's other considerable fragment of a novel:

> While each of the earlier novels had been, in some respect, an advance beyond its predecessors, none of them would, if broken off short at the eleventh [*sic*: *Sanditon* is broken off at the *twelfth*] chapter, have left us in such uncertainty as to the way in which it was going to develop; and her other piece of unfinished work, *The Watsons*, seems, by comparison, almost to foreshadow its own fulfilment.[2]

[1] E. M. Forster, "Jane Austen," *Abinger Harvest*, New York, 1936, 152.
[2] M. Lascelles, *Jane Austen and Her Art*, Oxford, 1939, 39.

As far as *Sanditon* has gone, uncertainty of development may, indeed, mean complexity of development (as distinguished from the imposed self-righteous simpleness of *The Watsons*), the kind of suspense generated by the problem of perception, by the peril of a point of view. We have already had from Jane Austen various illustrations of this peril: all of them, however, limited and qualified, in consequence of Catherine Morland's wide-eyed credulity, Elizabeth Bennet's overconfidence and deep involvement, Emma Woodhouse's blind wilfulness. In *Sanditon*, on the other hand, the peril and the irony depend on no patent defect in the protagonist— Charlotte Heywood is very nearly the neutral observer—and both survive and flourish nevertheless. The problem of perception has expanded, finally, beyond sharp qualification.

Since the problem is Charlotte Heywood's, since Charlotte *is* the point of view through most of the story, the two occasions on which she definitely is not are of special interest. The first exception occurs at the very outset, when we are introduced to Mr. Parker by way of the coach accident before Charlotte has even been heard of.

Now the opening scene is striking for reasons quite unrelated to point of view. It is, for one, Jane Austen's first beginning with anonymity and action rather than with names, ancestries, and a careful accounting of material circumstances: it has an immediate provocativeness only heightened by the irony with which the author immediately edges Mr. Parker's already characteristic remarks. The scene, moreover, very soon introduces the name and atmosphere of Sanditon, which is to be the proper home of the story; and this energetic introduction of Mr. Parker and his pet project into passive outlands establishes the centralness of Sanditon, symbolizes and foreshadows its power to draw back within it such necessary aliens—Charlotte certainly, Sidney Parker probably—as, together with its present inhabitants, will make up the significant figures of the story.

But the scene is also striking because it does not violate the problem of perception shortly to be set up. Mr. Parker is the only figure of the story so unequivocal and unsurprising as to require no mediation through a point of view. What he is, he is obviously; what he thinks, he says, and what he thinks and says is always very simple. His first remark after the accident fixes him as an optimist:

> ". . . never mind, my Dear. . . . It c^d not have happened, you know, in a better place.—Good out of Evil.— The very thing perhaps to be wished for. We shall soon get releif. . . ." (s 3)

We find out soon that it was his hasty misreading of a news-paper advertisement which led him into the bad road responsi-ble for the accident; and, soon after, that this hasty, optimistic reader of advertisements (in 1817, advertisement-reading it-self appearing new-fangled and eccentric enough to the rural middle-class and gentry) knows a sure cure for his sprained ankle—perhaps, indeed, a panacea:

> ". . . A little of our own Bracing Sea air will soon set me on my feet again.—Depend upon it my Dear, it is exactly a case for the Sea. Saline air & immersion will be the very thing.— My sensations tell me so already." (s 10)

Mr. Parker is a "projector," a property speculator enthusias-tically devoted to his own speculation, spell-bound by the promise of Sanditon, the place that plays mistress to his im-passioned lover:

> ". . . Nature had marked it out—had spoken in most intelligible Characters—The finest, purest Sea Breeze on the Coast—ac-knowledged to be so—Excellent Bathing—fine hard sand— Deep Water 10 yards from the Shore—no Mud—no Weeds— no shiney rocks—Never was there a place more palpably de-signed by Nature for the resort of the Invalid—the very Spot which Thousands seemed in need of. . . ." (s 14f.)

And when he and the narrative are ready to be handed over to Charlotte, the author's comment carefully reminds us not only of his candor but of his transparency:

> All that he understood of himself, he readily told, for he was very openhearted;—& where he might be himself in the dark, his conversation was still giving information, to such of the Heywoods as could observe. (s 20)

The other occasion on which Charlotte is not the point of view, the only occasion on which Jane Austen takes over once Charlotte has been presented, occurs much later, when Sir

Edward Denham has voluminously informed Charlotte of his taste in novels. The author steps in here to explain this taste and—with a further omniscience even more destructive of the point of view—to relate it to Sir Edward's plans for Clara Brereton. If the intervention represents only a temporary straightforward sketch by which in the first draft the author reminds herself of what she must later dramatize and align with the point of view, it nevertheless appears strangely out of place in a work otherwise already dramatized. The fact is that Jane Austen is finally resisting the extraordinary conventional pressure, the moral imperative in effect, to which in her published novels she has always yielded, that actual seduction or the planning of seduction must never be represented comically; and the pressure still retains enough force to oblige her to treat the prohibited material with an authoritative external irony, a conscious defiance as it were, before she can discipline herself to mediate the irony through her chosen point of view.[3]

Her explication of Sir Edward is, then, the breaking of a taboo as in *Persuasion* the infusion of personal feeling is the breaking of (or the growth out of) a taboo. It is, moreover, very funny as a "burlesque of the conventional catastrophe of the sentimental novel":[4]

> Sir Edw:'s great object in life was to be seductive.—With such personal advantages as he knew himself to possess, & such Talents as he did also give himself credit for, he regarded it as his Duty.—He felt that he was formed to be a dangerous Man—quite in the line of the Lovelaces. . . . it was Clara whom he meant to seduce.—Her seduction was quite determined

---

[3] Miss Lascelles has finely documented the use which the author makes of Sir Edward in blowing away the convention; but she persists in regarding it as merely a literary convention, which Jane Austen picked up from Richardson and never questioned till now merely for lack of another usable catastrophe (*ibid.*, 82f.). That the convention, however, had for Jane Austen mainly a moral, a social sanction may be indicated by the exuberance with which she flouts it in her *juvenilia* and *Lady Susan* (both of which she wrote with no notion of publication) and, on the other hand, the severity with which she observes it, even to the point of damaging or ruining her story (as in *Sense and Sensibility* and *Mansfield Park*), in her published novels. From the scope that *Sanditon* implies, it, like *The Watsons*, seems to have been begun, at least, with the idea of publication in mind.

[4] *Loc.cit.*

on. Her Situation in every way called for it. She was his rival in Lady D.'s favour, she was young, lovely & dependant. . . . He was armed against the highest pitch of Disdain or Aversion.—If she could not be won by affection, he must carry her off. He knew his Business.—Already had he had many Musings on the Subject. If he *were* constrained so to act, he must naturally wish to strike out something new, to exceed those who had gone before him—and he felt a strong curiosity to ascertain whether the Neighbourhood of Tombuctoo might not afford some solitary House adapted for Clara's reception;—but the Expence alas! of Measures in that masterly style was ill-suited to his Purse, & Prudence obliged him to prefer the quietest sort of ruin & disgrace for the object of his Affections, to the more renowned.— (s 110ff.)

And if, also, the description is not worked consistently into the fabric of the novel, it remains notable as the latest large sign of personal liberation, of the full release of powers—a release presaged by the intense fulfillment of *Emma*, and in a very different manner already signalized in the expanding world of *Persuasion*.

Elsewhere in *Sanditon* Jane Austen is not impelled, by a sense of icon-smashing or for any other reason, to justify her story in her own person, however amusingly. Except for a moment to comment on Charlotte's susceptibility to Sir Edward's attentions:

I make no apologies for my Heroine's vanity.—If there are young Ladies in the World at her time of Life, more dull of Fancy, & more careless of pleasing, I know them not, & never wish to know them. (s 85)

the author neither obstructs Charlotte's vision nor intrudes her own; and the comedy of appearances proceeds through the agency of a heroine uniquely armed—by her perceptiveness, her position as an outsider, her lack of involvement with anyone at Sanditon—to penetrate the appearances she will meet.

Being an outsider has, of course, its preliminary disadvantages if one's guide and only source of information, until the circle has been reached, is as garrulous and genially undiscriminating as Mr. Parker. The opportunity of seeing a new world quite freshly is not given to Charlotte, for everything and everyone have their premature introduction through him as he brings his guest homeward. Still, Charlotte already suspects that as a transparent medium Mr. Parker admits light only from himself, that from others he admits almost exclusively that minimum of facts with which people furbish up their appearances. Once she has come face to face with the new world, she must begin to measure his easy enthusiasms against reality; and it is not long before she recognizes that reality is never so simple and seldom so pleasant.

Mr. Parker's first subject is Lady Denham; and his account of her is very full, even to mentioning the widespread belief that of her two marriages the first was for money and the second for a title. Yet Mr. Parker can explain away such trifling details, by reference to the fact, as he sees it, of her abundant amiability:

> "There is at times . . . a little self-importance—but it is not offensive;—& there are moments, there are points, when her Love of Money is carried greatly too far. But she is a good-natured Woman, a very goodnatured Woman,—a very obliging, friendly Neighbour; a chearful, independant, valuable character. . . ." (s 34)

Nor does Charlotte's own impression, on meeting Lady Denham, differ appreciably from his, except to be still more favorable:

> . . . tho' her manner was rather downright & abrupt, as of a person who valued herself on being free-spoken, there was a good humour & cordiality about her—a civility & readiness to be acquainted with Charlotte herself, & a heartiness of welcome towards her old friends, which was inspiring the Good will, she seemed to feel . . . (s 74f.)

Her parsimony appears at first only quaint and amusing:

> ". . . Aye—that young Lady smiles I see;—I dare say she thinks me an odd sort of a Creature,—but *she* will come to care about such matters herself in time. Yes, Yes, my Dear, depend upon it, you will be thinking of the price of Butcher's meat in time— tho' you may not happen to have quite such a Servants Hall full to feed, as I have. . . ." (s 79)

Her unsolicited confidences to Charlotte, however, are less amusing, as she compliments herself on her shrewdness:

> ". . . I am not the Woman to help any body blindfold.—I always

take care to know what I am about & who I have to deal with, before I stir a finger. . . ." (s 96)

and on her generosity to the nephew of her second husband:

". . . when he died, I gave Sir Edwd his Gold Watch.—" She said this with a look at her Companion which implied it's right to produce a great Impression—& seeing no rapturous astonishment in Charlottes countenance, added quickly—"He did not bequeath it to his Nephew, my dear—It was no bequest. It was not in the Will. He only told me, & *that* but once, that he sh^d wish his Nephew to have his Watch; but it need not have been binding, if I had not chose it.—" (s 97)

She is, indeed, frank enough, in the unchallengeable supremacy of her position, to place before this young stranger the whole story of her affluence and the calls upon it, to warn Charlotte off the track of Sir Edward by

. . . giving a shrewd glance at her & replying—"Yes, yes, he is very well to look at—& it is to be hoped some Lady of large fortune will think so—for Sir Edwd *must* marry for Money. . . ." "Sir Edw: Denham, said Charlotte, with such personal Advantages may be almost sure of getting a Woman of fortune, if he chuses it."—This glorious sentiment seemed quite to remove suspicion. "Aye my Dear—That's very sensibly said cried Lady D— And if we c^d but get a young Heiress to S! . . ." (s 98f.)

and, by the end of her protracted monologue, which she interrupts now and then only as she may wring agreement from her auditor, to convince Charlotte of something not simple at all, not available to a first impression, but profoundly in the nature of a materialistic society:

"She is thoroughly mean. I had not expected any thing so bad.— Mr. P. spoke too mildly of her.—His Judgement is evidently not to be trusted.—His own Goodnature misleads him. He is too kind hearted to see clearly.—I must judge for myself.— And their very *connection* prejudices him.—He has persuaded her to engage in the same Speculation—& because their object in that Line is the same, he fancies she feels like him in others. —But she is very, very mean.—I can see no Good in her.—Poor Miss Brereton!—And she makes every body mean about her.— This poor Sir Edward & his Sister,—how far Nature meant them to be respectable I cannot tell,—but they are *obliged* to be mean in their Servility to her.—And I am Mean too, in giving her my attention, with the appearance of coinciding with her.—Thus it is, when Rich People are Sordid." (s 103)

This final judgment of Lady Denham embodies also Charlotte's last word on Sir Edward; and it is through a similar sequence of impressions that Charlotte has arrived at both. She first hears about Sir Edward, from Mr. Parker, as the likely heir of his aunt, and deserving of this enviable position:

> "He is a warm friend to Sanditon—said Mr Parker—& his hand w^d be as liberal as his heart, had he the Power.—He would be a noble Coadjutor! . . ." (s 37)

Again, Charlotte's impression on meeting him is very favorable:

> He came into the room remarkably well, talked much—& very much to Charlotte, by whom he chanced to be placed—& she soon perceived that he had a fine Countenance, a most pleasing gentleness of Voice, & a great deal of Conversation. She liked him. (s 84)

When she observes him glancing anxiously after Lady Denham and Clara, obviously more concerned about them than about her, she is

> . . . cured . . . of her halfhour's fever. . . . "Perhaps there was a good deal in his Air & Address; And his Title did him no harm." (s 86)

It soon becomes clear to her that he is in love with Clara; but this settles nothing for Charlotte except her "halfhour's fever." It is not till Sir Edward begins to speak at length to her that he begins to give himself away. He is, for example, a lover of the sea:

> The terrific Grandeur of the Ocean in a Storm, its glassy surface in a calm, it's Gulls & its Samphire, & the deep fathoms of it's Abysses . . . and she c^d not but think him a Man of Feeling—till he began to stagger her by the number of his Quotations, & the bewilderment of some of his sentences. (s 88f.)

Sir Edward is an admirer of Wordsworth and Campbell, a copious quoter of Scott—when he can remember the lines—and, as a man of sensibility, passionately devoted to Burns:

> ". . . If ever there was a Man who *felt*, it was Burns. . . ." (s 90)

When Charlotte, as a well brought up young lady, objects that though she has enjoyed much of Burns's poetry she is "not poetic enough to separate a Man's Poetry entirely from

his Character," (s 92) Sir Edward embarks on an almost
Shelleyan defense of genius against mere propriety:

> ". . . It were Hyper-criticism, it were Pseudo-philosophy to ex-
> pect from the soul of high toned Genius, the grovellings of a
> common mind.—The Coruscations of Talent, elicited by im-
> passioned feeling in the breast of Man, are perhaps incompat-
> ible with some of the prosaic Decencies of Life;—nor can you,
> loveliest Miss Heywood—(speaking with an air of deep senti-
> ment)—nor can any Woman be a fair Judge of what a Man
> may be propelled to say, write or do, by the sovereign impulses
> of illimitable Ardour." (s 92f.)

There is in literature perhaps no better illustration of the well-
bred response to social error than Charlotte's here:

> This was very fine;—but if Charlotte understood it at all, not
> very moral—& being moreover by no means pleased with his
> extraordinary stile of compliment, she gravely answered "I
> really know nothing of the matter.—This is a charming day.
> The Wind I fancy must be Southerly." (s 93)

Later, undismayed, Sir Edward expresses his preference in
novels:

> ". . . such as display Human Nature with Grandeur—such as
> shew her in the Sublimities of intense Feeling—such as exhibit
> the progress of strong Passion from the first Germ of incip-
> ient Susceptibility to the utmost Energies of Reason half-de-
> throned . . ." (s 106)

For, even before the author specifically explains him in her
own voice as her admission, and first great step toward demon-
strating, that sex can be treated comically, Sir Edward has
made it plain that he is in training to become a lady-killer; and
by the time his earliest self-exposure has ended, moral Charlotte (the author being no longer moral, but ironic) has decided, decorously, that

> He seemed very sentimental, very full of some Feelings or
> other, & very much addicted to all the newest-fashioned hard
> words—had not a very clear Brain she presumed, & talked a
> good deal by rote. (s 94)

There are, certainly, minor figures whose difficulty—at
least when Charlotte comes face to face with them—is very
minor, and who serve mainly to enforce her conviction that
Mr. Parker's judgment is quite untrustworthy, perhaps worth-

less. So Sir Edward's sister, whom Mr. Parker mentions merely as meriting, by her "very small provision," (s 36) Lady Denham's remembrance in her will: at first appearance,

> . . . a fine young woman, but cold & reserved, giving the idea of one who felt her consequence with Pride & her Poverty with Discontent . . . (s 84)

and later, as the would-be heiress,

> . . . the change from Miss Denham sitting in cold Grandeur in Mrs Parker's Drawg-room to be kept from silence by the efforts of others, to Miss D. at Lady D.'s Elbow, listening & talking with smiling attention or solicitous eagerness, was very striking—and very amusing—or very melancholy, just as Satire or Morality might prevail. (s 87)

Mr. Parker's hypochondriac sisters and brother are equally discoverable to Charlotte. Mr. Parker, of course, introduces them at the value they wish to have:

> ". . . They have wretched health, as you have heard us say frequently, & are subject to a variety of very serious Disorders. —Indeed, I do not beleive they know what a day's health is; —& at the same time, they are such excellent useful Women & have so much energy of Character that, where any good is to be done, they force themselves on exertions which to those who do not thoroughly know them, have an extraordinary appearance. . . ." (s 58)

and insists on reading to Charlotte Diana's letter in which, among other horrors, is presented a description of Susan's high susceptibility after some dental work:

> ". . . She can only speak in a whisper—and fainted away twice this morning on poor Arthur's trying to suppress a cough. . . ." (s 63)

Yet Charlotte hardly has time to be impressed by Mr. Parker's sympathetic evidence and commentary before she meets the three invalids themselves and learns that Diana is a very decisive, talkative, apparently quite healthy woman, who makes a business of officiousness, and who establishes the pattern of invalidism for her dominated sister:

> ". . . she has kept up wonderfully.—had no Hysterics of consequence till we came within sight of poor old Sanditon—and the attack was not very violent . . ." (s 116)

and her happily acquiescent brother, "Broad made & Lusty—

250

and with no other look of an Invalide, than a sodden complexion," (s 133) and, unlike his less gross and far more active sisters, "determined on having no Disorders but such as called for warm rooms & good Nourishment." (s 144)

Still, the Denhams and the hypochondriac Parkers are not complex; the Parkers, besides, are drawn so broadly (Jane Austen, being herself an invalid at the time, was, in this first draft, perhaps too close to the material) as to verge on, sometimes to slip over into, burlesque. The serious—in fact, as far as the fragment has gone, unsolved—aspects of Charlotte's problem of perception are elsewhere.

What kind of person, for example, is Mr. Parker's brother Sidney? Mr. Parker does not presume to understand him; he presents him as that

> ". . . someone in most families privileged by superior abilities or spirits to say nothing.—In ours, it is Sidney; who is a very clever Young Man,—and with great powers of pleasing.—He lives too much in the World to be settled; that is his only fault.—He is here & there & every where. . . ." (s 50)

He is, plainly, a social young man, "with his neat equipage & fashionable air." (s 50) He is so much the family wit that Mrs. Parker, otherwise quite subdued by Mr. Parker's effervescence, several times breaks into the conversation to ask her husband to repeat some amusing comment Sidney has made about one thing or another. Mr. Parker remarks that Sidney "pretends to laugh at my Improvements," (s 50) and that this "saucy fellow . . . will have it there is a good deal of Imagination in my two Sisters' complaints" (s 58): Sidney appears to be equally unimpressed by groans, speculation, and Sanditon. Charlotte does get to meet him briefly—our only sight of him in the book—as he arrives at Sanditon:

> Sidney Parker was about 7 or 8 & 20, very good-looking, with a decided air of Ease & Fashion, and a lively countenance. (s 166)

And that is all. The touch of stylization may be the author's first hint to Charlotte and the reader that Sidney is to be gradually revealed as a conceited, affected young man, not too unlike Sir Edward, beneath his fashionableness. He is, however,

clever—and perhaps heartless—enough to mock at his brother's enthusiasms and his sisters' imaginary debilities. He might
have been exposed as a worldly, unscrupulous trifler, like
Frank Churchill (the parallel would be very neat—even fatal
—if Clara Brereton were his Jane Fairfax). He may be a
fortune-hunter, destined to capture the newly arrived heiress,
Miss Lambe, out from under Lady Denham's vigilance on behalf of her nephew. Or he might have become, with an appropriate development of interest and affection, Charlotte's suitor,
since for the present he is the only one at all available in this
capacity, and since Jane Austen has never so far left her
heroine without a husband. In any case, the essence and the
fate of Sidney Parker, as Charlotte learns about him in the
time allowed her, remain complexly debatable and unpredictable.

Clara Brereton is another puzzle. Chosen as a companion
by Lady Denham (who is a distant relative) from the household in which she has lived in dependence and poverty, she is
now, Mr. Parker declares,

> . . . a general favourite;—the influence of her steady conduct &
> mild, gentle Temper was felt by everybody. The prejudices
> which had met her at first in some quarters, were all dissipated.
> She was felt to be worthy of Trust—to be the very companion
> who wᵈ guide & soften Lady D—who wᵈ enlarge her mind &
> open her hand.—She was as thoroughly amiable as she was
> lovely—& since having had the advantage of their Sanditon
> Breezes, that Loveliness was complete. (s 42)

At Charlotte's first meeting with her,

> . . . her appearance so completely justified Mʳ P.'s praise that
> Charlotte thought she had never beheld a more lovely, or more
> Interesting young Woman.—Elegantly tall, regularly hand-
> some, with great delicacy of complexion & soft Blue eyes, a
> sweetly modest & yet naturally graceful Address . . . (s 75)

Charlotte finds her a perfect novel-heroine, and builds up a
fancy in which Clara has to be abused by Lady Denham:

> Such Poverty & Dependance joined to such Beauty & Merit,
> seemed to leave no choice in the business. (s 76)

Yet Charlotte is sensible enough to accept evidence to the
contrary:

. . . while she pleased herself the first 5 minutes with fancying the Persecutions which *ought* to be the Lot of the interesting Clara, especially in the form of the most barbarous conduct on Lady Denham's side, she found no reluctance to admit from subsequent observation, that they appeared to be on very comfortable Terms.—She c^d see nothing worse in Lady Denham, than the sort of oldfashioned formality of always calling her *Miss Clara* [this is before Charlotte has had better evidence about Lady Denham]—nor anything objectionable in the degree of observance & attention which Clara paid. (s 76f.)

Charlotte discovers that Sir Edward is in love with Clara (though she does not discover, as we do, Sir Edward's crude design), without learning how Clara responds. Finally, while entering the grounds of Sanditon House on a visit to Lady Denham, Charlotte

. . . caught a glimpse . . . of something White & Womanish in the field on the other side;—it was a something which immediately brought Miss B. into her head—& stepping to the pales, she saw indeed—& very decidedly, in spite of the Mist; Miss B—seated, not far from her, at the foot of the bank which sloped down from the outside of the Paling & which a narrow Path seemed to skirt along;—Miss Brereton seated, apparently very composedly—& Sir E. D. by her side.—They were sitting so near each other & appeared so closely engaged in gentle conversation, that Ch. instantly felt she had nothing to do but to step back again, & say not a word. . . . It could not but strike her rather unfavourably with regard to Clara;—but hers was a situation which must not be judged with severity. (s 167f.)

With a single exception, this is all we learn about Clara. The exception occurs during the author's exposure of Sir Edward's design, when, in her omniscient stance, she remarks incidentally that

Clara saw through him, & had not the least intention of being seduced—but she bore with him patiently enough to confirm the sort of attachment which her personal Charms had raised. (s 111f.)

The exception, of course, is a very significant one, since it is our only direct knowledge of Clara, and since it indicates what has elsewhere been implied, that she is a totally aware and—if still in a rather neutral sense—calculating person. But the puzzle and the provocation remain.

It is certainly clear, by the end of the fragment, that Clara is not the conventional uncomplicated novel-heroine Charlotte imagined her to be. In the first place, she is making no effort to fend off, is perhaps even encouraging, the advances of a man who not only has wicked plans for her (about which she knows), but is silly and boring besides. She seems, at least, devotedly attached to a woman whose meanness and evil dominance over the lives of many people she cannot help observing. It is notable, moreover, that Lady Denham is a very wealthy and an old woman, who may well be persuaded by Clara's devotion to leave her a fine bequest, and whose probable major heir is the man whose attentions Clara does not dismiss or discourage.

Now, though these are suspicious appearances, it is possible that only appearances are against Clara. She may, for example, be biding her time among people she justly detests or merely tolerates until she can, like Jane Fairfax, be rescued by another Frank Churchill—say, Sidney Parker. She may be so overwhelmingly grateful to Lady Denham for her kindness as to deny or mitigate everything else about her, and to display more than mere good manners toward Lady Denham's nephew.

In this subsidiary comedy of inheritance, as in the large comedy of appearances, Clara's position has not yet been defined, remains in fact highly ambiguous. If we recall, however, how Sir Edward has been anatomized for us, it seems likely that he and Clara are destined to play out that comic sex intrigue suggested and abruptly dropped between Sir Walter Elliot and Mrs. Clay in *Persuasion*; that Jane Austen, having finally swept aside her most durable taboo, is ready to show the panting male and the calculating female, if not in action, at least in such poses as the female will allow the relationship to extend to in order to achieve some more significant goal—money, for example. Perhaps Clara is holding Sir Edward as a kind of reserve, in case she is unsuccessful in diverting most of Lady Denham's fortune to herself; perhaps she intends to marry him anyway to be certain of the money. If this is so, Clara has, of course, good reason for keeping things unresolved, since Lady Denham openly declares that Sir Edward must marry an heiress, and since Clara is probably not yet sure enough of her influence over the shrewd old woman to risk offending her. At all events, Charlotte had many things to learn and many incidents to wait for before she might have closed the book on Clara Brereton.

Over all these ambiguities impends the ambiguity of Sanditon, Mr. Parker's beloved Sanditon, which, he asserts, "was wanted, was called for," (s 14) on "the noblest expanse of Ocean between the South foreland & the Land's end," (s 44) concentrating in its most favored location all the well known advantages of a seacoast resort:

> The Sea air & Sea Bathing together were nearly infallible, one or the other of them being a match for every Disorder, of the Stomach, the Lungs or the Blood. . . . Nobody could catch cold by the Sea, Nobody wanted appetite by the Sea, Nobody wanted Spirits, Nobody wanted Strength.—They were healing, softing, relaxing—fortifying & bracing—seemingly just as was wanted —sometimes one, sometimes the other. (s 25)

It is true that Mrs. Parker gazes "with something like the fondness of regret" (s 45) at their former home, in a little valley they pass through on the way to Sanditon; that Charlotte observes its snugness and the cultivated sheltering beauty of its grounds; and that Mr. Parker must note, with an almost conscious nostalgia:

> ". . . This is my old House—the house of my Forefathers—the house where I & all my Brothers & Sisters were born and bred —& where my own 3 eldest Children were born—where Mrs P. & I lived till within the last 2 years. . . ." (s 43)

and reminiscently on, until he stops short with the Sanditon judgment: "Our ancestors, you know always built in a hole. . . ." (s 44)

There is an exposed impermanence both spiritual and physical, a lack of memory and sheltering solidity, about Sanditon; and, as Mr. Parker has just illustrated the former impermanence, so in a moment he absurdly confirms his wife's wistful evidence of the latter:

> ". . . The Hilliers [who now occupy the Parkers' old house] did not seem to feel the storms last winter at all.—I remember see-

ing Mrs Hillier after one of those dreadful Nights, when *we* had been literally rocked in our bed, and she did not seem at all aware of the Wind being anything more than common." "Yes, yes—that's likely enough. *We* have all the Grandeur of the Storm, with less real danger, because the Wind meeting with nothing to oppose or confine it around our House, simply rages & passes on—while down in this Gutter—nothing is known of the state of the Air, below the Tops of the Trees—and the Inhabitants may be taken totally unawares, by one of those dreadful Currents which do more mischief in a Valley, when they *do* arise than an open Country ever experiences in the heaviest Gale. . . ." (s 47f.)

When, however, Charlotte arrives at Sanditon, she can forget Mr. Parker's exaltation and her own cool skepticism to look at it for the first time, to get her single total vision of the place, fusing its commonness, its beauty, its false-fronted hopefulness, its equivocal promise all together with her own hopefulness and excitement at the prospect of novelty in a new world, as she stands

> . . . at her ample, Venetian window . . . looking over the miscellaneous foreground of unfinished Buildings, waving Linen, & tops of Houses, to the Sea, dancing & sparkling in Sunshine & Freshness. (s 56)

Through the rest of the story, this vision enriches and obscures the characters within the frame, enhances and justifies their transience and meanness, their profiting by the whole flimsy structure superimposed on grand surroundings, enhances also their lack of a history and their promise, even— as with mysterious unhistoried Clara and, perhaps, Sidney Parker—their grand, unfamiliar, impersonal, possibly dangerous beauty. For if one must after all disagree with E. M. Forster in his contention that *Sanditon* is a weak, reminiscent work, there should still be no doubt that, as he has also remarked, "topography comes to the front, and is screwed much deeper than usual into the story,"[5] that indeed it serves a unique purpose he may have failed to investigate.

Topography, the Romantic poets, and sex as comedy are, then, the three new ingredients of *Sanditon*; and for a novelist who has till now been content to describe surroundings with

---

[5] Forster, *op.cit.*, 154.

very little attention to their influence or symbolic value (Lyme, in *Persuasion*, is the only exception that comes to mind), whose "romantic" poets, in her novels at least, have been Cowper and Scott, and who has treated sex with the most severe, quarantining moralism or left it severely alone, they are significant by their presence merely. They are, however, more significant yet; they are functional: not, that is, ingredients at all, but elements of a compound entirely different and distinct in Jane Austen's work, a comedy of ambiguities depending not on the ingenuousness (as in *Northanger Abbey*) or the partiality (as in *Pride and Prejudice*) or the indulged stubbornness (as in *Emma*) of the observer, but on the ambiguities inherent in an unsettled place among a transient group, in a romantic setting among unromantic people, inherent in the relationships, in a materialistic society, between the monied and their possible inheritors, inherent also in the diverging personal pressures and social responsibilities of sex upon men and women in a society in which sex has become the ultimate, polarly remote, invisible stage of a narrow, a convention-hedged and convention-trapped road.

It is this expanding perception of the intrinsic equivocalness of her materials—of *all* her materials, the society of appearances she lives in and *all* the personal impulses conniving with or at war against it—to which Jane Austen has come in her final work, and where her irony finds its renewed and, at least potentially, most uninhibited opportunity; it is, in fact, her irony that is dynamic, changing or expanding at last into an authentically unrestricted (as collected and mediated through every variety of restricted) point of view, into the free, exploring, undefensive agent of perception. Jane Austen's personal growth in the last years, out of moral uneasiness and false conventional obligations, is still in the process of being rapidly translated into artistic growth, now into the freedom of reference, the unshirked weight of ambiguity, of *Sanditon* as just before into the avowed shaping emotion of *Persuasion*, into energies and directions still greatly unexplored. To such works as *Emma* and *Persuasion*, *Sanditon* may—if only in its brevity and incompleteness—seem an epilogue; but it makes its own path. It is a new work; in the midst of her last illness, three months before her death at the age of forty-one, Jane Austen was undertaking with fresh impulse another liberation.

APPENDIX I

BIBLIOGRAPHY
AND KEY TO EDITIONS USED

E : *Emma**

L I & II: Letters, ed. R. W. Chapman, 2 vols., Oxford, 1932.

LF : *Love and Freindship and Other Early Works* (ed. unnamed), London, 1922.

LS : *Lady Susan*, ed. R. W. Chapman, Oxford, 1925.

MP: *Mansfield Park**

NA : *Northanger Abbey**

P : *Persuasion**

PP : *Pride and Prejudice**

S : *Fragment of a Novel Written by Jane Austen January-March 1817* [*Sanditon*], ed. R. W. Chapman, Oxford, 1925.

SS : *Sense and Sensibility**

VF : *Volume the First*, ed. R. W. Chapman, Oxford, 1933.

VT : *Volume the Third*, ed. R. W. Chapman, Oxford, 1951.

W : *The Watsons*, ed. R. W. Chapman, Oxford, 1927.

* Five-volume edition, ed. R. W. Chapman, Oxford, 1923.

APPENDIX II

MRS. LEAVIS'S JANE AUSTEN

In the course of this study I have attempted to indicate my attitude, either by appropriate quotation and comment or by omission, toward most of the Jane Austen criticism. Mrs. Leavis's series of articles,* however, call for special attention because they do not lend themselves to incidental quotation in a study of this sort, and because they constitute the most iconoclastic, the most confidently documented, and the most comprehensive effort to describe Jane Austen's method and development.

What she proposes, first of all, is a "palimpsest" hypothesis of Jane Austen's method: that Jane Austen was writing and revising continually from the earliest *juvenilia* till *Sanditon* without the barren period (approximately, the decade after 1798) traditionally accepted, that "The novels as we know them are palimpsests through whose surface portions of earlier versions, or of other and earlier compositions quite unrelated, constantly protrude, so that we read from place to place at different levels," (I, 65) that most of the novels were in their first drafts epistolary, and that Jane Austen's genius lay in the most scrupulous revision, in her increasingly skilled and conscious selecting and reworking of the raw materials of her life, her reading in the novels of the time, her correspondence, and her (usually) epistolary first drafts into the novels as we know them.

The arguments which Mrs. Leavis presents and the chronology she proposes to support this hypothesis are imposingly detailed (for some objections to its implication of a steady continuity of artistic impulse to cover the "barren years," see above, Chapter V, note 5). Many of her aesthetic deductions from it, however, are less imposing. Thus: "*Emma* and *Mansfield Park* bristle with vestigial traits" (I, 65); *Mansfield Park's* "ill-assorted tone is vestigial," it arises because the book "was written up from *Lady Susan* but much later in life and in a different convention, with a correspondingly different attitude to its material" (I, 86); yet *Emma*, which has an identical relationship to *The Watsons* (according to Mrs. Leavis), is a "mature and artistically perfect novel." (I, 65) "The

* There are three, which for the purpose of reference through the rest of the Appendix, I shall designate respectively as follows: (1)—"A Critical Theory of Jane Austen's Writings," *Scrutiny*, X (June, 1941), 61-87; (II)— "A Critical Theory of Jane Austen's Writings: II 'Lady Susan into Mansfield Park,'" *Scrutiny*, X (October, 1941; January, 1942), 114-142, 272-294; (III)—"A Critical Theory of Jane Austen's Writings: III The Letters," *Scrutiny*, XII (Spring, 1944), 104-119.

dimmed and distant effect" of *Mansfield Park*, "the impression it gives of low spirits in its presentation, is due . . . to its being retold from letters" (II, 122): presumably, this explains the "dimmed and distant effect," "the impression of low spirits," we receive from *Pride and Prejudice*, another novel retold from letters. Jane Austen, she states "was decidedly not precociously mature as an artist" (I, 65); these are weasel words, and might be used, with a suitable clearing up of implications, about Mozart; but "Love and Freindship" may nevertheless pass as a precociously mature work. Everything in a later work must come from its early prototype: so Mrs. Leavis finds Maria and Julia Bertram out of place and unconvincing, they "confuse the contrasted values" of *Mansfield Park*, apparently because they may be traced back not to the prototypic *Lady Susan* but to "Lesley Castle" (II, 135); for Mrs. Leavis, faithful to her hypothesis, seems unwilling to accept Maria and Julia as quite adequate symbols of what happens when Sir Thomas's principles yield to his fatherly indulgence, she dismisses Lady Bertram as a mere self-indulgence of the author's and refuses to consider that the self-indulgence might be Sir Thomas's, she seems to think that in introducing such unpredicted characters the author has merely confused the values so simply and distinctly contrasted—Mrs. Leavis believes—in *Lady Susan*. (As a matter of fact, to be as exact as possible, it is I think impossible—let the reader of the article judge for himself—to make out exactly what Mrs. Leavis is getting at here: whether she means to emphasize that *Mansfield Park* is more complex, or more confused, or more complex *and* more confused, in its opposition of values than—it is Mrs. Leavis speaking—the "simple and consistent *Lady Susan*"; actually, she seems to be suspended between the hobby-horse of her hypothesis and the ground of plain specific criticism.)

Supplementing this hypothesis is Mrs. Leavis's contention that Jane Austen was a perfectly candid individual, "neither puritanical nor Victorian—she thought freely and knew no reason why she should conceal what she thought." (III, 107) Mrs. Leavis interrupts her documentation for a moment to remark, with a rather disarming honesty: "What she can have found objectionable in *The Spectator* is beyond conjecture" (III, 108); the critic is unwilling to qualify her myth of the free-wheeling Jane Austen even as she presents damaging evidence against it. "The advantage of seeing life unprotected by blinkers is apparent in the faculty it developed in her, that of taking stock of all kinds of experience and absorbing new kinds not only without being disconcerted or repelled but without having even to brace herself" (III, 108): one might retort that if Jane Austen did not have to brace herself it was because her alternative defenses of irony and convention were quite strong; at any rate, she never—at least before *Persuasion*—absorbed the experience of sensibility or passionate love, she examined both by the light of irony in order to reject them with laughter or refused to examine them at all as she rejected them with moral disapproval. "The occasional schoolmarmy effects of *Sense and Sensibility* . . . are only the result of artistic inexperience (for the same kind of points are made effectively in *Persuasion* without any impression of preaching) . . ." (ii, 115): the "for," of course, implies a relationship altogether undemonstrated; perhaps the "schoolmarminess" in *Sense and Sensibility* is there because Jane Austen is too defensive to absorb the experience of sensibility, perhaps by *Persuasion* her attitude, not her technique merely, has matured. "The unfeeling treatment of a Lydia Bennett [*sic*] or a Maria Rushworth . . . is the result of the letter-writer's unsympathetic attitude to all who lapse from an implied standard of great severity," says Mrs. Leavis (iii, 115), failing to explain why in the letters Jane Austen's treatment of sin—and of everything else—is ironic while toward Lydia and Maria she takes a tone of quite unironic moral indignation. "The lack of sincerity in ordinary social intercourse," says Mrs. Leavis, "is clearly one of the sources of irritation in her relations with the outside world" (iii, 116); yet, constantly exposing and mocking at this lack of sincerity, Jane Austen herself cannot make a straight statement of feeling about anything, she always—even and always in the extant letters to Cassandra—makes the devious ironic or conventional gesture. Of Cassandra and Jane Austen against their society, Mrs. Leavis observes that they were not "ignorant of it or shy of it, but . . . they had too much penetration to be comfortable in society and knew too much about the people they had to live among" (iii, 117): though why such knowledge should forbid a candid and freely experiencing person to express (or, presumably, to *feel*) even a hint of sympathy or involvement regarding his society and the people in it, is a problem which Mrs. Leavis not only fails to explain but seems altogether unaware of.

Mrs. Leavis's two large propositions are, then, that Jane Austen was a very slowly but quite steadily and consciously developing artist who extensively used the materials of her own life and of her reading, and that she was a person who saw life "unprotected by blinkers," "who thought freely and knew no reason why she should conceal what she thought." In other words, as a person Jane Austen was not only highly perceptive but without any inhibitions to hobble her perceptions; and as an artist her problems were strictly problems to be coped with on the level of conscious revision of still-to-be-worked biographical and literary materials. It seems to me that, as I have attempted to demonstrate in this study, the facts lie elsewhere, and that Mrs. Leavis's insistence on her propositions not only invalidates her study in general, but diverts our attention from her frequent fine specific insights, even her scholarship. So she points out the relationship of *Pride and Prejudice* to *Cecilia* and other areas of contact between Fanny Burney's novels and Jane Austen's. So, also, her account of the failure of moral tone in *Mansfield Park* is quite convincing: "This unnatural censure, to be found only in this novel, of Jane Austen's own standards of judgment, of her independence of outlook and her own instinctive values, is what the discerning reader finds intolerable. To deny his own light is the worst offence of which an artist can be guilty. But," Mrs. Leavis pauses with a complacent portentousness, "we can now understand how it came about" (II, 281); and she goes on to fill in her banal and dubious biographical particulars.

For Mrs. Leavis, the artist—Jane Austen at least—is a wholly conscious self-seeker, shedding irrelevances and crudenesses like so many skins off the artistic essence in the process of revision. Mrs. Leavis is perceptive enough to note, in passing, Jane Austen's characteristic cynicism, her failures of tone, her moralistic retreats, her resolutely omniscient irony at least in the earliest novels toward her "puppets," her distance which seems more than merely aesthetic; but she never seems to recognize that these qualities (together with what they imply: the lack or avoidance of emotion) are quite incompatible with the Leavis view of Jane Austen as the uninhibited and wholly conscious pre-Victorian (or post-Victorian) woman and artist. Jane Austen was not Victorian; but her society was becoming so, and as she was conditioned by that society from her childhood, so she was sensitive to its demands in her maturity. Her alternation between defiance and submission toward it—that is, between an ironic and a conventional view of her materials—is the central fact which Mrs. Leavis, hot on a peripheral or perhaps false trail, never comes near.

INDEX

INDEX

229, 230, 231, 239, 245, 257, 260

Churchill, Frank, 215, 221n., 252, 254

Woodhouse, Emma, 30, 161, 215, 219, 220, 223, 227, 228, 240, 242

Plan of a Novel and Other Notes, 35 & n., 171n.

Two Chapters of Persuasion, 51n., 217

Persuasion (Chapter VIII), 51, 81, 140n., 150, 241, 244, 245, 254, 257, 262

Elliot, Anne, 201

Sanditon (Chapter IX), 222, 260

Austen-Leigh, J. E., *A Memoir of Jane Austen*, 158n., 171, 194n., 216

Austen-Leigh, M. A., *Personal Aspects of Jane Austen*, 23 & n., 24n.

Austen-Leigh, R. A. and W., *Jane Austen: Her Life and Letters*, 37-39n., 101n.

Bailey, John, 221n.

Brontë, Charlotte, 36

Brooke, Frances, *Lady Julia Mandeville*, 5n.

Brooke, Henry, *The Fool of Quality*, 5n.

Brower, R. A., ixn., 119, 116n.

burlesque, 5, 17, 53

Burney, Fanny, 5, 9, 17, 36, 119, 263

Camilla, 22

Cecilia, 117, 125, 263

Evelina, 5, 9, 38n.

Burns, 248

Byron, 40n., 237

Campbell, Thomas, 248

Chapman, R. W., ix, 16n., 91n., 139, 140n., 160n., 172f., 199n., 216n.

Chesterton, G. K., 150n., 194n.

Clarke, Rev. J. S., 35n.

comedy, 2f., 36, 215f., 228-230

convention, middle-class, 1, 12, 15 & n., 16-19, 22, 29-31, 34-36, 46n., 78f., 91, 123-125, 130, 136-138, 144, 152, 154, 170-173, 175-177, 180, 206, 221f., 229-236, 257

Cowper, 88, 162, 257

Emerson, R. W., 36

Farrer, Reginald, ixn., 201, 202, 218

Fielding, Henry, 39n., 160

Joseph Andrews, 39n.

Tom Jones, 211n.

Fielding, Sarah, *David Simple*, 5n.

Firkins, O. W., 181n.

Flaubert, 219n.

Forster, E. M., ix, 35n., 209n., 241, 256

Garrod, H. W., 36

Goldsmith, 25

History of England, 23

Harding, D. W., ixn.

irony, 1-3, 5, 6, 7f., 11n., 12, 13, 17-19, 25, 30f., 34, 37, 38-40, 46, 48-54, 59, 91, 94f., 125, 178, 180, 202-206

James, Henry, 116n., 221n.

Johnson, Dr., 4

Johnson, R. B., 14f.

Lascelles, Mary, ixn., 4n., 16, 18, 41n., 45n., 90n., 111, 179, 207n., 215, 228, 231, 238n., 241, 244n.

Laura and Augustus, 5-19, 29n., 35

Leavis, (Mrs.) Q. D., 117, 139n., 140n., 260-263

Lee, Sophia, *The Recess*, 5n., 40

Lennox, Charlotte, *Harriet Stuart*, 5n.

Lewis, M. G., *The Monk*, 39f.; *Lovers' Vows*, 160

Lubbock, Percy, 219n.

Mackenzie, Henry, *The Man of Feeling*, 5, 6, 10n.

Maturin, C. R., *Melmoth the Wanderer*, 40n.

Meredith, George, 207n., 239, *The Egoist*, 239

Meynell, Alice, 36

Mitford, Mary Russell, 34f., 35n.

Moore, George, 91n.

Mozart, 261

parody, 6, 15, 17, 25, 37-39, 41n., 52f., 59, 60-63

Radcliffe, Mrs., 17, 37, 40, 42n.

The Italian, 44